We'Moon '04

Sueño Dorado
© *Cynthia Ré Robbins 2002*

GAIA RHYTHMS FOR WOMYN
POWER

WE DEDICATE WE'MOON '04 TO THE POWER OF PEACE

published by
Mother Tongue Ink

WE'MOON '04: GAIA RHYTHMS FOR WOMYN
SPIRAL, LAYFLAT AND UNBOUND EDITIONS © 2003

We'Moon Crone Editor/Acting We'Moonager: Musawa
Interim We'Moonager: Gwendolyn Morgan
Production/Graphic Design/Promotion: Meghan Garrity
E-Office/Editor/Production: Amy Schutzer
Office Co-Chiefs: Cherie Smythe, Mountain, Eaglehawk
MT Ink Matrix/staff: all of the above
Special Editor: Bethroot Gwynn
We'Moon Creatrix: Bethroot, Meghan, Musawa

Front cover art: *Sueño Dorado* © Cynthia Ré Robbins 2002
Back cover art: *Sekhmet* © Hrana Janto 1994
(See "Cover Notes" on page 4.)

Order direct from Mother Tongue Ink, publisher and distributor (see page 240), or call to order from one of our many fine wholesale distributors.

Disclaimer: Mother Tongue Ink does not take responsibility for views expressed by artists or writers in their work in **We'Moon '04** or for the outcome of readers' uses of astrological and herbal information contained herein. Caution: use at your own risk, with common sense and/or expert advise from professionals you trust.

Astro-data and ephemerides reprinted with permission from Astro Communications Services, Inc., P.O. Box 34487, San Diego, CA 92163-4487.

We'Moon '04 is printed in full color by Sung In Printing America, in South Korea, on New Leaf Reincarnation Matte coated paper with 1% of the paper cost going to breast cancer research (95# cover: 100% recycled, 50% post consumer waste, processed chlorine free/ 70# text: 50% recycled, 30% post consumer waste, elemental chlorine free). By using 15,776 pounds of post consumer waste, We'Moon saves 95 trees, 8574 lbs. of solid waste, 9434 gals of water, 12,305 kilowatt hrs. of electricity, 15,586 lbs. of green house gases, 24 cubic yards of landfill space.

As a moon calendar, this book is recyclable: every nineteen years the moon completes a metatonic cycle, returning to the same phase, sign, and degree of the zodiac. If you still have We'Moon '86 you can use it again this year (We'Moon '04 will be reusable in 2023)!

Mother Tongue Ink

P.O. Box 1395-A
Estacada, Oregon 97023 USA
Toll Free: 877-O WeMoon
(877-693-6666)
Phone: 503-630-7848
Fax: 503-630-7048
E-mail: matrix@wemoon.ws
URL: http://www.wemoon.ws

Power of Peace
© *Amarah K. Gabriel 2002*

We'Moon '04 (spiral binding)
ISBN: 1-890931-18-7 ($16.95)
We'Moon '04 (lay-flat binding)
ISBN: 1-890931-17-9 ($16.95)
We'Moon '04 Unbound (no binding)
ISBN: 1-890931-19-5 ($16.95)

Art and writing from the **We'Moon** '04 datebooks also appears in the wall calendar and greeting cards available from Mother Tongue Ink:

We'Moon on the Wall 2004
ISBN: 1-890931-20-9 ($12.95)
4 We'Moon Greeting Cards
ISBN: 1-890931-21-7 ($5.95)

JANUARY

S	M	T	W	T	F	S
				1	2	3
4	5	6	(7)	8	9	10
11	12	13	14	15	16	17
18	19	20	(21)	22	23	24
25	26	27	28	29	30	31

FEBRUARY

S	M	T	W	T	F	S
1	2	3	4	5	(6)	7
8	9	10	11	12	13	14
15	16	17	18	19	(20)	21
22	23	24	25	26	27	28
29						

MARCH

S	M	T	W	T	F	S
	1	2	3	4	5	(6)
7	8	9	10	11	12	13
14	15	16	17	18	19	(20)
21	22	23	24	25	26	27
28	29	30	31			

APRIL

S	M	T	W	T	F	S
				1	2	3
4	(5)	6	7	8	9	10
11	12	13	14	15	16	17
18	(19)	20	21	22	23	24
25	26	27	28	29	30	

MAY

S	M	T	W	T	F	S
						1
2	3	(4)	5	6	7	8
9	10	11	12	13	14	15
16	17	(18)	19	20	21	22
23	24	25	26	27	28	29
30	31					

JUNE

S	M	T	W	T	F	S
		1	(2)	3	4	5
6	7	8	9	10	11	12
13	14	15	16	(17)	18	19
20	21	22	23	24	25	26
27	28	29	30			

JULY

S	M	T	W	T	F	S
				1	(2)	3
4	5	6	7	8	9	10
11	12	13	14	15	16	(17)
18	19	20	21	22	23	24
25	26	27	28	29	30	(31)

AUGUST

S	M	T	W	T	F	S
1	2	3	4	5	6	7
8	9	10	11	12	13	14
(15)	16	17	18	19	20	21
22	23	24	25	26	27	28
(29)	30	31				

SEPTEMBER

S	M	T	W	T	F	S
			1	2	3	4
5	6	7	8	9	10	11
12	13	(14)	15	16	17	18
19	20	21	22	23	24	25
26	27	(28)	29	30		

OCTOBER

S	M	T	W	T	F	S
					1	2
3	4	5	6	7	8	9
10	11	12	(13)	14	15	16
17	18	19	20	21	22	23
24	25	26	(27)	28	29	30
31						

NOVEMBER

S	M	T	W	T	F	S
	1	2	3	4	5	6
7	8	9	10	11	(12)	13
14	15	16	17	18	19	20
21	22	23	24	25	(26)	27
28	29	30				

DECEMBER

S	M	T	W	T	F	S
			1	2	3	4
5	6	7	8	9	10	(11)
12	13	14	15	16	17	18
19	20	21	22	23	24	25
(26)	27	28	29	30	31	

2004

Labrys
© *Louise Chambers*
1989

( ) = NEW MOON, PST/PDT

( ) = FULL MOON, PST/PDT

Cover Notes

Front Cover Art:

Sueño Dorado (Golden Dream) © **Cynthia Ré Robbins 2002**
This oil painting by Cynthia Ré Robbins was inspired by a dream she had about returning home, in which her home was in ancient Mexico. She was returning by boat, but out of the sky. She was led back by a school of leaping dorado (dolphin) fish and porpoise, feeling an absolute joy at the prospect of coming home at last.

Back Cover Art:

Sekhmet ©**Hrana Janto 1994**
Sekhmet is considered the destructive aspect of the sun, distinct from Bast, the life-giving aspect of the sun. Sekhmet burns and scorches as the relentless desert sun. While contemplating painting Her, I could feel Her fierceness, Her beauty and passion as a primal force, and Her healing power through the fire of transformation.

What's New This Year

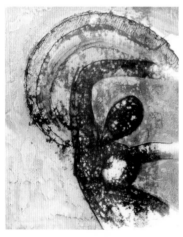

© *Deborah Koff-Chapin 2002*

What's new this year is **COLOR!** We have waited a long time to be able to bring forth the power of Iris, the Rainbow Goddess, to reveal the full beauty of **We'Moon** art in living color throughout the pages. For the best color reproduction, we are using a fine quality recycled paper that is slightly heavier. This is also the first **We'Moon** to sail across the ocean (as portended by our front cover image) where we found an excellent, affordable and ethical color printing option in South Korea.

Some changes in placement:
- Information on how to order **We'Moons** is given on page 240.
- World Time Zones and Signs and Symbols at a Glance are located just before the blank address/note pages for easy reference.
- Look for new and updated articles in the Introduction and Appendix.
- How to become a **We'Moon** contributor and how to order **We'Moon** products can be found on page 240.

TABLE OF CONTENTS

I. INTRODUCTION

Year at a Glance Calendar............3
Cover Notes............................4
What's New This Year 4
What is **We'Moon**? 6
How to Use this Book................9
Sun Signs 12
Moon Signs...........................15
The Eight Lunar Phases............18
Where's That Moon? 19
Lunar Rhythm 20
Wheel of the Year: Holy Days ...21

Keeping the Holidays 22
Southern Hemisphere Seasons...23
Herbs for We'moon 24
Flower Essences for Each Sign ...25
Eclipses 26
Mercury Retrograde 2004 26
Planetary Movements 2004.......27
Astrological Predictions 2004....27
Astro Trends 2004 28
Year of the Monkey 31
Introduction to the Theme........32

II. MOON CALENDAR

MOON I.............................. 39
MOON II............................. 49
MOON III 61
MOON IV 71
MOON V............................. 85
MOON VI 97
MOON VII 107

MOON VIII......................... 121
MOON IX 133
MOON X............................. 143
MOON XI 155
MOON·XII 167
MOON XIII.........................179

Calendar Pages feature

Astrological Predictions: Gretchen Lawlor; Holydays: Jessica Montgomery

III. APPENDIX

We'moon Ancestors 192
Copyrights/Contacts 193
Contributor Bylines/Index 193
Acknowledgments 203
Asteroids 204
Asteroid Ephemeris 206
Planetary Ephemeris...............207

Month at a Glance Calendars..213
Year at a Glance 2005 225
World Time Zones 226
Signs and Symbols..................227
Addresses/Notes 228
Ordering a **We'Moon** 240
Becoming a Contributor 240

Introduction and Appendix Page features

We'Moon Cycles: Musawa; **We'Moon** Astrologers: Gretchen Lawlor, Heather Roan Robbins, Sandra Pastorius, Susan Levitt, Beate Metz; Herbs and Flower Essences: Colette Gardiner and Gretchen Lawlor

We'Moon: Gaia Rhythms for Womyn is more than an appointment book, it's a way of life! **We'Moon** is a lunar calendar, a handbook in natural rhythm and comes out of international womyn's culture. Art and writing by we'moon from many lands give a glimpse of the great diversity and uniqueness of a world we create in our own image. **We'Moon** is about *womyn's spirituality* (spirit reality). We share how we live our truth, what inspires us, how we envision our reality in connection with the whole earth and all our relations.

Goddess Numbers
© *Sarah Teofanov 2002*

We'moon means "**women.**" Instead of defining ourselves in relation to men (as in *wo*man or *fe*male), we use the word *we'moon* to define ourselves by our primary relation to the natural sources of cosmic flow. Other terms we'moon use are *womyn, wimmin, womon, womb-one* ... **We'Moon** is a moon calendar for we'moon. As we'moon, we seek to be whole in ourselves, rather than dividing ourselves in half and hoping that some "other half" will complete the picture. We see the whole range of life's potential embodied and expressed by we'moon and do not divide the universe into sex-role stereotypes according to a heterosexual model. **We'Moon** is sacred space in which to explore and celebrate the diversity of she-ness on earth. The calendar is we'moon's space.

We'moon also means "**we of the moon.**" The Moon, whose cycles run in our blood, is the original womyn's calendar. Like the Moon, we'moon circle the Earth. We are drawn to one another. We come in different shapes, colors and sizes. We are continually transforming. With all our different hues and points of view, we are one.

We'moon culture exists in the diversity and the oneness of our experience as we'moon. *We honor both.* We come from many different ways of life. At the same time, as we'moon, we share a common mother root. We are glad when we'moon from varied backgrounds contribute art and writing. When material is borrowed from cultures other than our own, we ask that it be acknowledged and something given in return. Being conscious of our sources keeps us from engaging in the divisiveness of either *cultural appropriation* (taking what belongs to others) or *cultural fascism* (controlling creative expression). We invite every we'moon to share how the "Mother Tongue" speaks through her, with respect for both cultural integrity and individual freedom.

Gaia Rhythms: We show the natural cycles of the Moon, Sun, planets and stars as they relate to earth. By recording our own activities side by side with those of other heavenly bodies, we may notice what connection, if any, there is for us. The Earth revolves around her axis in one day; the Moon orbits around the Earth in one month ($29^1/_2$ days); the Earth orbits around the Sun in one year. We experience each of these cycles in the alternating rhythms of day and night, waxing and waning, summer and winter. The Earth/Moon/Sun are our inner circle of kin in the universe. We know where we are in relation to them at all times by the dance of light and shadow as they circle around one another.

The Eyes of Heaven: As seen from Earth, the Moon and the Sun are equal in size: "the left and right eye of heaven," according to Hindu (Eastern) astrology. Unlike the solar-dominated calendars of Christian (Western) patriarchy, the **We'Moon** looks at our experience through both eyes at once. The **lunar eye** of heaven is seen each day in the phases of the Moon as she is both reflector and shadow, traveling her $29^1/_2$-day path through the zodiac. The **solar eye** of heaven is apparent at the turning points in the sun's cycle. The year begins with Winter Solstice (in the Northern Hemisphere), the dark renewal time, and journeys through many seasons and balance points (solstices, equinoxes and the cross-quarter days in between). The **third eye** of heaven may be seen in the stars. Astrology measures the cycles by relating the sun, moon and all other planets in our universe through the star signs (the zodiac), helping us to tell time in the larger cycles of the universe.

Measuring Time and Space: Imagine a clock with many hands. The Earth is the center from which we view our universe. The Sun, Moon and planets are like the hands of the clock. Each one has its own rate of movement through the cycle. The ecliptic, a band of sky around the earth within which all planets have their orbits, is the outer band of the clock where the numbers are. Stars along the ecliptic are grouped into constellations forming the signs of the zodiac—the twelve star signs are like the twelve numbers of the clock. They mark the movements of the planets through the 360° circle of the sky, the clock of time and space.

Whole Earth Perspective: It is important to note that all natural cycles have a mirror image from a whole earth perspective—seasons occur at opposite times in the Northern and Southern Hemispheres and day and night occur at opposite times on opposite sides of the Earth as well. Even the Moon plays this game—a waxing crescent moon in Australia faces right (e.g., ☾), while in North America it faces left (e.g., ☽). **We'Moon** has a northern hemisphere perspective regarding times, holy days, seasons and lunar phases. See page 23 for a southern hemispere perspective on the seasons.

Whole Sky Perspective: It is also important to note that all over the Earth, in varied cultures and times, the dome of the sky has been interacted with in countless ways. The zodiac we speak of is just one of many ways that hu-moons have pictured and related to the stars. In this calendar, we use the tropical zodiac.

by Musawa © Mother Tongue Ink 1999

Star Thrower
© Marion Cloaninger 2001

How to Use This Book
Useful Information about the *We'Moon*

Time Zones: All aspects are in Pacific Standard/Daylight Time, with the adjustment for GMT and EDT given at the bottom of each page. To calculate for other areas, see "World Time Zones" (p. 226).

Signs and Symbols at a Glance is an easily accessible handy guide that gives brief definitions for commonly used astrological symbols (p. 227).

Pages are numbered throughout the calendar to facilitate cross referencing. See Table of Contents (p. 5) and Contributor Bylines and Index (pp. 193–203). The names of the days of the week and months are in English with additional foreign language translations included (Spanish, Dutch, Quechua and German).

Moon Pages mark the beginning of each Moon cycle with a two-page spread near the new moon. Each Moon page is numbered with Roman numerals (eg., **Moon III**) and contains the dates of that Moon's new and full moon and solar ingress.

Year at a Glance Calendar (p. 3), **Month at a Glance Calendar** (pp. 213–224) includes daily lunar phases.

Annual Predictions: For your astrological portrait for 2004 (starting with Aquarius), turn to Gretchen Lawlor's prediction for your sun sign. See "Astrological Predictions 2004" (p. 27) for page numbers by sign.

Holydays: There is a two-page holy day spread for all 2004 equinoxes, solstices and cross quarter days. These include feature writings by Jessica Montgomery, with related art and writing.

Planetary Ephemeris: Exact planetary positions for every day, (pp. 207–212). These ephemerides show where each planet is in a zodiac sign at noon GMT, measured by degree in longitude in Universal Time.

Asteroid Ephemeris: Exact positions of asteroids for every ten days are given for sixteen asteroids in the zodiac at midnight GMT on p. 206. See Beate Metz's "Asteroids, an Impetus for a New Connection" (p. 204) for more information.

Astrology Basics

Planets: Planets are like chakras in our solar system, allowing for different frequencies or types of energies to be expressed.

Signs: The twelve signs of the zodiac are a mandala in the sky, marking off 30° segments in the 360° circle around the earth. Signs show major shifts in planetary energy through the cycles.

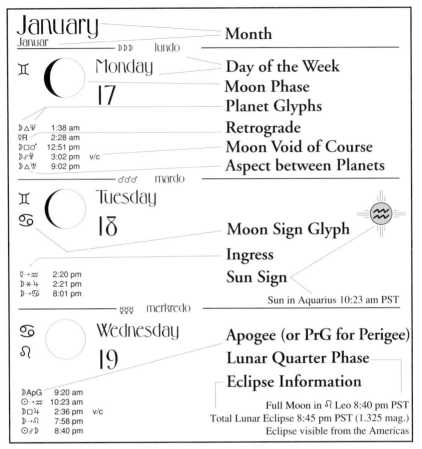

January
Januar ☽☽☽ lundo — Month
♊ ☽ Monday — Day of the Week
            Moon Phase
       17 — Planet Glyphs
                Retrograde
☽△♆ 1:38 am — Moon Void of Course
☿R   2:28 am
☽□♂ 12:51 pm
☽☍♀ 3:02 pm v/c — Aspect between Planets
☽△♅ 9:02 pm

♂♂♂ mardo
♊ ☽ Tuesday
♋   18 — Moon Sign Glyph
                Ingress
☿→♒ 2:20 pm Sun Sign
☽⚹♃ 2:21 pm
☽→♋ 8:01 pm Sun in Aquarius 10:23 am PST

☿☿☿ merkredo
♋ ○ Wednesday — Apogee (or PrG for Perigee)
♌   19 — Lunar Quarter Phase
                Eclipse Information
☽ApG 9:20 am
⊙→♒ 10:23 am Full Moon in ♌ Leo 8:40 pm PST
☽□♃ 2:36 pm v/c Total Lunar Eclipse 8:45 pm PST (1.325 mag.)
☽→♌ 7:58 pm Eclipse visible from the Americas
⊙☍☽ 8:40 pm

Glyphs: Glyphs are the symbols used to represent planets and signs.

Sun Sign: The Sun enters a new sign once a month (around the 20th or so), completing the whole cycle of the zodiac in one year. The sun sign reflects qualities of your outward shining self. For a description of sign qualities see "Sun Signs" (pp. 12–14).

Moon Sign: The Moon changes signs approximately every 2¹/₂ days, going through all twelve signs of the zodiac every 29¹/₂ days (the sidereal month). The moon sign reflects qualities of your core inner self. For descriptions see "Moon Signs and Transits" (pp. 15–17).

Moon Phase: Each calendar day is marked with a graphic representing the phase of the Moon. Although the Moon is not usually visible in the sky during the new or dark moon, we represent her using miniscule crescent moon graphics for the days immediately before and after the actual new moon or conjunction. [See related articles on pp. 18–19.]

Lunar Quarter Phase: At the four quarter points of the lunar cycle (new, waxing half, full and waning half) we indicate the phase, sign and exact time for each. These points mark off the "lunar week."

Day of the Week: Each day is associated with a planet whose symbol appears in the line above it (e.g., ☽☽☽ is for Moon: Moonday, Monday, Luna Day, lundi, lunes). The names of the days of the week are displayed prominently in English with translations appearing in the line above them. Four languages (Spanish, Dutch, Quechua and German) rotate weekly in this order throughout the calendar.

Eclipse: The time of greatest eclipse is given, which is not the exact time of the conjunction or opposition. Locations from where eclipses are visible are also given. For lunar and partial solar eclipses, magnitude is given in decimal form (e.g., 0.881 mag.), denoting the fraction of the moon's diameter obscured by the shadow of Earth. For total and annular solar eclipses, the duration of the eclipse in minutes and seconds is given. For more information see "Eclipses" (p. 26).

Aspects (□ △ ☍ ☌ ✳ ⊼): These show the angle of relation between different planets. An aspect is like an astrological weather forecast for the day, indicating which energies are working together easily and which combinations are more challenging. See "Signs and Symbols at a Glance" (p. 227) for a brief explanation of each kind.

Ingresses (→): Indicate planets moving into new signs.

Moon Void of Course (☽ v/c): The Moon is said to be void of course from the last significant lunar aspect in each sign until the Moon enters a new sign. This is a good time to ground and center yourself.

Apogee (ApG): This is the point in the orbit of a planet or the Moon that is farthest from Earth. At this time the effects of transits (when planets pass across the path of another planet) may be less noticeable immediately but may appear later on.

Perigee (PrG): This is the point in the orbit of a planet or the Moon that is nearest to Earth. Transits with the Moon or other planets when they are at perigee will be more intense.

Direct or Retrograde (D or R): These are times when a planet moves forward (D) or backward (R) through the signs of the zodiac (an optical illusion, as when a moving train passes a slower train which appears to be going backward). When a planet is in direct motion, planetary energies are more straightforward; in retrograde, planetary energies turn back in on themselves and are more involuted.

by Musawa © Mother Tongue Ink 2000

SUN SIGNS AND SUN TRANSITS

Each month the Sun pours its power and energy through the filter of a different sign. Our Sun's sign is at the core of our being, our source of power.

Tassi
© *Margot Foxfire 1998*

♈ **Aries (March 20–April 20):** Every spring, while the Sun is in Aries, it's time to remember what makes us passionate, to re-learn what we want and don't want. The Aries Sun imbues us with the courage to start over again as the Green world shoots into new life.

If you're born while the Sun was in Aries, your power comes from your ability to be direct and original, strong and willful. You're the primal rebel in us all, and can be a rascally, mischievous instigator. You may love a clear, clean fight for a good cause but your challenge is to move past mere rebellion and shift the paradigm; choose your own disciplines and become a leader.

♉ **Taurus (April 20–May 20):** For Taurus, earth is the energy. During the month of Taurus we find our power through our ability to sink deep roots and hold our position. It's time to explore the sensual potential of our body and the body of the Mother, as we garden, touch, build, sing, make love, strengthen and manifest.

If you were born while the Sun was in Taurus, your power comes from your grounded strength and your ability to bring a dream into the world of matter. You remind us that matter can be a sacred vessel: our bodies and our earth. Comfort renews you. Stubbornness and the search for security are your gifts and challenges.

♊ **Gemini (May 20–June 21):** While the Sun traverses Gemini, our power comes from our networks, diversity and the sisterhood. Gemini stimulates our ability to find sense, humor and poetry in the every day world. We search for the fresh breath of inspiration.

If you were born while the Sun was in Gemini, your power comes from your ability to invent and communicate. Your words weave the web; your challenge is to make sure they have meaning and to be diverse without being scattered. You can translate from one friend to another or from one culture to another and often can find the humor when others have lost theirs.

♋ **Cancer (June 21–July 22):** While the Sun swims through Moon-ruled Cancer, our power comes though deepening our roots. We grow stronger as we nourish connections with our chosen family and tribe, our body, our garden, our community and our temple's hearth. Ask what makes you feel truly safe in the world.

If you were born while the Sun was in Cancer, your strength comes from the archetype of the mother, whether you nurture and defend your career, culture, garden, art or children. Your gift is to teach us the power of guardianship but your challenge is to risk believing in your strength, rather than stay guarded behind your unique protective shell.

♌ **Leo (July 22–Aug. 23):** During the Leo Sun, our power comes from expressing ourselves. Live life to its fullest, celebrate your body's ripeness along with the ripening crops and culture.

If you were born while the Sun was in Leo, your power comes from your ability to be the hearth-fire. You can light up the room and warm souls, be a reason why people gather on a cold winter night as long as you can give as much attention as you ask for yourself. Your challenge is to listen deeply and call people together for good reason.

♍ **Virgo (Aug. 23–Sept. 22):** While the Sun is in Virgo, our power comes from our ability to harvest and sort the wheat from the chaff. It's time to critique our world, figure out what needs work or healing, then, make plans and blueprints for the year ahead. Wild craft herbs and prepare our health for autumn as we grow introspective.

If you were born while the Sun was in Virgo, your power comes from your ability to analyze and to ask us to look beneath the surface and think more deeply. You're a healing force as long as you don't get stuck on the weeds or problems—focus on solutions.

♎ **Libra (Sept. 22–Oct. 23):** While the Sun is in Libra, strengthen your relationship with all your two-legged, four-legged, winged and finned relations. Feed your partnership and creative process with romance. Our power now comes from balance and beauty and the search for peace through justice.

If you were born while the Sun was in Libra, your power comes from your ability to notice when we're in balance and when we're out of whack. You understand relationships and what's really in our hearts; you know what's fair and are willing to fight for it (though prefer a peaceful path). Your challenge is to remember yourself in the equation and not get lost in relationship.

♏ **Scorpio (Oct. 23–Nov. 22):** While the Sun burrows in Scorpio, we're empowered by our willingness to transform, to compost the old year as we peer into the shadows and face our fears. Mysteries fascinate and instruct us; we celebrate the day of the dead, dance with skeletons and go deep within our souls to find our desires.

If you're born with the Sun in Scorpio, your strength comes from your ability to use your intense, laser-like focus and curiosity to look past the easy answers and search out secrets. You remind us that sex is a mystery school. Your challenge is to balance your depth with a broad horizon.

♐ **Sagittarius (Nov. 22–Dec. 21):** While the Sun travels through Sagittarius, our joy and strength comes through celebration and by expanding horizons; both intellectually and through exploring the diversity of life and cultures. We give thanks for one another, weave our global network and value our connection to the organic world.

If you're born with the Sun in Sagittarius, your power comes from your ability to speak out with disarming frankness and your restless curiosity of mind and body. Life for you is a journey; it is research. Your challenge it to learn how to stick out the work, rather than move on to greener pastures.

♑ **Capricorn (Dec. 21–Jan. 20):** While the Sun is in Capricorn, we remember our roots: the routines and rituals that connect us to our past and to biological or chosen family. We grow as we take stock of ourselves and organize for the year ahead.

If you were born while the Sun was in Capricorn, your power is in your backbone—your ability to stay strong and practical even when a storm hits. You help us take a dream and bring it into form with leadership and organization. Your challenge is to make sure you have a worthy goal.

♒ **Aquarius (Jan. 20–Feb. 18):** While the Sun is in Aquarius, our power comes from the collective. It's time to find allies and take your philosophy into political and cultural action.

If you're born while the Sun is in Aquarius, your power comes from your ability to network, to theorize and to gather community. You can stand back and offer an objective perspective, see the effects of the one on the whole. Your challenge is to know what you feel and build intimacy as well as collectivity.

♓ **Pisces (Feb. 18–March 20):** While the Sun is in Pisces, our power comes from our ability to dream and feel. We are sensitized to the quiet voice of wakening plants and stirring visions. We become newly aware of what hurts and what heals and can be moved to compassionate action.

If you were born while the Sun was in Pisces, your strength is found in your sensitivities and imagination. Your courage is supple—like willow that bends in a storm—and you feel every quiver on life's web. Your challenge is to take action towards your vision.

by Heather Roan Robbins © Mother Tongue Ink 2003

Moon Signs

Moon Goddess
© *Jan Salerno 1992*

The moon speaks directly to our spirit. It describes the daily pulse and the emotional matrix we walk through. As the moon changes sign every 2$^1/_2$ days, the filters on our inner world change. Let the garden be a metaphor for any project you want to nourish. Our own moon sign indicates our personal, spiritual lineage and our emotional prime-directive.

The **Moon in ♈ Aries** asks us to wake up and remember who we truly are, even if it bothers those we love or work for. Tempers, tears and passions run hot. It's a great time for digging new beds, moving boulders, weeding or pest removal, but put a hold on planting. The Moon in Aries woman searches for fire, fierce independence and her own voice. She may need to learn patience and cooperation. She appreciates our fire.

The **Moon in ♉ Taurus** asks us to discover what nurtures us and how to grow deeper roots. We can almost feel the mud oozing between our toes, awakening our senses and sensuality and growing our stubbornness. It is time to cultivate our material resources, our homes and our body. Plant anything you want to grow strong and fertile. The Moon in Taurus womon searches for stability and sensuality. She may need to learn mobility. She offers us comfort, beauty and solid presence.

15

The **Moon in ♊ Gemini** quickens our nervous system. Build a web of understanding—network, absorb new information. Speak to your plants, trim, but avoid planting. The Moon in Gemini woman wants to understand, she lives and breathes communication. She may need to learn to honor stillness and concentration. She translates for us, questions us.

With the **Moon in ♋ Cancer** our feelings take the lead. Cancer encourages the wisdom rising out of our oceanic unconscious through moods and feelings. Ground in the magic of our home as a temple. Ask what needs protecting and feeding. Plant, fertilize and water your garden. The Moon in Cancer woman searches for what nurtures her soul and the world's. She may need to learn to carry her security with her. She respects our deepest feelings, eases our past fears.

With the **Moon in ♌ Leo** we have the guts to be visible and bring culture to life. In your garden or life, arrange, glorify and weed the extraneous so your star can shine, but don't plant or fertilize. The Moon in Leo woman came here to dramatize and ritualize her world. She may need to learn to find the sacred in the mundane. She offers us celebration and fascination and honors our self-expression.

The **Moon in ♍ Virgo** asks us to consider what needs healing, what needs composting. It's time to study, learn, train, organize and turn our compassion into pragmatic action. Don't get stuck in your head. Weed, prune, ammend your garden with nutrients and companion planting. Plant and care for medicinal herbs. The Moon in Virgo woman came here to diagnose and heal her soul and the world's. She needs to learn to celebrate the beauty in each of us. She offers us practical compassion and ancient wisdom.

Moon in ♎ Libra highlights the magic of the dance of inter-relatedness—friendly, romantic and searching for a way to connect. Libra asks us to treat those around us as equals and make sure our politics and art, our lovemaking and our networks integrate. Tend to the beauty of the garden, cultivate, but don't plant. The Moon in Libra woman came here to feel the beauty in cooperation. She may need to learn to hear her own voice under conflict. She offers us bone-deep kindness, mediation and justice.

With the **Moon in ♏ Scorpio**, dig deep. Scorpio weaves the visible and invisible worlds together. We see through and into the roots. Direct this energy away from obsession and towards creation. Sexuality can be potent, musky. Dig in your garden, plant roots, feed the soil and compost. The Moon in Scorpio woman came here to find herself in solitude first and then through transformative action with others. She may need to learn flexibility. She offers us a fearless guide to the inner worlds as she midwifes all transitions.

Moon in ♐ Sagittarius brings out our inner-Artemis; we need to roam, to explore in body and in soul. Our curiosity intensifies. Check out untraveled territory and connect with the organic world. Have a long talk with the animals in your garden. Work the soil but hold off on the planting. The Moon in Sagittarius woman came here to explore. She needs to learn to hold still and work through a challenge. She offers us radical acceptance.

Moon in ♑ Capricorn brings planning magic and takes your ideas, giving them form and hope. We can tap into the inner wisewoman—ask how form, ritual, organization or tradition can serve. Trim, prune, plant slow-growing seedlings and make sure you and your garden have enough water. The Moon in Capricorn woman came here to accomplish and understand compassionate leadership. She may need to learn to respect other rhythms and to love herself, not just what she does. She offers us constructive determination and practical support.

The **Moon in ♒ Aquarius** expands our circles and offers the magic of collaboration; spirit and politics weave together. We can get too farsighted now and need to stay aware of others' feelings. Let go of assumptions and find new, unusual allies. A time to gather plants, mulch, prune and talk to your garden. The Moon in Aquarius woman came here to understand group dynamics. She may need to learn to be comfortable with emotional intimacy. She offers us a global perspective and collaboration.

With the **Moon in ♓ Pisces** we feel the world with compassion, heightened senses and strong imagination. We need quiet time in the temple or back under our covers to deal with sensory overload. A time to vision, listen to inner voices, allow creative juices to flow and touch each other with new awareness. Plant, transplant, water, fertilize. Moon in Pisces woman came here to feel everything; she may need to filter impressions and find her deep strength. She offers us insight, imagination, and subtle, compassionate medicine while encouraging our vision.

by Heather Roan Robbins © Mother Tongue Ink 2000

THE EIGHT LUNAR PHASES

As above, so below. Look into the sky and observe which phase the Moon is in. Then you will know where you are in the growth cycle of each lunar month. The phase that the moon was in when you were born reflects your purpose, personality and preferences.

The **new moon** is like a SEED planted in the earth. We cannot see her but she is ready to grow, full of potential and energy for her new journey. We'moon born during the new moon are impulsive, passionate and intuitive. They are risk takers and pioneers.

The **crescent moon** is the SPROUT. The seed has broken through the earth and reaches up as she ventures from the dark, moist earth she has known. We'moon born during the crescent moon must break from the past to create their own destiny.

The **first quarter moon** is the GROWTH phase. Roots go deeper, stems shoots up and leaves form as she creates a new strong body. We'moon born during the first quarter moon live a full active life—old structures are cleared away providing room for new development.

The **gibbous moon** is the BUD of the plant, the pulse of life tightly wrapped, wanting to expand. For we'moon born during the gibbous moon, their talents lie in the ability to refine, organize and purify. They are seekers, utilizing spiritual tools as guides on their path.

She opens and blossoms during the **full moon** into the FLOWER, with the desire to share her beauty with others. We'moon born during the full moon enjoy companionship and partnership and desire to merge deeply. Fulfillment and illumination are their goals.

As we go into the darkening phase of the **disseminating moon**, we get the FRUIT of the plant's life cycle—the fruits of wisdom and experience. For we'moon born during the disseminating moon, life must have meaning, purpose. They enjoy sharing their ideas with others.

The **last quarter moon** is the HARVEST phase—the plant gives her life so that others may continue theirs. We'moon born during the last quarter have a powerful internal life of reflection, transformation. They can assume different roles while balancing their internal and external worlds.

The **balsamic moon** is the COMPOST phase, when the nutrients remain in the soil, providing nourishment for the next new seed. We'moon born during the balsamic moon possess the potential to be wise, insightful, understanding and patient. They are prophetic and unique.

by Susan Levitt © Mother Tongue Ink 2000

WHERE'S THAT MOON?

Why is the Moon sometimes visible during the day? And why does the Moon sometimes rise very late at night? The answers lie in what phase the Moon is in, which reflects the angle between the Sun and Moon as seen from Earth. For each of the eight Moon phases, the angle between the Sun and Moon progresses in 45° increments. Each phase lasts approximately 3–4 days of the moon's entire 29$^1/_2$ day cycle.

The **new moon** (or dark moon) rises at sunrise and sets at sunset. Astrologically, the Sun and the Moon are in *conjunction*. Because the Sun's light overpowers the nearby Moon in the day, and the Moon is on the other side of the Earth with the Sun at night, she is not visible in the sky at all.

The **crescent moon** (or waxing crescent moon) rises midmorning and sets after sunset. She is the first visible sliver of Moon seen in the western sky in the late afternoon and early evening.

The **first quarter moon** (or waxing half moon) rises around noon and sets around midnight. Astrologically, the Moon is *square* to the Sun. She is visible from the time she rises until she sets.

The **gibbous moon** rises midafternoon and sets before dawn. She is the bulging Moon getting ready to be full, visible soon after she rises until she sets.

The **full moon** rises at sunset and sets at sunrise. Astrologically, the Sun and Moon are in *opposition* (ie., opposite each other in the sky and in opposite signs of the zodiac). She is visible all night long from moonrise to moonset.

The **disseminating moon** is the waning full moon getting visibly smaller. She rises midevening and sets midmorning. She is visible from the time she rises almost until she sets.

The **last quarter moon** (or waning half moon) rises around midnight and sets around noon. Astrologically, the Moon is *square* to the Sun. She is visible from the time she rises until she sets.

The **balsamic moon** (or waning crescent moon) rises before dawn and sets midafternoon. She is the last sliver of Moon seen in the eastern sky in the dawn and in the very early morning.

by Susan Levitt © Mother Tongue Ink 2000

LUNAR RHYTHM

Everything that flows moves in rhythm with the Moon. She rules the water element on earth. She pulls on the ocean's tides, the weather, female reproductive cycles, and the life fluids in plants, animals and people. She influences the underground currents in earth energy, the mood swings of mind, body, behavior and emotion. The Moon is closer to the Earth than any other heavenly body. The Earth actually has two primary relationships in the universe: one with the Moon who circles around her and one with the Sun whom she circles around. Both are equal in her eyes. The phases of the Moon reflect the dance of all three: the Moon, the Sun, and the Earth, who together weave the web of light and dark into our lives. No wonder so much of our life on earth is intimately connected with the phases of the Moon!

The preceeding articles about the Moon and her cycles (pp. 18 and 19) correspond to the chart below.

by Musawa © Mother Tongue Ink 2003

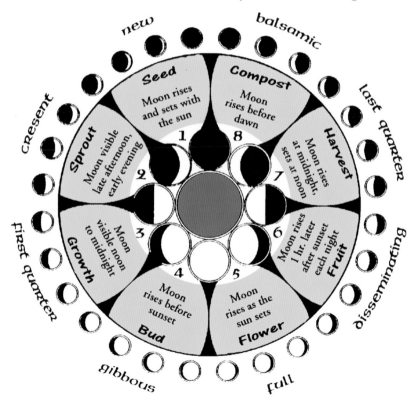

THE WHEEL OF THE YEAR: HOLY/HOLIDAYS

The seasonal cycle of the year is created by the tilt of the Earth's axis, leaning toward or away from the Sun, north to south, as the Earth orbits the Sun. Solstices are the extreme points all over the world when days and nights are longest or shortest. On equinoxes, days and nights are equal in all parts of the world. The four cross-quarter days roughly mark the midpoints in between solstices and equinoxes. These natural turning points in the Earth's annual cycle are the holidays we commemorate in **We'Moon**. We use the dates in the ancient Celtic calendar because it most closely approximates the eight spokes of the wheel of the year. **We'Moon '04** features Jessica Montgomery's interpretation of the holydays (names and dates in bold as follows). To try to represent the holy/holidays of the world's cultures would fill our pages. Since the seasonal celebrations of most cultures cluster around these same natural turning points, with similar universal themes, we leave it up to you to fill in your own.

Dec. 21: Solstice/Winter: the dwindling and return of the light—Kwanzaa (African-American), Soyal (Hopi), Santa Lucia (Scandanavian), Cassave/Dreaming (Taino), Chanukah (Jewish).

Feb. 2: Imbolc/Mid-Winter: celebrations, prophecy, purification, initiation—Candlemas (Christian), New Years (Tibetan, Chinese, Iroquois), Ground Hog's Day (American), Tu Bi-Shevat (Jewish).

Mar. 19: Equinox/Spring: rebirth, fertility, eggs, resurrection—Passover (Jewish), Easter (Christian), Festivals of the Goddess: Eostare (German), Astarte (Semite), Persephone (Greek).

May 1: Beltane/Mid-Spring: blossoms, planting, fertility, sexuality—May Day (Euro-American), Root Festival (Yakima), Ching Ming (Chinese), Whitsuntide (Dutch).

June 20: Solstice/Summer: sun, fire festivals—Niman Kachina (Hopi), Sundance (Lakota), Goddess festivals: Isis (Egypt), Litha (N. Africa), Yellow Corn Mother (Taino), Ishtar (Babylonian).

Aug. 2: Lammas/Mid-Summer: first harvest, breaking bread, goddesses of abundance: Green Corn Ceremony (Creek), Corn Mother (Hopi), Amaterasu (Japan), Hatshepsut's Day (Egypt).

Sept. 22: Equinox/Fall: gather and store, ripeness, goddesses: Tari Pennu (Bengal), Old Woman Who Never Dies (Mandan), Chicomecoatl (Aztec), Black Bean Mother (Taino).

Oct. 31: Samhain/Mid-Fall: underworld journey, ancestor spirits, Hallowmas/Halloween/Festivals of the Dead around the world, Sukkoth (Jewish harvest/wine festival).

© *Mother Tongue Ink 2003* Sources: *The Grandmother of Time* by Z. Budapest, 1989; *Celestially Auspicious Occasions* by Donna Henes, 1996; and *Songs of Bleeding* by Spider, 1992

KEEPING THE HOLIDAYS

The sacred holidays are the eight points of power in the cycle of seasons that define a calendar year: Winter Solstice, Imbolc (Candlemas), Spring Equinox, Beltane (May Day), Summer Solstice, Lammas, Fall Equinox, Samhain (Hallowe'en/All Hallow's Eve). These magical eight points on the circle of the year mark times when the relationships between the Sun, Moon and Earth are particularly powerful and can be felt or experienced by us most profoundly. At

4 Wands
© Motherpeace, a pseudonym of
Vicki Noble and Karen Vogel, 1981

these times, whether we are conscious of the holiday or not, we all have stronger experiences, bigger dreams and more intense impressions of the invisible energies and forces. In other words, the holidays exist whether we recognize them or not.

The Sacred Calendar is a visible image superimposed over the invisible structure that holds reality in place in our world. Marking the eight magical spots on the calendar year and celebrating them in some way is part of the Old Religion of the Goddess, which is active again today in the Women's Sprituality movement. These are the witches' "high holidays," and are recognized and honored in addition to the monthly New Moon and Full Moon. The Solstices and Equinoxes are noted in our modern calendars as the beginning days of winter, spring, summer and fall; and the "cross quarter" days that fall in between them are claimed by Pagans and Christians alike . . . they are included on the Julian calendar as church (and sometimes public) holidays.

A profound way of tuning into the powers and practices of the worldwide culture of the Mother Goddess is to honor her ancient calendar of eight magical sacred holidays. It is not really necessary to "do ritual" on the sacred holidays, since if you simply make the space in your life to observe and pay attention, the holidays will "do" you. Tuning into the "play of the dakinis" will allow them to spontaneously appear in your life as synchronicities and supernatural events, which tend to take place at a higher frequency around the holidays.

© Vicki Noble1998, excerpt adapted from
Motherpeace and the Sacred Holidays (Bear & Co., 2003)

A Southern Hemisphere Look at the Seasons

As you turn the calendar pages through the wheel of this year, **We'Moon** seasonal Holydays are interpreted from a Northern Hemisphere perspective. Summer and Winter, Spring and Fall are at opposite times of the year than in the Southern Hemisphere. If you live in the Southern Hemisphere, you might want to transpose descriptions of the Holydays to match the seasons in your area. To give a whole earth perspective, we are including the seasons (*Killa*) in Quechua, the most common Amerindian language spoken by millions of people in the Andes. 75% of the people of Bolivia today identify as indigenous and 12 million people speak Quechua. We are also including Quechua as one of the four languages rotating through the calendar pages.

Summer

end December–January: *Qhapaquintiraymi killa*—festival of the hummingbird (time of many flowers) month—starts the first new moon after the December Solstice and lasts the whole period of the moon.
end January–February: *Qhapmiy killa*—season of the rain month
end February–March: *Jatunpuquy killa*—large production month

Fall

end April–May: *Pachapuquy killa*—harvest of the earth month
end May–mid June: *Ariwaki Killa*—festival of the moon month

Winter

mid June–mid July: *Aymuray killa*—festival of the sun month
mid July–early August: *Chakraqunakuy killa*—obtaining Earth month
early August–early September: *Chakrayapuy killa*—preparing the Earth month

Spring

early September–early October: *Tarpuy killa*—planting month
early October–November 1: *Pawqarwara killa*—season of green month
November 2–December 2: *Ayamarqay killa*—festival of the souls month

The Quechuan's Incan roots promote the worship of the Pachamama, the Earth Mother. Their lives are governed by her cycles. This is seen even in the Quechua names of the month. Killa means both month and Moon . . . In the Southern Hemisphere, not only the seasons are opposite; the Moon is inverted too! Just as the Quechua language and its spelling changes in different regions, so may the interpretation and significance.

by Katrina Klemens © Mother Tongue Ink 2003

HERBS FOR WE'MOON

Women healers have always been at the heart of self-empowerment. They kept the knowledge of plants alive down through the generations. Women were the midwives of birth and death, a part of the community. During the Middle Ages the healer became a professional from outside the community—one who was part of a system based on profit. In this era of globalization and destruction of traditional communities it is vital that we re-empower ourselves in our healthcare. Certainly herbs can be used to help reweave a community based on hope and trust. Using the elemental types of earth, air, fire and water as guidelines is one way to start to work with herbs in your life.

We'moon who have a strong earth component (Capricorn, Taurus, Virgo) tend to be stable and reliable. Health challenges can revolve around a tendency towards slowing and stiffening. Empower yourself by stretching and cultivating flexibility. Mild digestive stimulants such as dandelion tea also help the liver and kidneys. If you tend to be cold add a little ginger or cinnamon to the blend.

Strong air types (Aquarius, Gemini, Libra) are quick and very mentally active. Support includes grounding and nervous system tonics. Oatstraw is one herb used as a nerve builder. It can be used as tea and is high in minerals including calcium to help our muscles and bones stay strong.

Fiery women (Aries, Leo, Sagittarius) are creative and inspirational. Health challenges can come in the form of a hot dry constitution. Spending time near water and using cooling herbs such as chickweed helps to support the blood, kidneys and liver. It can be used fresh in teas and is great in salads or as a cooked green.

We'moon who are strong water types (Pisces, Cancer, Scorpio) tend to be intuitive and flexible. Health challenges tend to revolve around being susceptible to cold and pollutants. Invoking magical protection and boundary work can be helpful. Immune support is important. Treat yourself to some fresh Shitake mushrooms regularly. Cooked slowly in soup, they are warming and immunity-building.

Remember that you are more than just your sun sign. Use the type of support that seems to fit you best. Talk to other plant We'moon and share what you've learned. Let's rebuild a web of healing.

by Colette Gardner © Mother Tongue Ink 2003
*Artwork: **The Healing Power of Nature** ¤ Kami McBride 2002*

FLOWER ESSENCES FOR EACH SIGN: 2004

Flower essences* are natural healing remedies with a profound capacity to soothe overstressed nerves, restore emotional equilibrium and mind-body well being. They do this gently, without sedating, working well in collaboration with other medications.

One universal remedy for 2004 is ELM, used when feeling overwhelmed, unequal to the tasks required to survive and be of help in a highly stressed global climate. It brings faith and confidence in self, in helpful alliances with others and with Spirit. Use it with your own Sun sign essence (see below) to make your own specific healing tonic.

I recommend the Bach and FES Essences as they are widely available.

Aries: Sage provides necessary detachment and reflection to align action with right timing.

Taurus: Trumpet Vine brings easy active and dynamic projection of self to others.

Gemini: Cosmos to be a conduit of higher wisdom through clear and coherent words.

Cancer: Milkweed nourishes the core self so the ego feels safe and relaxed, with no need for aggressive defense.

Leo: Honeysuckle for learning from the past while releasing it.

Virgo: Goldenrod to bring a unified, healthy Self to group situations.

Libra: Quince to stand firm in your authority while remaining open to innovative ideas.

Scorpio: Canyon Dudleya for gently adjusting efforts into alignment with highest principles and needs of the future.

Sagittarius: Sagebrush for safely shedding old identity and habits which are no longer appropriate.

Capricorn: Calendula to encourage warm and generous communication skills in personal relationship work.

Aquarius: Lavendar to integrate highly stimulated energy body with physical body.

Pisces: Walnut for protection when initiating a new phase in the journey.

by Gretchen Lawlor © Mother Tongue Ink 2003

ECLIPSES AND THE POWER OF PERSPECTIVE

When the Sun (self-consciousness), the Moon (unconscious awareness) and the Earth (our embodied Soul) become aligned with each other at the Nodes of the Moon, eclipses occur in opposite seasons and signs. The Sun and Moon appear visually the same size from our perspective and this perceived equality catalyses paradoxical perceptual shifts. Eclipses cast light in dark places, trigger revealing reversals and evolutionary jumps. Integrate the eclipse degrees into your birth chart to see where you will experience transformational glimpses of your shadow. As the Moon slips in front of the Sun on these new moon days, our past motives are unmasked, exposing inner authenticity—ready or not. On April 19th: a partial Solar eclipse at 29° Aries. On October 13th: a partial Solar eclipse at 21° Libra. At these full moons, look for the dark side of the Earth, cutting through appearances and foreshadowing things yet to come. On May 4th: a total Lunar eclipse at 15° Scorpio. On October 27th: a total Lunar eclipse at 5° Taurus.

*See dates in calendar for times and areas of visibility.

by Sandra Pastorius © Mother Tongue Ink 2003

MERCURY RETROGRADE—RE-SOURCING THE MUSE

Three or four times a year, Mercury, planetary muse and mentor of our mental and communicative lives, appears to reverse its course. This retrograde movement back through the signs symbolizes our return to the source of understanding and the creative repositioning of ourselves as communicators. Use Mercury re-sourcing periods to entertain your inner "winged-footed messenger" and ponder your power to make the connections necessary for invoking your world. Mine any melancholy for magical meaning. Tools using "alternating current" may also experience re-polarizing. Use patience. Enjoy the down time.

On Jan. 6th, at the same degree as galactic center (26° Sagittarius), Mercury turns direct. Muse on the big picture and give reverence to the perennial philosopher within. When Mercury retrogrades again from April 6th to 30th, we can contemplate our intentions more deeply. Remember, silence holds power and our words aim that power. Signal sensitively. August 9th to Sept. 2nd gives us pause, allowing us to re-trace our steps. Use physical reenactments to symbolically re-claim aspects of your past and allow for re-empowerment. Review messages when synapses shift from Nov. 30th to Dec. 19th and practice renewed resilience and balanced expression. Solstice Blessings.

by Sandra Pastorius © Mother Tongue Ink 2003

ASTROLOGICAL PREDICTIONS 2004

Every year I aspire to be even better at providing each one of you an overview of the year ahead. This time I used a long time oracular love of mine, tea leaf readings, to catch an image for each of the 12 signs. Sitting with my harper/bard friend Mara Gray, I drank many cups of tea while she transcribed what I saw. From this and a multitude of sky maps, I offer you these navigational aids for your journey 2004.

by Gretchen Lawlor © Mother Tongue Ink 2003

♒	p. 51
♓	p. 63
♈	p. 73
♉	p. 87
♊	p. 99
♋	p. 109
♌	p. 123
♍	p. 135
♎	p. 147
♏	p. 159
♐	p. 171
♑	p. 183

Astro Trends 2004:
Oracular Gems from *We'Moon* Astrologers

In 2004 we shift to a more introspective, protective, potentially more connected time as Saturn and Uranus move together through water signs while Jupiter expands earthy Virgo. It's time to explore the power of family, belonging and the power of our tribe, however we define it.

As 2004 begins, grounding, lesson-filled Saturn is in the early degrees of Cancer—the sign of home, ocean, the Mother. It challenges us to expand our concept of home until it encompasses the globe or we'll see more territorial, self-protective behavior. Saturn is joined in Cancer by two asteroids of healing and nurturance, Hygia and Ceres, who nudge us to heal our relationships with our family of choice or blood and begin to form new networks of family around the globe. Strength comes from remembering we are all family and feeling fiercely protective of our home,

Coatlique
© *Hrana Janto 1995*

this Earth. Redefine, reclaim the concept of homeland security. ⬅

In September 2004, the asteroid Toutatis passes closer to Earth than any other asteroid or comet has for 60 years. Mythologically, Toutatis is an early Celtic variation on Mars who protected the tribe, handicrafts and invention and forces us to look at the question of tribe and security. We may want to nest but we must stay involved in the big nest, rebuilding the whole global community and defusing old lines of tribal warfare.

Expect new political emphasis on family values; lead the redefinition of family. Watch for a potential regressive move back to family values of the 1950's and its gender typing and restriction of reproductive freedom. Continue to redefine family more inclusively, inventively. Work within your bioregion to shape communities by ecosystems, including human and nonhuman members. Reach across international boundaries and create grassroots coalitions around nurturance and support that belie sectarian efforts.

To stay healthy and avoid co-dependence within this global family (something which needs attention in 2004), start with yourself. Think of a crab, the symbol of Cancer. To change shape we need to dissolve some old forms, old skeletons. For this we'll need a flexible shell, a good sense of personal boundaries rather than give into the Cancerian desire to disappear into our shell. Practice self-nurturance. Look to reviving traditions, celebrations, foods and comforts from our own lineages and explore other such paths, finding and sharing strength in all these simple forms of nourishment.

Cancerian issues will bear fruit; reform child welfare agencies, conditions for the elderly, emergency shelters and education. Water will be key. Defend water rights, the rights of water creatures, rights of all beings to have access to healthy water. Feed the homeless. Investigate food: food quality, genetic engineering and food as medicine.

Jupiter in Virgo/Saturn in Cancer could bring cuts in standard medical care, though this can also restore the role of nurturing in healing. Medicine will increasingly emphasize good quality nursing, natural healing and the use of herbs and healthy food to maintain health. This is a great year to grow your garden or expand the organic farm. It is more powerful to work in depth rather than spread yourself thin in either food or projects. "Don't plant more than you have water for," is an old Navajo saying.

With both Saturn and Uranus now firmly in water signs it's time to rebuild emotional connections. A sense of loneliness and desire for deeper intimacy can nudge us out of our safe caves and push us to deeper connection with family, beloveds and with our own souls. Uranus in Pisces brings a new spiritual focus, developing our intuition and need for fantasy and magic.

As Mercury hovers near Pluto at the start of 2004, we reevaluate and may have to cut some losses. Forward motion picks up through February and releases stubborn/entrenched tensions; find something worthy to put your muscle behind; rebuild your community foundations, home, self or line of work. Reorganize power structures as Saturn leaves retrograde and turns direct March 7. Strut your stuff; use the personal authority you've built; portfolio your natural wisdom.

Late March is a turbulent, feisty time—watch our for real misuse of power as Pluto retrogrades and Mars squares Uranus. Fight the good fight! Whether it is your work with Amnesty International, the animal shelter, to save a river, stop a war or conquer your own illusions, ask what calls you to be a conscientious warrior for good cause.

A Solar Eclipse April 19, at 29 degrees Aries (while Mercury retrogrades) could bring mistakes that lock into conflict unless we proceed with love and caution. Work to balance the Aries needs of the individual with the Libran need to be fair to others.

Jupiter sextiles Saturn at the beginning of May and encourages rapport between the Jupiterian principles of expansion and Saturnine contraction, bipartisan cooperation. This is a subtle aspect: it's easy to miss the opportunities unless you go look for them. Tap into your own wisdom and investigate new enterprises.

Pre-dawn June 8, 2004 Venus will move across the face of the Sun (opposed Pluto) a very rare event, visible in Europe, Africa and Asia; a sky altar invoking global peace, compassionate action, energizing our passion, creativity and willingness to fight for what we love.

Early August we deal with power issues; power-over vs. empowerment as Jupiter squares Pluto. Pay attention, be willing to be held accountable and hold others to their responsibilities. Work towards empowerment of the individual and the community; we're ripe to make great progress if we can be patient and get the timing right.

In September the chaotic, inventive Toutanis hurtles through our skies as Jupiter shifts sign into Libra. If there's fear around you, remind people that miracles also happen at such unusual times. Jupiter in Libra brings auspicious alliances, encourages our romantic side and gives a boost to justice and social awareness. Support skyrockets for political action to protest unfair legislations and to balance inequalities.

Jupiter trines Neptune in November and encourages us to free our imagination and free ourselves from addictions, including addiction to fossil fuels. Science and imagination collaborate to envision new possibilities. Artistic and creative inspiration soars. If we choose to listen, new songs emerge and old ones revive to feed hope and nourish our spirits so we can resolve formerly intransigent problems.

by Heather Roan Robbins and Gretchen Lawlor © Mother Tongue Ink 2003

THE YEAR OF THE MONKEY 2004

The year of the Monkey begins on the new moon of January 21, 2004. (Chinese new year begins the second new moon after winter solstice.) Monkey year is a time of power, courage, action, anarchy and true devotion to even the wildest of schemes. Success can be attained in business, politics and real estate. Everyone wants

¤ Ba'ella Bo Conlan 1998

to work the shrewdest angle, get the best deal and win big. Now is the time to start new endeavors, for they are destined to succeed under Monkey's influence. But woe be it to the dull or slow-witted: Monkey will steal all the peanuts and leave nothing but empty shells.

We'moon born in Monkey years (1908, 1920, 1932, 1944, 1956, 1968, 1980, 1992, 2004, 2016, 2028) are ingenious, sharp, alert, extremely talented, entertaining, mercurial and aggressive. Uninhibited, she rarely gets embarrassed by anything. She is free to express herself fearlessly in all areas of life. In addition to mental alertness, Monkey possesses physical stamina and strength. Powerful Monkey gals embody strong leadership potential. She must be the leader because she won't allow anyone else to tell her what to do. Monkey is good with her hands and has skill and dexterity with machines. In short—Monkey can do anything. A Monkey we'moon succeeds by accepting her powerful nature and applying it to achievement in the world.

In relationships, Monkey is generous, sensitive and loves to help others. She can be romantic and playful. Yet she may treat relationships as games and has trouble staying committed for an extended period of time. Impatient Monkey gets bored easily and is constantly looking for excitement, stimulation and new games. She runs hot and cold in relationships and has devised a rigid personalized caste system of judging others. Either you are high on Monkey's list and a valued player, or you're not; either you contribute to Monkey's advancement, or you don't.

Astute Monkey must be aware not to indulge in monkey mind: jump to a branch, peel a banana, take a bite, drop it; jump to the next branch, peel a banana, take a bite, drop it—on and on in a useless cycle. Monkey experiences many flashes of brilliant insight. May she use them wisely and not suffer from monkey-mind tail chasing.

Monkey correlates to the Western sign Leo.

by Susan Levitt © Mother Tongue Ink 2003

INTRODUCTION TO THE THEME: POWER

Power is an on-going theme for **We'Moon**. With the Great Mother in **We'Moon '03**, we highlighted the power of nature; in **We'Moon '04** the focus is on the nature of power. Nature embodies exquisite powers of diversity, balance and interconnection. The interaction of elemental powers—air, fire, water, earth—create, sustain and transform the living planet. Of all Earth's creatures, "Man" is the only one who seeks to rule over nature and who often abuses even his own kind, in public and private realms. When control over others is the only power people know, we are caught up in endless power struggles. The cost, in terms of human and planetary destruction, is enormous. How can we transform patriarchal power over? What alternative forms of power do we use? What ancient/new sources or different cultural models can we draw from? In a world where abuse of power is so prevalent, we look to womyn to redefine, model and practice power in life-affirming ways.

Every year we divine our theme from the stages of spiritual empowerment represented by the Major Arcana in Tarot (based loosely on the card with that year's number). The Great Mother theme ('03) was our version of the Empress (III); the Power theme ('04) is based on

Fire Chant
¤ *Robyn Waters 1996*

the Emperor card (IV). In reclaiming power as a potentially positive force in the world, we stretch to embrace a womyn-inspired rendering of "the Emperor." We re-envision Her as an Empowerer whose strength transcends the polarity of "Emperor" and "Empress." Rather than construe these two energies as male or female, patriarchal vs. matriarchal, we claim both as complementary aspects of a greater power. The Empowerer balances both left and right brain, yin and yang, heart and head, receptive and active, being and doing. We are most in our power when we come from wholeness and create balance from the dynamic tension between polarities.

On the world stage, the "balance" is held by destructive force. During the Cold War, the balance of power was maintained by mutual fear of annihilation with each "Super Power" possessing enough weaponry to destroy life on Earth. Antagonists may shift but new enemies must always be available to hold that equation. Now with only one "Super Power" left, the War of Terror/Anti-Terror takes the balance of destructive powers to a new level. Imperial might puffs itself up to war against elusive, uncontrollable agents of the powerless who wield a formidable new weapon: that fear of death is no deterrent. Polarizations escalate. The real needs of people for sustenance, safety, health are sacrificed to the desperations of Control and the violent reactions it engenders.

The Emperor has no clothes! The people begin to shout and their voices are growing louder around the world. In the middle of putting together this **We'Moon**, we participated in a Peace March in Portland, Oregon, with 25,000 people of all ages and stripes. Although we had no illusions that our protest would reach the inner chambers of the war councils of this nation, we came away from it feeling empowered. Grave as the issues are, people were singing and laughing and dancing in the streets, holding up signs that spoke truth to the official lies with great humor and wisdom. In our world at that moment, the Empowerer held sway and the nakedness of the Emperor's dominion was exposed.

Grave as the issues are, **We'Moon** continues to offer a parade of we'moon celebrating and sharing the vitality of life force, connecting with what empowers us and expressing our humor and wisdom in creative ways. We cannot know what new expressions of a world in trouble may be facing us in the year 2004 when the words and images we select now will appear on these pages. As we introduce the theme, we wave signs that speak truth to the deceptions of the Emperor's rule. Expose the structure of power! Those in power cannot define reality for us! Their self-interests are not ours! Let's stop taking it out on each other! Don't demonize—organize!

Our work to confront and challenge the powers that be is not driven by impulse to ascend to the throne; reversing roles would just perpetuate the same old disempowering pattern. We would rather overturn the patriarchal paradigm of power itself, reaching for empowerment that connects people with one another, balancing individual needs with community spirit and honoring the interconnected web of life. Leadership can be effective, confident, efficient and offer service to the greater good.

In **We'Moon '04**, we name the 12 astrological signs as guiding spirits for the 13 Moon themes. We have placed the art and writing in conscious association with the different doorways to power symbolized by the signs of the zodiac. During the first moons/months of this year, the Sun enters a new sign around the time of the new moon, and that sign is key to our reflections on power; for example, fiery Aries sparks youthful, sometimes rebellious power. Themes in later months feature aspects of two signs, because we honor both solar and lunar cycles and they do not keep a synchronous pace. For example, soon after the Sun and new moon are conjunct in Libra, the Sun moves into Scorpio. Our Libra/Scorpio Moon, then, evokes love and balance, and begins to speak as well of deep sensual mysteries. The dance of Sun and Moon completes a full circle of powerful possibilities through the year.

We are especially delighted to show, this year for the first time, the full power of **We'Moon** art in living color! Sky indigo, ocean blue, fire red, sun yellow, forest green enrich the natural cycles that carry we'moon through the year with the full spectrum of elemental power. Refracting the subject of Power itself through the metaphor of color, we are inspired beyond black and white thinking about the nature of power.

We'moon imagine power in wonderfully varied and nuanced ways with the art and writing in **We'Moon '04**. Some speak directly to the Emperor's realm, the public sphere where enormities of corporate and state power imperil the world. They call for protection of forest and water, for justice toward imprisoned women, for community actions toward world peace. We'moon write of prayer and drum, of everyday gardens and poems, precisely as ways to counter the rapacious machines of greed and war. The simple acts of recycling a paper bag, talking to neighbors, eating a communal meal are steps toward mending the world fabric.

We'Moon '04 gives us stories and images that come from womyn's deep connection to life-force. The power that women can bring to the world is life-affirming, not necessarily because of qualities inherent in femaleness, but because we are socialized in most all cultures toward heart and community. We celebrate that sphere of influence as a site of strong power, where generations of women have presided over life transitions from birth to death, have cooked and quilted, farmed and nursed with strength of muscle, will, humor, devotion.

These pages delight in the power of womyn's body—her curves, her sensual joys, her fertility—as well as her abilities to run races and build houses. She speaks with sassy and determined tones and will not be confined to her traditional realms of influence. She creates brilliant works of art, using voice, hands, imagination with creative authority. Both alone and with others, she opens to the power of Spirit with meditation and ceremony. The empowered woman who speaks in **We'Moon '04** trusts her own inner guidance, regardless of judgments from others. She is her own angel, bruja, muse, genius, priestess, witch.

She sets her sail to catch the fiercesome wind, she rides the great waves. Nature is our power source, our teacher. When we learn to move as one with life-force, we are empowered; we become Empowerers. Pass it on! With this **We'Moon**, we invoke renewal and wholeness. We raise power to send where it is most needed for the healing of Earth and all our relations. **We'Moon** Power. Share it! Spread it around! It's no secret: the more you have, the more you have to give. Blessed Be!

by Musawa and Bethroot Gywnn © Mother Tongue Ink 2003

Kwan Yin
© Molly Sullivan 2002

Calling Down the Power

of the moon

the night

the dakini who dance

creation to chaos

the gopi who dance

the universe into being

mother earth

her dance among the stars

I am

she says

power of volcano

and beast

and storm and love and land

lightning, lamp, bubble, cloud

and girl and woman and man

and all things

living and passing

I am

tidal wave

and orgasm

and delight

and ten million clouds

and ten billion stars

the energy

the center

the dynamo

I am

the push behind

being and begetting

existing and enduring

I am the great axle

on which the stars rotate

come join hands with me now

in this circle now

while the drums play

and may every breath

you breathe

bring you

power

Embrace
© *Deborah Koff-Chapin 1992*

December 2003 ☉☉☉ Intichaw

♏
♐ 🌑

Sunday

21

♏
♐

☽→♐ 12:16 am
☽✳♀ 12:25 am
☽△♂ 4:54 am
☉✳♅ 3:34 pm

☽✳♆ 6:23 pm
♀☍♄ 10:34 pm
☉→♑ 11:04 pm

Lakeville
Circle
Beloved Sarah

Solstice

Sun in Capricorn 11:04 pm PST

The Castle
© Eaglehawk 2000
top left

Waterbirth
© Marleen Grommers 1997
bottom

Steamy Rendez-vous
© Lilian de Mello 2002
top right

MOON I. CAPRICORN

December 23–January 21

New Moon in ♑ Capricorn Dec. 23, Full Moon in ♋ Cancer Jan. 7, Sun in ♒ Aquarius Jan. 20

December

dezember

———))) Montag ———

♐︎
♑︎

Monday

22

☽PrG	3:50 am
☽□♃	5:56 am
☽☌♀	8:18 am
☽⚹♅	11:29 am v/c
☽→♑︎	11:55 pm

——— ♂♂♂ Dienstag ———

♑︎

Tuesday

23

☉☌☽	1:43 am
☽□♂	6:29 am
☽☌☿	2:04 pm
☽☍♄	4:30 pm

Family Return
Hornell

——— ☿☿☿ Mittwoch ———

New Moon in ♑︎ Capricorn 1:43 am PST

♑︎

Wednesday

24

☽△♃	5:52 am v/c

——— ♃♃♃ Donnerstag ———

♑︎
♒︎

Thursday

25

☽→♒︎	12:13 am
♀⚹♂	5:29 am
☽⚹♂	9:07 am
☽☌♀	9:17 am
☽☌♇	7:20 pm

——— ♀♀♀ Freitag ———

♒︎

Friday

26

☿□♂	12:53 am
☽⚹♀	10:18 am
☉☌☿	5:11 pm

Pele
© *Hrana Janto 1992*

≈
♓

Saturday
27

☽☌♅	2:57 am	v/c	☽⚹☿	10:02 am
☽→♓	3:10 am		☉⚹☽	1:16 pm
☿PrG	3:55 am		☽△♄	9:07 pm

Family Return
Sunt...

♓

Sunday
28

☽☍♃	1:11 pm	
☽□♀	4:03 pm	v/c

December/January

Worldwide,
Women wake from
centuries' forced slumber,
Awesome energy stretching
into actions of awareness.

excerpt © Nola Ann Conn 2002

♓
♈

Monday
29

♀⚻♄	12:38 am
☽→♈	10:08 am
☽□♅	12:19 pm
☉□♂	9:55 pm

Family Return Lainey / Milton

ⓞⓞⓞ　martes

♈

Tuesday
30

♅→♓	1:14 am	☽⚹♆	8:36 am
☽ⓞ♂	1:55 am	♀ⓞ♆	9:19 am
☉□☽	2:03 am	☿⚹♅	11:30 am
☽□♄	5:09 am	☿→♐	11:53 am
☽⚹♀	8:31 am		

Family Return Lainey / P-town

Waxing Half Moon in ♈ Aries 2:03 am PST

☿☿☿　miércoles

♈
♉

Wednesday
31

☽△♀	2:00 am
♄PrG	8:37 am
☉☍♄	12:57 pm
☽△☿	6:27 pm	v/c
☽→♉	9:02 pm
☽⚹♅	9:11 pm

P-town

♃♃♃　jueves

♉

Thursday
1

♂□♄	12:22 pm
☽⚹♄	4:34 pm
☉△☽	7:22 pm
☽□♆	8:44 pm

P-town

January 2004

♀♀♀　viernes

♉

Friday
2

| ☽□♀ | 3:28 am |
| ☽△♃ | 11:21 am | v/c |

Return to Milton

Wild Women Protect the Forest
© *Amarah K. Gabriel 1996*

ħħħ sábado

♉
♊

Saturday
3

☽→♊ 9:58 am
☽□♅ 10:21 am
☽ApG 12:21 pm
♃R 3:57 pm

⊙⊙⊙ domingo

♊

Sunday
4

☽⚹♂ 9:14 am
☽△♆ 10:00 am
☽△♀ 11:33 pm

visited V & T

Tea, Scones & Football

S called BR's small car accident

MOON I

January
januari

☽☽☽ maandag

♊ ♋

Monday
5

☽□♃	12:21 am	♀⊼♃	7:09 am	
♂✶♆	1:05 am	☽☍☿	3:14 pm	v/c
☽☍♇	3:53 am	☽→♋	10:38 pm	
♃△⚷	4:47 am	☽△♅	11:14 pm	

♂♂♂ dinsdag

♋

Tuesday
6

☿D 5:44 am
☽☌♄ 5:03 pm
♀✶♇ 6:44 pm

☿☿☿ woensdag

♋

Wednesday
7

☽□♂ 12:33 am
☉☍☽ 7:40 am
☽✶♃ 12:00 pm v/c

Full Moon in ♋ Cancer 7:40 am PST

♃♃♃ donderdag

♋ ♌

Thursday
8

☽→♌ 9:38 am

♀♀♀ vrijdag

♌

Friday
9

☽☍♆ 8:39 am
☉△♃ 10:59 am
☽△♂ 1:39 pm
☉☌⚷ 10:44 pm

Jo-burg Summit

Feminine Solar Power
¤ *Parimal Danielle Tonossi 2002*

There was a lot of talking at the World Summit on Sustainable Development in Johannesburg. We listened, we spoke, we wondered . . . what has the human species done to its habitat? In Soweto, we gave our minds a rest and let our hearts feel. Inside magical Khayalendaba village, created by Zulu traditional healer, Vusamazulu Credo Mutwa, Nomkhubulwane, the all-powerful female goddess, Mother of All, spoke to us. She said, "Do not wait for the 'big' guys to agree on the path the world should take . . . keep up the real work at the grassroots, from the heart of the earth, because I see what you are doing, and, together, we will heal this earth."

¤ *Tanya Pergola 2002*

ħħħ zaterdag

♌
♍  Saturday
10

☽△♀ 1:25 am
☽☍♀ 9:31 am
☽△♅ 2:00 pm v/c
☽→♍ 6:37 pm
☽☍♅ 7:35 pm

☉☉☉ zondag

♍ Sunday
11

☽✳ħ 11:06 am

*Anne K's Ph.D. Party
3-5 Parents in
Cambridge*

January
Qhapaqintiraymi Killa

Power has been
asphyxiated by CONTROL!
POWER lies within each being.
It is always there.
excerpt ¤ Debráe Firehawk

───))) Killachaw ───

♍ Monday
12

☽☌♃	5:18 am
☽□♀	9:10 am
☉△☽	10:59 am

─── ♂♂♂ Atichaw ───

♍
♎ Tuesday
13

☽□♅	12:01 am	v/c
☽→♎	1:38 am	
☽□♄	5:11 pm	
☽△♆	11:20 pm	

─── ☿☿☿ Quyllurchaw ───

♎ Wednesday
14

☿→♑	3:02 am	
☽☍♂	8:56 am	
♀→♓	9:16 am	
☽⚹♀	2:52 pm	
☉□☽	8:46 pm	v/c
☿⚹♅	10:53 pm	
♀☌♅	11:23 pm	

Waning Half Moon in ♎ Libra 8:46 pm PST

─── ♃♃♃ Illapachaw ───

♎
♏ Thursday
15

☿⚹♀	12:41 am
☽→♏	6:33 am
☽△♅	7:48 am
☽⚹♅	8:24 am
☽△♀	8:35 am
☽△♄	9:10 pm

─── ♀♀♀ Ch'askachaw ───

♏ Friday
16

♂⚻♃	1:56 am
☽□♆	3:29 am
☽⚹♃	2:18 pm

P purpose, protests, pressure, persist, peace, prevail, proud, paradigm-shift

O owning, onus, orders, organize, outraged, overcome, on-demand, openings, OM

W willful, wishes, words, witchcraft, wisdom, warriors, watchful, we-mean-it, Womyn

E energy, effects, everywhere, eternal, experience, equality, exalted, ecology

R ready, raging, rectify, recall, recourse, relentless, rhythm, rainbow

© Nola Ann Conn 2002

ʰʰʰ K'uychichaw

♏ ⚹
♐

Saturday
17

♄ApG	2:29 am	
☉⚹☽	3:48 am	v/c
☽→♐	9:18 am	
☽□♅	10:41 am	
☽□♀	3:53 pm	

⊙⊙⊙ Intichaw

♐

Sunday
18

☽⚹♆	5:35 am	
♂□♄	11:26 am	
☽□♃	3:46 pm	
☽△♂	6:42 pm	
☽☌♀	7:58 pm	v/c

To My Daughters

I'll tell you about power:
We are born with the potential
for every daughter we will ever have
embedded like pearls in the dark flesh of our ovaries.
You were already there, in me,
while I was yet curled within my mother, as she was,
inside my great-grandmother;
each mother birthing her grandchildren, through her pelvis,
ivory cradles protecting secret worlds within our own seas,
worlds of fierce hearts and minds beyond knowing.
Is there a greater power than holding the entire
universe in your belly?
All of Creation? What about our own galaxies pouring forth?
The summoning of all that is love
and alive into our very breasts, our marrow,
our coursing blood, a luminous milky way
so bright it blinds, with all the power and force of life,
heaven meeting earth, giving to those worlds we hold,
that we see in the irises of our daughters' eyes.

MOON II. AQUARIUS
January 21–February 20
New Moon in ♒ Aquarius Jan. 21, Full Moon in ♌ Leo Feb. 6, Sun in ♓ Pisces Feb. 18

Finding Our Way Through the Dark
© Molly Sullivan 2002

January
enero

♐
♑
Monday
19

☽→♑	10:24 am	
☽PrG	11:33 am	
☽⚹♅	11:56 am	
☽♂♉	7:36 pm	
☽⚹♀	9:14 pm	
☽☍♄	11:43 pm	

Bur Oak Acorn
© Lorena Babcock Moore 1996

♑
Tuesday
20

♂△♀	2:02 am	
☉→♒	9:42 am	
☽△♃	4:19 pm	
☽□♂	9:34 pm	v/c

Sun in Aquarius 9:42 am PST

♑
♒
Wednesday
21

♀△♄	2:04 am	
☽→♒	11:11 am	
☉♂☽	1:05 pm	
☿☍♄	8:59 pm	

Lunar Imbolc
New Moon in ♒ Aquarius 1:05 pm PST

♒
Thursday
22

☽♂♆	7:46 am	
☽⚹♀	10:32 pm	

♒
♓
Friday
23

Jackie's B-Day

☽⚹♂	1:33 am	v/c
☽→♓	1:29 pm	
☽♂♅	3:28 pm	

Year at a Glance for ≈ AQUARIUS (Jan. 20–Feb. 18)

The Aquarian image for 2004 is "a figure contemplating a wildly spinning orb in her lap." Over the last seven years the structures upon which you have depended have changed unexpectedly and repeatedly, altering you down to the cellular level. You cannot ignore the fact that you have a physical body. You are not just a whirling collection of sparkling possibilities and you need stillness to let your physical body align with your transformed energy body. Your bones and muscle groups require adjustment and mineral replenishment now in order to be good support for a more active 2005. Destructive habits are easily released this year, assisted by the skills of a good healer, counselor or coach. Fasting and detoxing will loosen the hold of habitual, mechanical responses and ready you for new inspirations coming later in the year.

Follow internal and external messages of a repetitive nature, i.e. the ones that come up over and over. Ignore occasional wishful thinking, if they are good impulses their frequency will increase. Search out situations where your originality is an asset. Apprentice yourself to geniuses in your field; they will be generous in passing on their secrets. Spend time in those settings, even if as a volunteer for now. You'll benefit from an unexpected vacancy if you're there on the spot.

Focus upon learning to show up, to work with an economy of effort and get out swiftly. This frees up time to return to stillness and sitting, an activity of primary importance in helping you to integrate the forms of the past with the visions of of the future.

by Gretchen Lawlor © Mother Tongue Ink 2003

The Water Bearers
© Durga Bernhard 2001

ħħħ   sábado

ℋ ● **Saturday**
24

☾△♄	3:15 am
☾⚹☿	8:58 am
☾♂♀	10:48 am
☾☍♃	9:30 pm

☉☉☉   domingo

ℋ ●
♈   **Sunday**
25

| ☾□♀ | 3:09 am | v/c |
| ☾→♈ | 7:06 pm | |

January/February

januari/februari ☽☽☽ maandag

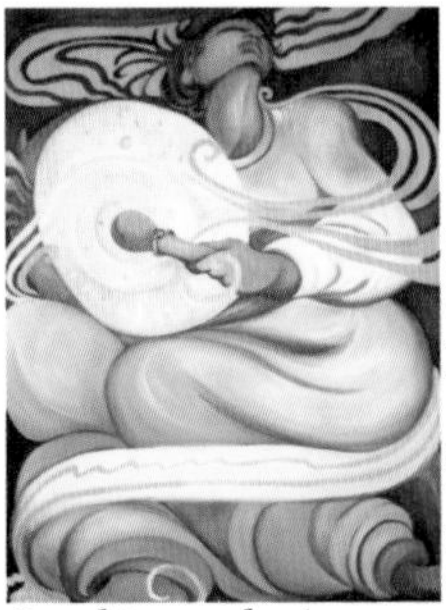

© Toni Truesdale 2000

Speaking to the Ancestors

♈

Monday
26

☉✶☽ 6:14 am
☽□♄ 9:38 am
☽✶♆ 6:54 pm
☽□☿ 10:29 pm

♂♂♂ dinsdag

♈

Tuesday
27

☽△♀ 11:49 am
☽☌♂ 8:59 pm v/c
☉⊼♄ 10:25 pm

☿☿☿ woensdag

♈
♉

Wednesday
28

☽→♉ 4:46 am
☽✶♅ 7:33 am
☽✶♄ 7:56 pm
☉□☽ 10:03 pm

Waxing Half Moon in ♉ Taurus 10:03 pm PST

♃♃♃ donderdag

♉

Thursday
29

♀☍♃ 4:01 am
☽□♆ 6:14 am
☿△♃ 10:09 am
☽△♃ 4:34 pm
☽△☿ 5:27 pm
☽✶♀ 6:04 pm v/c

♀♀♀ vrijdag

♉
♊

Friday
30

☽→♊ 5:18 pm
☽□♅ 8:27 pm

All aspects in Pacific Standard Time; add 3 hours for EST; add 8 hours for GMT

The GrandMother Drum Project

The GrandMother Drum, a seven foot diameter, kettle shaped drum was born at 4:00 am on June 5, 2001, after thirteen years of prayer, ceremony and physical labor by the Alaskan community.

© Barbara Shugg 2001

Grandmother Drum

The vision of the GrandMother Drum was received from indigenous Grandmothers as the first international, multicultural, interactive "world drum" dedicated to promoting Unity, Peace and Life, healing the separation between all Earth's children. According to many traditional prophecies, "when the grandmothers begin to speak, the earth will heal."

According to these Grandmothers, we are in conflict outside because we are in conflict inside. Healing, they say, must happen within ourselves first. World peace can happen only through inner peace, becoming that which we are seeking outside ourselves. The GrandMother Drum is a living, beating symbol from the hearts of the grandmothers that we are all one people, that Mother Earth is our one country, that love is stronger than fear and that peace and freedom are the birthrights of all humanity.

excerpt ¤ Suraj Holzwarth 2002

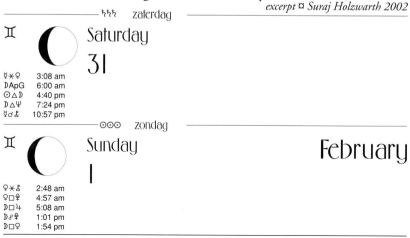

ካካካ zaterdag

♊ Saturday
31

☿⚹♀	3:08 am
☽ApG	6:00 am
☉△☽	4:40 pm
☽△♆	7:24 pm
☿♂♄	10:57 pm

☉☉☉ zondag

♊ Sunday
1

February

♀⚹♄	2:48 am
♀□♀	4:57 am
☽□♃	5:08 am
☽☍♀	1:01 pm
☽□♀	1:54 pm

February
Qhaqmiy Killa

♊
♋

Monday
2

☉☌♆ 1:29 am
☽✳♂ 4:56 am   v/c
☽→♋ 6:03 am
☽△♅ 9:25 am
♆ApG 10:49 am
☽☌♄ 8:35 pm

Imbolc/Candlemas

♂♂♂   Atichaw

♋

Tuesday
3

♂→♉ 2:04 am
☽✳♃ 4:28 pm

☿☿☿   Quyllurchaw

♋
♌

Wednesday
4

☽△♀ 7:39 am
☽☍♅ 9:53 am   v/c
☽→♌ 4:50 pm
☽□♂ 6:54 pm

♃♃♃   Illapachaw

♌

Thursday
5

☽☍♆ 5:30 pm

♀♀♀   Ch'askachaw

♌

Friday
6

☉☍☽ 12:47 am
♂✳♅ 1:22 am
☉⊼♃ 6:54 am
☽△♀ 9:38 am   v/c
☿→♒ 8:20 pm

Full Moon in ♌ Leo 12:47 am PST

ALL ASPECTS IN PACIFIC STANDARD TIME; ADD 3 HOURS FOR EST; ADD 8 HOURS FOR GMT

Scrying the World
© Diane Porter Goff 1999

Imbolc

Imbolc arrives with the first hints of spring. Also called Candlemas, Imbolc honors quickening life force as winter gives way and days slowly lengthen. Celebrated in Britain as the feast day of St Brigid, Imbolc is associated with her qualities as the triple patron of healing, poetry and smithcraft. What is curled and silent begins to unfurl; what is still begins to stir. Like flame in a rising wind, energies spark and sway.

Build on the healing power of Brigid's day by calling forth gifts that lay dormant in those beings dear to you. Place the names of your beloveds in a special container and draw one name at a time to be the recipient of an invocation to quickening. Light a candle, chant the name and imagine the potential of this greening soul as an unstoppable force, enriching the entire universe with unique talents and strengths. In circle or solo, throughout the day of Imbolc or every day from new moon to full, call forth the best and brightest in each other. Good will and sympathetic joy are as real as the sap singing in the trees and as potent.

by Jessica Montgomery © Mother Tongue Ink 2003

One
by one,
in tiny
increments,
candle
by candle,
gesture
by effort,
wish
by prayer,
concern
by care,
we feed
the life-fires
of the soul
and light
the infinite
universe,
little
by little
from within.

¤ *Donna Henes 2002*

Inner Power
© *Holli Zollinger 2002*

some steps

First, redefine the word power.
Delete all negative associations.
True power is not our government,
nor the illusionary corporate web
but something entirely ours.
We can access our own power
of positive creation with a subtle
connection between sight and insight.

Second, find a blend that works
right now, do it and let it go.
Keep the inside and the outside
connected and stay open.
Soon you will find yourself
in the company of others
with whom you can build community.
Keep dreaming and talking to your neighbors.
This is where you will find true power.

¤ *J. Davis Wilson 2002*

───────────── ʰʰʰ K'uychichaw ─────────────

♌
♍

Saturday
7

☽→♍ 1:03 am
☽☌♅ 4:37 am
☽△♂ 5:53 am
☽⚹♄ 1:55 pm

───────────── ☉☉☉ Intichaw ─────────────

♍

Sunday
8

☽☌♃ 7:51 am
♀→♈ 8:20 am
☽□♀ 4:23 pm   v/c

February

Februar

♍︎
♎︎

Monday
9

)→♎︎ 7:12 am
)☍♀ 9:24 am
☿□♂ 1:08 pm
)△☿ 2:41 pm
)□♄ 7:30 pm

♎︎

Tuesday
10

)△♆ 6:32 am
☉⚹♀ 7:56 pm
)⚹♀ 9:35 pm
☉△) 9:42 pm v/c

♎︎
♏︎

Wednesday
11

☿⚼♄ 7:40 am
)→♏︎ 11:58 am
)△♅ 3:47 pm
)☍♂ 9:42 pm
)△♄ 11:49 pm

♏︎

Thursday
12

)□♅ 1:56 am
)□♆ 10:55 am
)⚹♃ 4:27 pm

♏︎
♐︎

Friday
13

☉□) 5:39 am v/c
)→♐︎ 3:35 pm
♂⚹♄ 4:50 pm
)□♅ 7:33 pm

Waning Half Moon in ♏︎ Scorpio 5:39 am PST

ALL ASPECTS IN PACIFIC STANDARD TIME; ADD 3 HOURS FOR EST; ADD 8 HOURS FOR GMT

Walking with You

Tonight as I walk
Past the moon in the dark
I realize I'm walking with you.
With millions of long walking women
With silvery, moon walking women
With willowy, lake walking women
With you.
I know as I lose all sight of myself
And I smile and I spy on the world,
I am safe in the steps of my infinite walk
As the long line of women unfurls.
I shudder in mists and in dusks at the lake
But I'm strong in this line with you
I wait and I watch and I wish in the dark
But I'm sure that I feel all of you.
As we walk on our own, in our boots and spare time
In our feet and our moods and our need
Remember the line
And how far it winds
Walk in strength
Past the moon
Walk as we.
I thank you for walking with me.

© Sioux Patullo 2001

ħħħ   Samstag

♐

Saturday
14

♀□ħ	1:58 am
☽△♀	3:08 am
☽⚹☿	11:46 am
☽⚹Ψ	2:12 pm
☽□♃	7:06 pm

☉☉☉   Sonntag

♐
♑

Sunday
15

☽☌♀	4:32 am		☽→♑	6:14 pm
☿☌Ψ	9:43 am		☽⚹♅	10:20 pm
☉⚹☽	12:20 pm	v/c	☽PrG	11:39 pm

I am my own angel

I am my own angel.
No flutter of wings
but something within
directs my steps,
turns me away from harm,
gives me dreams,
works while I sleep,
like the elves in the fairy tale
who did the shoemaker's work
overnight,
like the magical assistants
who dig up the gold of consciousness
under the hearth,
or who warn of danger.

I am my own fairy godmother
who appears in moments of crisis,
who comforts my tears,
& finds the right clothes
for me to wear to the ball
or a poetry reading.

I am my own wizard,
conjuring deeds from intentions,
poems from words,
flowers from seeds.

¤ *Karen Ethelsdattar 2002*

MOON III. PISCES
February 20–March 20
New Moon in ♓ Pisces Feb. 20, Full Moon in ♍ Virgo March 6, Sun in ♈ Aries March 19

What I Seek, Now Seeks Me
© *Catherine Holmes 2001*

February
febrero

♑

Monday
16

♄   5:23 am
△♂   8:23 am
□♀   10:05 am
△♃   9:00 pm   v/c

power haiku 4
Subtle power, doze
dream of a healthy planet
wakes me to action.
   ¤ *J. Davis Wilson 2002*

♑
♒

Tuesday
17

☿⊼♃   12:00 am
☽→♒   8:27 pm

♒

Wednesday
18

☽□♂   1:02 pm
☽✶♀   4:53 pm
☽☌♆   7:12 pm
☉→♓   11:50 pm

♓

Sun in Pisces 11:50 pm PST

♒
♓

Thursday
19

☽☌☿   5:45 am
☽✶♀   9:34 am   v/c
♀✶♆   10:09 pm
☽→♓   11:27 pm

♓

Friday
20

☉☌☽   1:18 am
☽☌♅   4:07 am
☽△♄   10:47 am
☿✶♀   1:42 pm
☽✶♂   7:10 pm

New Moon in ♓ Pisces 1:18 am PST

ALL ASPECTS IN PACIFIC STANDARD TIME; ADD 3 HOURS FOR EST; ADD 8 HOURS FOR GMT

Year at a Glance for ♓ PISCES (Feb. 18–March 20)

Change is upon you Pisces, as Uranus, agent of awakening and the unexpected has just committed to its journeys through your sign until 2011. Periods of restlessness and dissatisfaction will alternate with moments of inspired originality. 2004 will contain moments of pure brilliance, sparked by new ways of presenting yourself to the world. Pace yourself, you need plenty of time and opportunity to experiment in this process of reinventing yourself.

The image for Pisces 2004 is "the warrior of faith, ready to confront a dark, shadow image, a ghost from your past or your dreams who holds an old power over you." You will not have to confront this alone, and in fact would miss out on extraordinary opportunity if you isolate yourself. Someone will offer to help you to safely, skillfully and courageously confront and close on the past: a therapist, lawyer, business partner, even a romantic companion. Through this work, power, vitality and creativity is restored. You will be more available to live well, for something much deeper—either artistically or romantically—to emerge. 2004 is a year for collaborations, an unexpected fortunate alliance benefiting both parties. Existing relationships will either expand to allow for your changing self or end amicably.

In the next seven years Pisces will be working more and more with the collective terrors we are all encountering in our dreams and imaginations. You are the dream healer, capable of releasing the collective mind from old enslavements. Use your healing gifts in oblique ways, both releasing the past and inspiring the future through music, dance, movement, art, meditation or prayer.

by Gretchen Lawlor © Mother Tongue Ink 2003

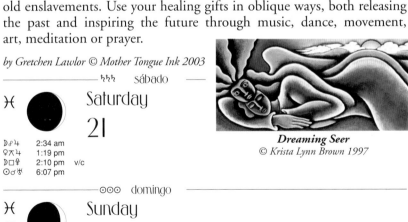

Dreaming Seer
© Krista Lynn Brown 1997

ħħħ   sábado

♓ ● Saturday
21

☽☍♃	2:34 am
♀⊼♃	1:19 pm
☽□♀	2:10 pm v/c
☉♂♅	6:07 pm

☉☉☉   domingo

♓ ● Sunday
♈ 22

☽→♈	4:45 am
☽□♄	4:40 pm
♅ApG	5:26 pm

February
februari

The Muse Listening
The Muse is listening for
a silence she can erupt through.
An emptied mirror
she can reflect in.
excerpt © Lorraine Schein 2002

ⅅⅅⅅ   maandag

♈

Monday
23

☽✶♆   6:08 am
☽☌♀   1:53 pm
☽△☿   10:02 pm

♂♂♂   dinsdag

♈
♉

Tuesday
24

☽✶☿   10:55 am   v/c
☽→♉   1:30 pm
♂□♆   1:32 pm
☽✶♅   7:18 pm

☿☿☿   woensdag

♉

Wednesday
25

☉✶☽   1:30 am   ☿ApG 10:46 am
☽✶♄   2:04 am   ☽□♆   4:39 pm
☿→♓   4:58 am   ☽☌♂   6:05 pm
☉△♄   8:15 am   ☽△♃   6:55 pm   v/c

♃♃♃   donderdag

♉

Thursday
26

♂△♃   7:12 am
☿☌♅   10:21 am

♀♀♀   vrijdag

♉
♊

Friday
27

☽→♊   1:22 am
☽□♅   7:40 am
♀△♀   8:34 am
☽□♉   9:18 am
☉□☽   7:24 pm

Waxing Half Moon in ♊ Gemini 7:24 pm PST

ALL ASPECTS IN PACIFIC STANDARD TIME; ADD 3 HOURS FOR EST; ADD 8 HOURS FOR GMT

Prairie Lilith

© Carol Wylie 2002

—— ♄♄♄ zaterdag ——

♊ **Saturday**
28

☽ApG	2:43 am	☿△♄	5:23 pm
☽△♅	5:29 am	♀□♇	6:53 pm
☽□♃	6:57 am	☽☌♀	10:13 pm

—— ☉☉☉ zondag ——

♊
♋ **Sunday**
29

☽⚹♀	2:08 am	v/c
☽→♋	2:12 pm	
☽△♅	8:44 pm	

March

Jatunpuquy killa

-----))) Killachaw -----

Monday
1

☽☌♄	2:52 am
☽△☿	8:58 am
☉△☽	1:27 pm
☽⚹♃	6:35 pm

----- ♂♂♂ Atichaw -----

Tuesday
2

| ☽⚹♂ | 1:45 am |
| ☽□♀ | 7:42 pm | v/c |

----- ☿☿☿ Quyllurchaw -----

Wednesday
3

☽→♌	1:18 am
♃⚼♆	4:12 pm
☉☌☿	5:43 pm
☿☍♃	7:36 pm
☉☍♃	9:05 pm

----- ♃♃♃ Illapachaw -----

Thursday
4

♃PrG	1:16 am
☽☍♆	3:50 am
☽□♂	2:02 pm
☽△♀	6:56 pm

----- ♀♀♀ Ch'askachaw -----

Friday
5

☽△♀	9:13 am	v/c
☽→♍	9:18 am
♀→♉	10:12 am
☽☍♅	3:40 pm
☽⚹♄	8:39 pm

ALL ASPECTS IN PACIFIC STANDARD TIME; ADD 3 HOURS FOR EST; ADD 8 HOURS FOR GMT

Dandelions

I believed they made wishes
come true
even for me
even for my neighborhood
I searched alone
because no one believed
in my front yard fantasies
among street sounds
barking dogs
and arguing neighbors
I pulled them up
closed my eyes tight
and I blew and blew
and the dandelions
traveled in the air
on ghetto notes
and floated between
rented houses
and hanging clothes
peeling bill boards
and buildings

Blue Jean Faerie
¤ *Trenah 2002*

because I blew and I believed
No, these dandelion's seeds
never touched the ground
they stuck to the wings of sparrows
and floated into space among the stars
because I blew and I believed
I blew and I believed
I knew my wishes would come
because I was taught to dream.

¤ *Jackie Joice 1998*

ᚻᚻᚻ K'uychichaw

♍ ( ) Saturday

6

D☌♃ 9:46 am
☉☍D 3:14 pm
D☍♅ 8:41 pm
D△♂ 10:47 pm

Full Moon in ♍ Virgo 3:14 pm PST

☉☉☉ Intichaw

♍ ( ) Sunday
♎

7

D□♀ 12:49 am v/c
♄D 8:51 am
D→♎ 2:31 pm
☿⚹♂ 5:41 pm

March
März

Rainy Season Power
Rain is rocking me.
Rain is washing my thoughts.
Rain is endless.
There's nothing I must do.
excerpt ¤ Sue Silvermarie 2002

☽☽☽ Montag

♎

Monday
8

☽□♄ 1:25 am
☿□♀ 1:52 am
☽△♆ 2:58 pm
♀⚹♅ 6:37 pm
♂⚻♀ 6:46 pm

♂♂♂ Dienstag

♎ ♏

Tuesday
9

☿⚹⚷ 4:17 am
☽⚹♀ 4:43 am v/c
☽→♏ 6:03 pm

☿☿☿ Mittwoch

♏

Wednesday
10

☽△♅ 12:28 am
☽☍♀ 2:50 am
☽△♄ 4:45 am
☽⚹♃ 4:16 pm
☽□♆ 6:13 pm

♃♃♃ Donnerstag

♏ ♐

Thursday
11

♀⚹♄ 3:44 am
☉△☽ 6:17 am
☽☍♂ 10:35 am
☽PrG 7:56 pm
☽△☿ 8:11 pm v/c
☽→♐ 8:57 pm

♀♀♀ Freitag

♐

Friday
12

☿→♈ 1:44 am
☉□♀ 2:57 am
☽□♅ 3:32 am
♂△⚷ 10:41 am
☽□♃ 6:40 pm
☽⚹♆ 9:10 pm

The Well of Remembrance

Come to the Well of Remembrance.
Here have women sacrificed the memories that overflow
In both mourning and joy
In all times and places.

Now it is your turn to pour into it your libations—
A grandmother's feathery hair
A daughter's pink-painted toenails
Fierce years of labor wasted and
Angry seconds of agony pain.
The Well is constructed of millennia of
Hands held around sacred groves, quilting bees,
birthing stools, and teal Formica kitchen tables.
It can hold all you offer to it.

Now it is your turn to take from it what you need—
All the water that has flowed from women's
Eyes, mouths, wombs
Has saturated to the earth's bones,
Has seethed next to our planet's molten core,
Has evaporated and risen then fallen again into
Your cupped hands as cool rain.
Taste one tear from each of your ancestresses.
It is their wish that you drink deeply and
be as mighty as all their memories
distilled into one swallow.

¤ *Carolyn Lee Boyd 2002*

──────── ♄♄♄ Samstag ────────

♐
♑

Saturday
13

☽☌♀	10:37 am	
☉□☽	1:01 pm	v/c
☽→♑	11:51 pm	

──────── ☉☉☉ Sonntag ────────

Waning Half Moon in ♐ Sagittarius 1:01 pm PST

♑

Sunday
14

☽⚹♅	6:41 am	☉⚹♇	1:55 pm
☽□♅	7:17 am	☽△♀	5:08 pm
☽☍♄	10:39 am	☽△♃	9:14 pm

Bruja

Yo soy una Bruja de la ciudad. I am an urban witch. I did not grow up as my sisters of the mountains, forests and jungles; communing with earth's wilderness, nature and wildlife. I grew up around the hard, dry desperate, thirsty patches of earth that are the crossroads of Hecate. I grew up in rush hour traffic on the intricately woven matrix of freeway after freeway, a dizzying web spun out of control of even Grandma Spider Herself. My childhood playgrounds were hot black molten asphalt erupting with the mysteries of Pele in the heat of July in Los Angeles, the city of lost angels. Even as a very little niña, as far back as I can remember I knew I was a brujita. I felt the vibrations of magic in the things around me. In my head I understood the world as allegory, mythology. The parables I heard in church, temple, synagogue, bedtime stories. I saw everything as mythical, signs, symbols, real, very real; yet curiously unconfirmed by a cynical world I refused to join. A world I sometimes feel lost in as a grown Bruja. A mostly unacknowledged Priestess, I create my own world. My inner reality, a world where all is Sacred. I am Sacred. A world where the beauty in Spirit is worshipped, the Body and Breath Divine. Touch is a sacred healing ritual and a symphony of the voices of the unacknowledged are heard all the way up to the Heavens. In such a world there is no room for fear or shame. When I go out into the world as a Woman Warrior, a Bruja, I hold this inner world in my breast, my armour, my shield against a world at war against itself. My inner knowledge is my survival, my protection against the world's ability to render me nearly invisible and silent. I believe in this inner world. I believe in myself. I believe in creating sacred space for it in the outer world. I believe this is the basis for Revolution. Hermanas, Rise up and believe in the power of your own magic!

¤ *Celestina Pearl 2002*

MOON IV. ARIES

March 20–April 19

Sun in ♈ Aries March 19, New Moon in ♈ Aries March 20, Full Moon in ♎ Libra April 5

Oya

© *Hrana Janto 1992*

March
maart

Monday
15

☿□♄	7:57 am	
☉✶☽	8:08 pm	
☽△♂	9:34 pm	v/c

♈
♒

Tuesday
16

☽→♒	3:10 am	
♀△♃	6:00 pm	
☽✶☿	6:56 pm	

♒

Wednesday
17

☽□♀	1:00 am	
☽♂♆	4:08 am	
☽✶♀	5:46 pm	

♒
♓

Thursday
18

☉✶♂	1:47 am	
☽□♂	4:15 am	v/c
☽→♓	7:26 am	
☿☌♃	9:31 am	
☽♂♅	2:56 pm	
☽△♄	6:47 pm	
♀□♆	7:02 pm	

♓

Friday
19

☽☍♃	4:48 am	
☽✶♀	10:26 am	
☿✶♆	5:22 pm	
☉→♈	10:49 pm	
☽□♀	11:17 pm	

Equinox

♈

Sun in Aries 10:49 pm PST

ALL ASPECTS IN PACIFIC STANDARD TIME; ADD 3 HOURS FOR EST; ADD 8 HOURS FOR GMT

Year at a Glance for ♈ ARIES (March 20–April 20)

The image received for Aries 2004 is "a very tall figure bowing from the waist being guided by a smaller figure nestled at the larger's belly." Hold yourself in check, you have a sense of something important coming through you, an inspiration whose time has not quite come. A deeper core self has needs which must be considered first. Develop a stable home for yourself. Identify your deepest wishes and desires regarding where do you belong? Where can you feel safe and secure? How could your home be a more healthy and supportive base of operations for you? Your core self responds best to images rather than words—make a collage of your dreams and longings. Display it as a constant reminder of essential considerations.

Progressive visions need modest starts. Consider all developments as they impact your personal life. This is a good year to fine-tune a project or dream to make it really work well. Keep projects simple or close to home; lay good foundations from which they can expand in their right time. Both physical and emotional healing work are particularly effective this year, clearing habits and attitudes established in your early years, replacing them with simple affirming routines and attitudes that are likely to take hold and endure.

September onwards there will be invitations to collaborate— mutually beneficial alliances that unleash possibilities you could not manifest alone. A project or alliance which starts in 2004 is likely to remain in your life for a long time—make sure it's something/someone that will ultimately make your world bigger, not smaller.

by Gretchen Lawlor © Mother Tongue Ink 2003

© *Lynn Dewart 2000*

New Moon in ♈ Aries 2:41 pm PST

───────── ♄♄♄　zaterdag ─────────

♓
♈
Saturday
20

☽⚹♂	12:57 pm	v/c
☽→♈	1:29 pm	
☉♂☽	2:41 pm	
♂→♊	11:39 pm	

───────── ☉☉☉　zondag ─────────

♈
Sunday
21

☽□♄	1:26 am
☽⚹♆	4:37 pm
☽♂♉	11:49 pm

Sneaky Spring

Spring sneaked up
    and grabbed me once again!
All winter:
    dark days, wakeful nights, weary and confused,
I planned an early move—
    escape myself and all that mired me to my misery;
Then a golden daffodil popped the ground
    and flaunted herself at my fears,
Joined forces with a spiderwort
    that bared her violet beauty right before my eyes!
Have they no shame?
    tempting me to stay, taunting me to take a trowel
    and puncture the planet, poke seed into soil
        and reconnect with hope?
Sneaky spring!
    foiling all my efforts to run from unreality—
Offering instead, in showy silence, a timeless birth canal—
And passageway to peace.

© Elsie Williams 1998

Spring Equinox

Equinox (equal night) marks a point of dynamic balance as dark and light synchronize along the path of the Sun. From Spring Equinox onward, day overtakes night. Imagine the relief the warming of the land would bring without artificial heat and light. Once upon a time, our ancestors called forth the living goddess as a matter of life and death. Celebrate the power of the living goddess with a joyful procession to your local wilderness. Build an altar from what is at hand: stone, feather, woven branch, stump, stoop, glittering glass. Even in cities, elementals dance ceaselessly. Surely, lamppost remembers the mountain and sidewalk remembers the sea—nothing is separate from her mystery. Take turns invoking the living goddess one sense at a time: see her, smell her, taste her, hear her, feel her. When her presence is undeniable, tell the dark and light stories of the year: twilight tales of winter passed and bright prophesies of the soon-to-be. Stand in balance, brimming with contradictions, embodied and volatile. Call forth the living goddess as if she matters, bringing her spark into every cell, every act, every hope. Close with gratitude, leaving the altar as a sign of sanctification and readiness for the growing season.

by Jessica Montgomery © Mother Tongue Ink 2003

Mother Nature at the Age of Three

¤ *Robyn Waters 1993*

March
Jatunpuquy killa

— ☽☽☽ Killachaw —

♈
♉

Monday
22

☽△♀ 7:14 am   v/c
☽→♉ 10:10 pm

— ♂♂♂ Atichaw —

♉

Tuesday
23

☽⚹♅ 6:53 am
☽⚹♄ 10:52 am
☽△♃ 8:35 pm

— ☿☿☿ Quyllurchaw —

♉

Wednesday
24

☽□♆ 2:49 am
♀R 7:09 am
☿△♀ 12:41 pm
☽☌♀ 2:29 pm   v/c

— ♃♃♃ Illapachaw —

♉
♊

Thursday
25

☽→♊ 9:35 am
☽☌♂ 3:36 pm
☽□♅ 6:54 pm
☉⚹☽ 9:29 pm

— ♀♀♀ Ch'askachaw —

♊
Friday
26

☽□♃ 8:14 am
♀⚻♀ 8:19 am
☉□♄ 3:15 pm
☽△♆ 3:19 pm
☿□♇ 7:52 pm
☽ApG 10:57 pm

ALL ASPECTS IN PACIFIC STANDARD TIME; ADD 3 HOURS FOR EST; ADD 8 HOURS FOR GMT

Riding Trixie

She's a barely tamed beast; 1200 sexy cc's of screaming red roadrocket, sleek lines, throaty pipes, 140 horses of surging arm straightening speed on two wheels.

I mount her with due respect. She can be unforgiving if I'm complacent. Attentive, my slight adjustments control her direction; we move as one.

On a sultry July night, I jet eastward, wearing boots, tight jeans and a clinging red top that show the curve of my breasts, my back tattoo and my thick black braid sweeping across it.

Toward the rising yellow moon, I sing songs to the grandmother inside my helmet, my mirrors reflecting the pink, lavender and blue-gray tones of the setting sun.

I am alert, fully alive and filled with an emotion that unites strength, freedom and pure bliss. I smell hay fields and blackberries. Warm wind rushes at me, bathing me in the earth's breath.

People respond to my energy and are drawn to look. I smile back at them all. I wave to children in backseats of sedans. I wave at hooting young boys flashing hand gestures.

When young women look, I hope they see in me that there are no limits, only those we make ourselves. Women who take risks can reap great rewards, we can fly, in and out of our dreams.

excerpt ¤ K. Marie Bender 2002

———————————— ꛬꛬꛬ K'uychichaw ————————————

♊
♋

Saturday
27

☽☌♀	6:40 am	
☽⚹♅	2:44 pm	v/c
☽→♋	10:23 pm	

———————————— ⊙⊙⊙ Intichaw ————————————

♋

Sunday
28

☽△♅	7:59 am
♂□♅	9:40 am
☽☌♄	11:55 am
⊙□☽	3:48 pm
☽⚹♃	8:25 pm

Waxing Half Moon in ♋ Cancer 3:48 pm PST

March/April

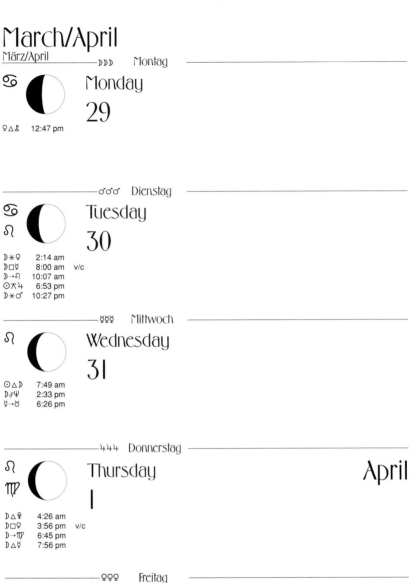

⟂⟂⟂ Montag

♋

Monday
29

♀△♄ 12:47 pm

σσσ Dienstag

♋
♌

Tuesday
30

☽⚹♀ 2:14 am
☽□☿ 8:00 am v/c
☽→♌ 10:07 am
☉⊼♃ 6:53 pm
☽⚹♂ 10:27 pm

☿☿☿ Mittwoch

♌

Wednesday
31

☉△☽ 7:49 am
☽☍♆ 2:33 pm
☿→♉ 6:26 pm

♃♃♃ Donnerstag

♌
♍

Thursday
1

☽△♇ 4:26 am
☽□♀ 3:56 pm v/c
☽→♍ 6:45 pm
☽△☿ 7:56 pm

April

♀♀♀ Freitag

♍

Friday
2

☽☍♅ 3:49 am
☽⚹♄ 7:16 am
☽□♂ 9:07 am
☽☌♃ 1:40 pm

ALL ASPECTS IN PACIFIC STANDARD TIME; ADD 3 HOURS FOR EST; ADD 8 HOURS FOR GMT

© *Sharon Virtue 2002*

Transformation

♍
♎ ☽

Saturday
3

♀→♊   6:57 am
☽□♀   10:24 am   v/c
☽→♎   11:52 pm

♎ ○

Sunday
4

☉⚹♆   12:06 am
☽△♀   2:05 am
☽□♄   12:52 pm
☽△♂   4:54 pm

Daylight Savings Time begins 2:00 am PST

MOON IV   79

April

abril

♎︎ **Monday**

5

☽△♆ 2:14 am
☉☌☽ 4:03 am
☽⚹♀ 2:26 pm v/c
♂□♃ 10:16 pm

Eve in the Garden
© *Sharon Virtue 1997*
Full Moon in ♎︎ Libra 4:03 am PDT

♎︎
♏︎ **Tuesday**

6

☽→♏︎ 3:24 am
☽☌☿ 6:35 am
☽△♅ 11:59 am
☿R 1:27 pm
☽△♄ 3:11 pm
☽⚹♃ 8:06 pm

♏︎ **Wednesday**

7

☽□♆ 4:06 am v/c
☽PrG 7:17 pm

♏︎
♐︎ **Thursday**

8

☽→♐︎ 4:50 am
☽☌♀ 12:43 pm
☽□♅ 1:32 pm
☽□♃ 9:13 pm

♐︎ **Friday**

9

☽☌♂ 12:53 am
♀□♅ 2:51 am
☽⚹♆ 5:36 am
☉△☽ 2:28 pm
☽☌♀ 5:30 pm v/c

The Power of No

The power of no
is like the night heavens
in which the power of yes glows:
a crescent, a quarter, a full moon.

The power of no
is like dark waters
in which swim many yeses—
the porpoise, the whale, the ships,
the little & big fishes.

The power of no
is the shadows
into which the streetlight
pools & flows.

The power of no
is why I can say
yes & yes & yes.

¤ *Karen Ethelsdattar 2002*

♐ ♄♄♄ sábado
♈ **Saturday**
10

☽→♈	6:33 am
☽△♅	8:30 am
☽⚹♅	3:34 pm
☽☍♄	6:55 pm
☽△♃	11:00 pm

☉☉☉ domingo
♈ **Sunday**
11

☉△♀	10:35 am	
☉☐☽	8:46 pm	v/c

Waning Half Moon in ♈ Capricorn 8:46 pm PDT

April
april

☽☽☽ maandag

Monday 12

♑ ♒

☽→♒ 9:33 am
☽□☿ 9:53 am
☿→♈ 6:23 pm

♂♂♂ dinsdag

Tuesday 13

♒

☽△♀ 12:39 am
☽△♂ 11:43 am
☽☌♆ 11:52 am
♂△♆ 3:02 pm

☿☿☿ woensdag

Wednesday 14

♒ ♓

☽⚹♇ 12:20 am
♀□♃ 1:57 am
☉⚹☽ 5:14 am
☽⚹☿ 12:27 pm v/c
☽→♓ 2:24 pm

♃♃♃ donderdag

Thursday 15

♓

☽☌♅ 12:25 am
☽△♄ 4:12 am
☉□⚷ 7:30 am
☽☍♃ 7:34 am
☽□♀ 9:41 am
☽□♂ 8:23 pm

♀♀♀ vrijdag

Friday 16

♓ ♈

☽□♇ 6:43 am v/c
☉☌☿ 6:05 pm
☽→♈ 9:24 pm

All aspects in Pacific Daylight Time; add 3 hours for EDT; add 7 hours for GMT

meditation on women in prison

I'm thinking hard,
like rocks, like lead, like the heaviness of boulders and planets
about the lives of women, caged goddesses
I'm thinking of the families that get crushed to glass dust
when their mothers, daughters, sisters, lovers
are systematically stolen from their lives
placed in roughness and a cold structure
designed to tear away their sense of life, connection, power
I'm thinking weighty thoughts
about my freedom being pitted against their isolation and pain
thinking of how white supremacist capitalism
tells me i can't quite have my freedom
if poor and working class women
and women of color have theirs.

I'm thinking hard
ishtar and kali thoughts, medusa thoughts
of throwing off the behemoth lies and greed
turning to stone the real criminals
I'm thinking of how to build a movement
where people can feel the rage of being made unwittingly
into racists, into materialists, into imperialists
I'm thinking of how women are soul and dance
I'm thinking women are power
and I'm moving to tear the walls down
and know the gorgeous stories of women free.   ¤ *Elizabeth Roberts 2001*

—————————— ♄♄♄ zaterdag ——————————

♈ ⬤ Saturday

17

☽□♄ 12:05 pm
☽⚹♀   9:16 pm

—————————— ☉☉☉ zondag ——————————

♈ ⬤ Sunday

18

☽⚹♆   2:05 am
☽⚹♂   7:40 am
☿□♅   2:53 pm
☽△♀   3:21 pm
☽☌☿ 10:32 pm

Genies

I squeeze the mud, press the coils and rub, and rub and rub,
an earthen pot,
a place to pour into and from,
a strong container,
a small world made of clay,
round and smooth about the size of a womb after giving birth. The opening just big enough that a newborn's head might squeeze through.

A pot, a container, a place to store grain.

There are genies in these pots, big women rising from their open mouths. The women, large and luscious, no longer contained by the smallness of these vessels. Powerful women rising into the air, rising up from their earthy containers, lifting out of the ordinary, demanding to be seen. They make a scene, they cause a stir. Women, like children, used to being seen not heard, expected to serve not deserve, expected to remain in their places not rise above.

Huge women with hearts in their hands and snakes in their bellies rising up and out into life. Women have been defined by containers too small for us for too long and now is the time for the restraints to fall away. It is time for the mouths to open and the spirit to ascend to the light. Women, like sweet fragrance, rising up into the air, changing the scent wherever they unfurl themselves from within the small safe spaces they have been incubating.

An unbounded passionate expression of power and peace, love, fear, grief and rage. Unleashed she is an awesome thing to behold.

I squeeze the mud, press the coils and rub and rub and rub.

¤ *Katey Branch 2002*

MOON V. TAURUS

April 19–May 18

New Moon in ♈ Aries/♉ Taurus cusp April 19, Sun in ♉ Taurus April 19, Full Moon in ♏ Scorpio May 4

Butterfly Woman
© *Patricia Mary Brown 2000*

April

Pachapuquy Killa

☽☽☽ Killachaw

♈
♉

Monday

19

☉☌☽ 6:21 am v/c
☽→♉ 6:43 am
☉→♉ 10:50 am
☽✶♅ 5:57 pm
☽✶♄ 10:20 pm
☿PrG 11:07 pm

New Moon in ♈ Aries 6:21 am PDT
Partial Solar Eclipse* 6:33 am PDT
Sun in Taurus 10:50 am PDT

♂♂♂ Atichaw

♉

Tuesday

20

☽△♃ 12:50 am
☽□♆ 12:36 pm v/c

☿☿☿ Quyllurchaw

♉
♊

Wednesday

21

♀△♆ 7:17 am
☽→♊ 6:10 pm

♃♃♃ Illapachaw

♊

Thursday

22

☽□♅ 5:57 am
☽□♃ 12:37 pm

♀♀♀ Ch'askachaw

♊

Friday

23

☽△♆ 12:57 am
☽☌♀ 3:34 am
☽☌♂ 1:30 pm
☽☍♇ 2:42 pm
☽✶☿ 4:22 pm v/c
☽ApG 5:19 pm

*Eclipse visible from Antarctica, Southern Africa and Madagascar

Year at a Glance for ♉ TAURUS (April 20–May 21)

The Taurus image for 2004 is "you stand as spokesperson for a group of people who are gathered behind you, whispering with great concern amongst themselves." A willingness to use your voice on behalf of others, particularly the dispossessed, is of great importance this year. Focus on a specific area, gather knowledge and bring it to the awareness of others through speaking, writing or teaching. Organize your ideas carefully and communicate them creatively, using bold images to potently illustrate your message. A simple twist of fate, a conversation, an invitation, etc., this year, exposes you to an amazing collection of true individuals who open your eyes to fresh new possibilities. A sense of fear or isolation shifts as you connect with others equally devoted. There's a wider spectrum of possible roles here to try on than you could have ever made up on your own—it's a good time to try on some new hats. Show these people all that Taurean determination and resourcefulness—they need it.

An ongoing challenge is to consciously identify your bottom line in a job or money issue. There will be a point where you must choose to disconnect and move on if you cannot resolve a stalemate. If you do not choose, fate may step in and decide for you. A series of eclipses this year, in April, May and October help Taurus shift, revealing new work or better conditions by the end of the year. A creative boldness to you invites relationships with lovers and children. You censor yourself less, able to revel in the easy playfulness of the moment.

by Gretchen Lawlor © Mother Tongue Ink 2003

MoBoko
© Toni Truesdale 2001

ħħħ K'uychichaw

♊
♋

Saturday
24

☽→♋	6:56 am	☽△♅	6:58 pm
♂☍♀	11:13 am	☿⚹♂	9:30 pm
☉⚹☽	5:21 pm	☽♂ħ	11:54 pm

⊙⊙⊙ Intichaw

♋

Sunday
25

☽⚹♃	1:18 am
☉⚹♅	1:40 pm
☿△♀	3:14 pm

April
April

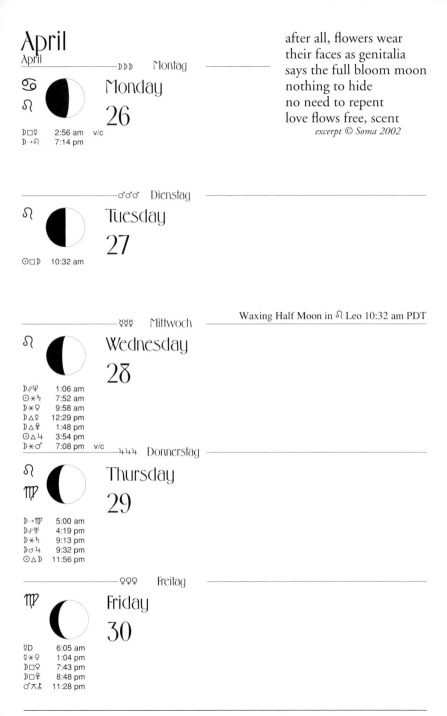

after all, flowers wear
their faces as genitalia
says the full bloom moon
nothing to hide
no need to repent
love flows free, scent
excerpt © Soma 2002

—— ☽☽☽ Montag ——

♋
♌

Monday
26

☽☐☿ 2:56 am v/c
☽→♌ 7:14 pm

—— ♂♂♂ Dienstag ——

♌

Tuesday
27

☉☐☽ 10:32 am

—— ☿☿☿ Mittwoch ——

Waxing Half Moon in ♌ Leo 10:32 am PDT

♌

Wednesday
28

☽☍♆ 1:06 am
☉⚹♄ 7:52 am
☽⚹♀ 9:58 am
☽△☿ 12:29 pm
☽△♀ 1:48 pm
☉△♃ 3:54 pm
☽⚹♂ 7:08 pm v/c

—— ♃♃♃ Donnerstag ——

♌
♍

Thursday
29

☽→♍ 5:00 am
☽☍♅ 4:19 pm
☽⚹♄ 9:13 pm
☽☌♃ 9:32 pm
☉△☽ 11:56 pm

—— ♀♀♀ Freitag ——

♍

Friday
30

☿D   6:05 am
☿⚹♀ 1:04 pm
☽☐♀ 7:43 pm
☽☐♀ 8:48 pm
♂⚻♇ 11:28 pm

ALL ASPECTS IN PACIFIC DAYLIGHT TIME; ADD 3 HOURS FOR EDT; ADD 7 HOURS FOR GMT

Sexual Power
© *nicole lori mamann 2002*

6 Disks
© *Motherpeace, a pseudonym of Vicki Noble and Karen Vogel, 1981*

Choosing

I choose the power of the blood that has flowed
Through all the women
With whom I am linked

I choose the knowledge of women's hands
Working the earth
Midwifing miracles.

I choose the gentleness of women's skin
Opening sweetly
To a loving touch.

¤ *Jenny Yates 1984*

Beltane

Traditionally a fertility festival, Beltane is associated with maypoles, circle dances, bonfires and making love in the fields—ancient rites, encouraging the land to bear abundantly. In our age, while land is forced to bear year-round and unchecked growth eats the earth from under us, we'moon commit to conscious fertility and sustainable abundance.

Celebrate alchemical power with an irresistible seduction of the wild divine. Create a temple of sensual opulence, an altar of earthly delights heaped with love offerings to favorite non-human beings. Call the four directions in their most delicious forms: torch song for the lilting east; snake dance for the smoldering south; sweet nectar for the juicy west; kisses passed round for the embodied north. Light a fire or use the fire of rhythm, breath, pulse. Is it the Moon we most adore or a tenacious weed in an unlikely place or the sea or a spider? Woo each in turn and receive the rising heat of the season in response.

Dedicate Beltane to the pan-erotic: expansive, exuberant, joyful or fierce, let crackling passion take the night. In the red coals of morning is the warmth that endures, the fiery flower that soon becomes fruit.

by Jessica Montgomery © Mother Tongue Ink 2003

ħħħ Samstag

♍︎ ☽
♎︎

Saturday
1

May

Beltane

☽□♂	4:31 am	v/c
☽→♎︎	11:03 am	
♃⚹ħ	1:31 pm	
⚷R	9:10 pm	
♀☍♇	11:07 pm	

☉☉☉ Sonntag

♎︎ ☽

Sunday
2

☽□ħ	2:30 am
☽△♆	1:16 pm
☽☍♅	11:27 pm

May
mayo

♎
♏

Monday
3

☽✶♀ 12:10 am
☽△♀ 1:05 am
☽△♂ 9:49 am   v/c
☽→♏ 1:38 pm
☽△♅ 11:50 pm

Night Sky

¤ Shoshana Rothaizer 2000

♏

Tuesday
4

☽✶♃ 4:12 am
☽△♄ 4:37 am
☿△♀ 10:53 am
☉☍☽ 1:33 pm
☽□♆ 2:36 pm   v/c
♃D 8:07 pm

Lunar Beltane
Total Lunar Eclipse* 1:30 pm PDT (mag 1.309)
Full Moon in ♏ Scorpio 1:33 pm PDT

♏
♐

Wednesday
5

☉□♆ 5:49 am
☽→♐ 2:08 pm
☽PrG 9:23 pm

♐

Thursday
6

☽□♅ 12:12 am
☽□♃ 4:24 am
☽✶♆ 2:43 pm

♐
♑

Friday
7

☽♂♀ 1:00 am
♂→♋ 1:45 am
☽△♅ 2:54 am
☽☍♀ 4:50 am   v/c
☽→♑ 2:17 pm
☽☍♂ 2:50 pm

---

*ECLIPSE VISIBLE FROM SOUTH AMERICA, EUROPE AND AFRICA

Reclaiming the Woman of Iron and Fire

I am the proud female owner of muscles!

It saddens me how girls and women are discouraged from developing our natural physical strength, even as we celebrate the emotional strength it takes to be a whole woman in a patriarchal society. Many of us have reclaimed our hearts of iron and our minds of fire but not the fire and iron of our bodies.

As a hiker, gardener, handy-woman, rock climber, weight lifter and dancer, I celebrate the power of my flesh! Through it, I feel connected to generations of women. In her eighties, my grandmother still repaired her own roof and plumbing, and her forearms rippled from decades of kneading bread. My great aunt Luise, 95, takes an almost daily five-mile walk. Despite multiple sclerosis, my mother cruises around on her three-wheeled bike at near-light speed. My cousin Deirdre just turned 50, but she out-hikes younger folks and could probably lift a car. We're all "built tough," more like fire hydrants than like kites, meant to anchor ourselves in earth, not to get launched into the wind.

I delight in the power of the mind, which can bring stars and cells home to us. However, I also feel fulfillment in the exertion of the body. Wimmin, grrrls everywhere, we're born into this glorious, sprawling, unapologetic flesh—let's build ourselves to be as sturdy, courageous, loving, curious, questing, and unafraid as we can be, in these wondrous womoon bodies!

¤ *Margaret Hammitt-McDonald 2002*

ꜣꜣꜣ   sábado

♑ Saturday

♉

☽✶♅ 12:35 am
☽△♃ 4:48 am
☽☍♄ 5:49 am
☉△☽ 9:10 pm

☉☉☉   domingo

♑ Sunday

♒ 9

☽□♅ 6:03 am v/c
☽→♒ 3:46 pm

May
mei

maandag

≈

Monday

10

☿✶♀ 4:47 pm
☽♂♆ 6:06 pm

© Cosima Hewes 1994

♂♂♂ dinsdag

≈
♓

Tuesday

11

☉□☽ 4:04 am
☽✶♀ 5:07 am
☽△♀ 11:44 am
☽✶♉ 12:31 pm v/c
☿□♄ 6:23 pm
☉⚻♀ 6:29 pm
☽→♓ 7:52 pm

Waning Half Moon in ≈ Aquarius 4:04 am PDT

☿☿☿ woensdag

♓

Wednesday

12

☽△♂ 1:32 am
☽♂♅ 7:29 am
☽☍♃ 12:06 pm
☽△♄ 1:53 pm

♃♃♃ donderdag

♓

Thursday

13

☽□♀ 11:20 am
☉✶☽ 2:44 pm
☽□♀ 7:14 pm v/c

♀♀♀ vrijdag

♓
♈

Friday

14

☽→♈ 3:02 am
☽□♂ 11:57 am
☽□♄ 10:30 pm

ALL ASPECTS IN PACIFIC DAYLIGHT TIME; ADD 3 HOURS FOR EDT; ADD 7 HOURS FOR GMT

Women Build Houses!

Building close to the earth with respect for the Mother! You can smooth the mortar to perfection, but I love the parts un-smoothed, where you can see people's fingerprints, the mark of the effort and devotion to community. Working together to build a community of hand-made homes, built with Love.

I feel so empowered, as a single mom of a two-year-old to come this far (with no carpentry experience!) to build my own house!

So empowered and loved to be in a community that helps me to realize my dreams and visions.

¤ *Pamela Ewasiuk 2002*

Sheetrock'in Sister
¤ *Deborah Jones 2002*

———— ♄♄♄   zaterdag ————

♈

Saturday
15

♀⊼♇	4:15 am
☽⚹♆	8:27 am
☽△♀	8:27 pm
☿→♉	11:54 pm

———— ☉☉☉   zondag ————

♈
♉

Sunday
16

☽⚹♀	5:17 am	v/c
☉△♃	6:22 am	
☽→♉	12:57 pm	
☽♂☿	2:11 pm	

Stone Words

I put a stone into my mouth
And it sat there like a word
Unable to be moved
Unable to be swallowed
Unable to be said
Flat like a word.
I waited
Like the earth . . .
Then centuries of burial, denial, aboriginal
Came speaking through the stone
Like a lizard through the dust
With a rhythm that is rising, uplifting and surviving
Not stampeding, nor receding, nor rushed
The stone it was speaking
And I could taste its words
Round and unprotected like the earth.
We are stepping on the stones
We are stepping on their words . . .
Words that live outside, that can climb and can forgive
Words that have eyes, that can remember and can live
Words that came from sound and from wave and from wind
Words that came from cave and from color and from wing
Words that have power, ancestors, skin.
I can only send paper
Real speaking is stone
Round like the earth
Where words are at home

MOON VI. TAURUS/GEMINI
May 18–June 17
New Moon in ♉ Taurus May 18, Sun in ♊ Gemini May 20, Full Moon in ♐ Sagittarius June 2

Meeting
© *Linda Chido 2001*

May

Ariwaki Killa

♉

Monday

17

☽⚹♂	1:26 am	☽⚹♄	9:42 am
☽⚹♅	1:54 am	♂△♅	10:28 am
♆R	5:13 am	♀R	3:28 pm
☽△♃	7:02 am	☽□♆	7:28 pm

© Linda Ann Brunner 2002

Sky Woman

♉

Tuesday

18

☉☌☽	9:52 pm	v/c

New Moon in ♉ Taurus 9:52 pm PDT

♉
♊

Wednesday

19

☽→♊	12:47 am
☽□♅	2:07 pm
☽□♃	7:29 pm

♊

Thursday

20

☽△♆	7:55 am
☉→♊	9:59 am
☽☍♀	8:14 pm

Sun in Gemini 9:59 am PDT

♊
♋

Friday

21

♀⚻♇	2:34 am	
☽ApG	5:00 am	
☽☌♀	5:13 am	v/c
☽→♋	1:35 pm	
☿⚹♅	3:43 pm	
♂⚹♃	8:05 pm	

ALL ASPECTS IN PACIFIC DAYLIGHT TIME; ADD 3 HOURS FOR EDT; ADD 7 HOURS FOR GMT

Year at a Glance for ♊ GEMINI (May 21–June 21)

Gemini, your image this year is "the dancing shaman." You are a bridge between past and future, spirit and earth. Uranus, planet of radical genius, hums at the apex of your chart all year. As you dance, you hold a lightning rod. With your remarkable mental agility you capture some divine spark, some progressive vision. Share it with contagious enthusiasm. If you've been going solo, change to teamwork. Likewise, if you've been working with others, try being an independent agent. Ride the cutting edge of your field or surprise everyone and jump the tracks, i.e. move into a different field where you offer a refreshing new perspective.

Even with all of this creative sparking, your resources may seem to limit you. Nurture yourself generously with simple things. Claim your imagination, your eclectic style, as a most treasured jewel. Identify exactly what you need to do your Work and let the universe help. Practice accepting gifts and support—especially from your family. Don't leave your genius to flap in the imaginal winds or to come out in ways you had not intended (genius = originality, a fresh perspective, to bring about new life; also high fertility if you want to conceive children this year). Capitalize upon a family trait, or natural gift you take for granted. Take chances and especially in November–December be willing to be inspired by Spirit. If relationships aren't deep this year, don't bother. Geminis are true oddballs. This irritates, even infuriates people. Confrontations provide opportunities to give others what they need while getting your own needs met. This is deep chess—stay with it.

by Gretchen Lawlor © Mother Tongue Ink 2003

───────── ꜩꜩꜩ K'uychichaw ─────────

♋ 🌑 **Saturday**
22

☽△♅	3:04 am
☽⚹♉	4:28 am
☽⚹♃	8:36 am
☽☌♂	9:14 am
☽☌♄	11:58 am	v/c

─────○○○ Intichaw ─────

♋ 🌑 **Sunday**
23

| ☿△♃ | 5:51 pm |

Wild Sisters
© Patricia Mary Brown 1998

May
März

☽☽☽ Montag

♋ ♌

Monday
24

☽→♌ 2:07 am
☉✶☽ 9:46 am
♂☌♄ 10:39 pm

Ink from a Stone

Women hear the beauty of silence.
Women hear melodious life.
Women extrude poetry from nothing.

excerpt ¤ Elizabeth Roberts 1998

♂♂♂ Dienstag

♌

Tuesday
25

☽□☿ 12:28 am
☿✶♄ 1:39 am
☿✶♂ 3:33 am
☽☍♆ 8:33 am
☽△♇ 8:10 pm

☿☿☿ Mittwoch

♌ ♍

Wednesday
26

☽✶♀ 2:42 am v/c
☽→♍ 12:52 pm

♃♃♃ Donnerstag

♍

Thursday
27

☉□☽ 12:57 am
☽☍♅ 1:36 am
☽☌♃ 7:09 am
☉□♅ 9:43 am
☽✶♄ 10:46 am
☽✶♂ 1:18 pm
☽△☿ 5:42 pm
☿□♆ 6:14 pm

Waxing Half Moon in ♍ Virgo 12:57 am PDT

♀♀♀ Freitag

♍ ♎

Friday
28

☽□♇ 4:37 am
☽□♀ 9:17 am v/c
☽→♎ 8:22 pm

© Katheryn M. Trenshaw 2000

Under Northern Lights

 ♎

Saturday
29

☉△☽	11:47 am
☽□ħ	5:16 pm
☽□♂	9:45 pm
☽△Ψ	11:18 pm

♎

Sunday
30

☽⚹♀	9:21 am	
☽△♀	12:09 pm	v/c
☉□♃	5:34 pm	

MOON VI

May/June
mayo/junio

Mind's Eye Shield
© Maya Dobroth 1989

Monday
31

♎︎
♏︎ ☾

☽→♏︎	12:08 am
♂⚻♆	7:42 am
☿⚹♀	8:10 am
☽△♅	11:19 am
☽⚹♃	4:37 pm
☽△♄	8:05 pm

Tuesday
1

♏︎ ☾

☽□♆	1:20 am	
☽△♂	2:08 am	
☽☌♅	2:15 pm	v/c

June

Wednesday
2

♏︎
♐︎ ○

☽→♐︎	12:52 am	
☽□♅	11:36 am	
☽□♃	4:56 pm	
♀☍♇	6:24 pm	
☿△♄	7:22 pm	
☉☍☽	9:20 pm	

Full Moon in ♐︎ Sagittarius 9:20 pm PDT

Thursday
3

♐︎ ☾

☽⚹♆	1:05 am	
☽PrG	6:13 am	
☽☍♀	9:39 am	
☽☌♇	10:12 am	v/c

Friday
4

♐︎
♑︎ ☾

☽→♑︎	12:12 am
☽⚹♅	10:55 am
☽△♃	4:30 pm
☽☍♄	8:07 pm

ALL ASPECTS IN PACIFIC DAYLIGHT TIME; ADD 3 HOURS FOR EDT; ADD 7 HOURS FOR GMT

There is a Day

There is a day, morning sunshine or driving rain,
when you realize spells won't keep you safe,
after all, that your heart
will still break, let in both dark and light,
when you discover which rules to break
and which to keep, not because they are rules
but because they are yours—

> your way of life, your way
> toward life.

There is a day when writing a poem
is working in the garden,
watching sparrows dart above the trees,
or holding someone you love,
when words (despite the irony
of making these lines)
take a rest for a while
in the hollow of the soul
nesting   cupped around the body
> of the world.

© Ellen S. Jaffe 2002

ℏℏℏ   sábado

♑   Saturday
5

♌⚹♂   5:28 am   v/c
☿→♊   5:47 am
☉△♆   8:40 am

☉☉☉   domingo

♑   Sunday
♒   6

☽→♒   12:10 am
☽△☿   2:54 am

June

juni

———— ⟩⟩⟩ maandag ——————————————

♒

Monday

7

☽☌♆	1:27 am
☉△☽	4:25 am
☽△♀	6:42 am
☽⚹♀	11:09 am v/c
♀PrG	11:59 pm

———— ♂♂♂ dinsdag ——————————————

♒
♓

Tuesday

8

☉☌♀	1:43 am
☽→♓	2:38 am
☽□♅	2:08 pm
☽☌♅	2:34 pm
♀□♅	5:05 pm
☽☍♃	9:31 pm

———— ☿☿☿ woensdag ——————————————

♓

Wednesday

9

☽△♄	1:48 am
♂⚹♀	5:29 am
☽□♀	8:59 am
☉□☽	1:02 pm
☽□♀	4:03 pm
☽△♂	4:37 pm v/c

Waning Half Moon in ♓ Pisces 1:02 pm PDT

———— ♃♃♃ donderdag ——————————————

♓
♈

Thursday

10

♀PrG	4:16 am
♅R	8:47 am
☽→♈	8:49 am
☿□♃	4:51 pm

———— ♀♀♀ vrijdag ——————————————

♈

Friday

11

☉☍♀	5:26 am
☽⚹♅	7:56 am
☽□♄	10:13 am
☽⚹♆	1:46 pm
☽⚹♀	2:40 pm

ALL ASPECTS IN PACIFIC DAYLIGHT TIME; ADD 3 HOURS FOR EDT; ADD 7 HOURS FOR GMT

Ritual

¤ Abby Wentworth 2002

♈
♉

Saturday
12

☽△♀	12:44 am		☿☌♀	4:24 pm
☉⚹☽	2:24 am		☿△♆	6:05 pm
☽□♂	4:31 am	v/c	☽→♉	6:37 pm
♀△♆	10:08 am			

♉

Sunday
13

☽⚹♅	8:05 am
☽△♃	4:52 pm
☽⚹♄	9:52 pm

Where Does Power Come From?

"Grandmother Eagle, where does power come from?" asked the small child. "Oh, that is easy to say," replied the old woman. "It is in the leaves and roots and flowers of the plants that Mother Earth has for us. You can use these for food, for medicine, for inspiration, or for ritual. They are very powerful."

The child wondered what her Aunt Lily would say. "Can you please tell me where power comes from?" "Certainly, my child. It is in the stones that Mother Earth has for us. Healing stones and weapon stones and meditation stones and all of them bring power."

The child asked her oldest sister, Luna, "Tell me please, where does power come from?" "Ah, that is a great secret, but I will share it with you. It is in the water that Mother Earth has for us. Water to drink and water to grow plants with and water to bathe in and water for healing purposes. That is the true power."

One day when the child was leading the sheep back to the house, she noticed that one of the lambs was limping. She sat on the ground and cradled the lamb in her lap while she tried to think of what to do. She had no plants, no stones and no water. She could only stroke the lamb lovingly until it fell asleep in her embrace. Soon it grew dark. She could hear her mother calling and before long her mother found them sitting in the pasture.

The child said, "I am sorry to have caused you worry, but I had to stay with this lamb because it was hurt. I didn't have any plants or stones or water so I had no power to help it." The lamb awoke, made a little "bahhh" sound, stood up on its spindly legs and began to walk. The lamb was no longer limping. "Mother how could this be? I had no power to heal this lamb. What happened?"

Her mother embraced the child. "My Dear One," she said, "You had the power inside you, where all power comes from. You had a loving heart." The child listened carefully and remembered the wisdom of her mother.

¤ *Linda Kerby – Spiral Crone 2002*

MOON VII. GEMINI/CANCER

June 17–July 17

New Moon in ♊ Gemini June 17, Sun in ♋ Cancer June 20, Full Moon in ♑ Capricorn July 2

Samovila with the Spirits of the Forest

© Sandra M. Stanton 1999

June
Aymuray killa

 ♉

Monday
14

☽□♆ 12:52 am
☽⚹♂ 7:34 pm v/c

 ♉
♊

Tuesday
15

☽→♊ 6:44 am
☿☍♀ 8:07 am
☉⚻♇ 11:11 am
♂☍♇ 1:32 pm
☽□♅ 8:29 pm

♊

Wednesday
16

☽□♃ 6:01 am
☽☌♀ 9:12 am
☽△♆ 1:29 pm

♊
♋

Thursday
17

☽☍♀ 12:51 am
☿⚻♇ 4:46 am
☽ApG 8:59 am
☽☌♉ 10:14 am
☉☌☽ 1:27 pm v/c
☽→♋ 7:37 pm

New Moon in ♊ Gemini 1:27 pm PDT

♋

Friday
18

☽△♅ 9:20 am
☉☌☿ 2:24 pm
☽⚹♃ 7:28 pm

ALL ASPECTS IN PACIFIC DAYLIGHT TIME; ADD 3 HOURS FOR EDT; ADD 7 HOURS FOR GMT

Year at a Glance for ♋ CANCER (June 21–July 22)

Cancer's evocative image for this year is "a shoe embellished with roses." Roses are flowers of love, warming the heart, softening the emotions, soothing anxiety and returning the body to its own safe center. Shoes suggest ownership—you may be standing in another's shoes but must make your own heartfelt additions. You are trying to differentiate from the past. This year make life rosier by marking it with your own imaginative signature. Cancer, so soft and tender inside, uses a hard shell to provide a distinct shape and feeling of safety. You have a strong sense of the spirit world but the danger for you is the concretizing of spirit through isms: alcoholism, institutionalism, fundamentalism, nationalism. What you're really being called to comes from strengthening the center of your tender soul, not from the reactive defense of your shell.

This year all your progress in the world is dependent upon the quality of your personal life. Your home reflects the state of your heart, and, the well-being of your heart is the crucial source of everything else in your life. Make your home beautiful; fill it with roses, make it peaceful, safe and nourishing. From this place of comfort analyze past efforts. Old attitudes have become barriers towards further growth. Cancer is a water sign and must move with the tides and currents of change. The challenge is to be in and of, not against. You know how to be at home in a big sea. When you follow your deepest instincts you have much to share about how to live in a world of great diversity.

by Gretchen Lawlor © Mother Tongue Ink 2003

Mother and Child
© Anna Oneglia 1992

———————— ㅅㅅㅅ K'uychichaw ————————

♋ 🌑 **Saturday**
19

☽♂♄	12:37 am
♀□♃	2:29 am
☿ApG	6:09 am
☿→♋	12:49 pm

———————— ⊙⊙⊙ Intichaw ————————

♋
♌ 🌑 **Sunday**
20

☽♂♂	3:46 am	v/c
☽→♌	8:05 am	
⊙→♋	5:57 pm	

Solstice

Sun in Cancer 5:57 pm PDT

Durga
© *Sandra Stanton 1995*

Solstice/Soul-Stitch

Wielding harpoon needles of sunray fire she
carves into and out the tattered fineries
of stratosphere rumpled like a

broken heart.

In her curvilinear spin, she tilts out,
harpoon-handed, mending soul to itself and
also sky. Dipping, a precipice of fire,
even with the longest light,
heat's promise of the days to come:
when the turning light and the inferno
will wield healing, clearing us hotly.
Solstice is cautery, fierce piercing;
Earth turns us to be annealed by fire.

¤ *Marna 1995*

Summer Solstice

Solstice rolls in and the livin' is easy. The heart of the earth
opens and fullness is everywhere. This longest day of the year
drenches us in sweetness as we lean into the light, heliotropic.
Winter is a distant rumor: the beat of the planet thrums now,
now, now. Generosity is the power to cultivate in the shimmering
days. As easily as seed becomes blade and blade becomes grain,
we give ourselves away, undiminished. Wealth is generosity of
body. Compassion is generosity of heart. Creativity is generosity of
imagination. Love is generosity of spirit.

Whatever blesses us, we pass it along. Gather with friends to
create a celebration that nurtures and enlivens the community. Call
a circle, raise energy with voice and rhythm, share a feast of golden
foods and ask: how may we serve? Good work, bright words, healing
hands, open doors: the means vary with the needs of the group
but the source is the same. Ceaseless, radiant, unrequited—we
become as the sun, shining for all.

by Jessica Montgomery © Mother Tongue Ink 2003

June
Juni

DDD — Montag

♌

Monday
21

☽⚹♀ 6:00 am
☽☍♆ 2:00 pm

The world is starving
for the wisdom of our
natural internal rhythms.
Honoring the power of
our blood cycles
will change everything.
excerpt ¤ Kami McBride 2002

♂♂♂ — Dienstag

♌
♍

Tuesday
22

☽△♀ 12:54 am v/c
☿△♅ 3:11 pm
☽→♍ 7:10 pm
☉⚹☽ 11:16 pm

☿☿☿ — Mittwoch

♍

Wednesday
23

☽☍♅ 8:07 am
☽⚹☿ 11:38 am
♂→♌ 1:50 pm
☽□♀ 3:02 pm
☽☌♃ 6:57 pm
☽⚹♄ 11:48 pm

♄♄♄ — Donnerstag

♍

Thursday
24

♄☊♆ 9:40 am
☽□♀ 10:19 am v/c

♀♀♀ — Freitag

♍
♎

Friday
25

☽→♎ 3:50 am
☽⚹♂ 5:45 am
☿⚹♃ 9:48 am
☉□☽ 12:08 pm
☽△♀ 9:50 pm

Waxing Half Moon in ♎ Libra 12:08 pm PDT

All aspects in Pacific Daylight Time; add 3 hours for EDT; add 7 hours for GMT

Mi Hermana My Sista Mi Sangre

We bleed power
so celebrate your flow
magic woman
full figured moons
still happen
We be the ripe fruit
of this corroding earth
mango lips
and apricot eyes
pineapple hips
and coconut thighs
tread through
these rotten streets
we heavy steps
and spit in the eyes
of injustice
Dig in the earth
with your hands
lift up, revive
Our temple
is our choice
We are sacred
We are bad.

¤ *Jackie Joice 1996*

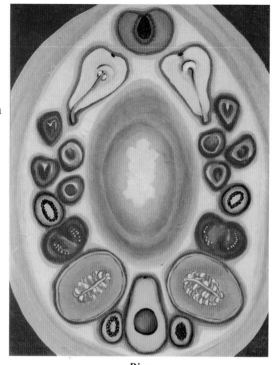

Ripe
¤ *Becki Hoffman 2001*

ħħħ   Samstag

Saturday
26

☽□♅	5:48 am	☿⊼♆	1:11 pm
☽△♆	6:56 am	☽⚹♀	4:41 pm v/c
☽□♄	7:26 am	♅♂♄	5:07 pm

⊙⊙⊙   Sonntag

Sunday
27

☽→♏	9:13 am
☽□♂	1:31 pm
⊙△♅	5:55 pm
☽△♅	8:37 pm
⊙△☽	8:49 pm

June/July
junio/julio

☽☽☽ lunes

Goodness of Cabbage
© Amarah K. Gabriel 2002

♏

Monday 28

☽✶♃ 7:18 am
☽□♆ 10:31 am
☽△♄ 11:31 am
☽△☿ 5:57 pm v/c

♂♂♂ martes

♏ ♐

Tuesday 29

☿⊼♇ 6:12 am
☽→♐ 11:15 am
♀D 4:15 pm
☽△♂ 5:31 pm
☽□♅ 9:59 pm

☿☿☿ miércoles

♐

Wednesday 30

☽☍♀ 2:45 am
☽□♃ 8:37 am
☽✶♆ 11:10 am
☽☌♇ 7:53 pm v/c

♃♃♃ jueves

♐ ♑

Thursday 1

July

☿☍⚷ 3:42 am
☽→♑ 11:01 am
☽PrG 4:10 pm
☽✶♅ 9:25 pm

♀♀♀ viernes

♑

Friday 2

☉☍☽ 4:09 am
☽△♃ 8:24 am
☽☍♄ 12:17 pm

Full Moon in ♑ Capricorn 4:09 am PDT

ALL ASPECTS IN PACIFIC DAYLIGHT TIME; ADD 3 HOURS FOR EDT; ADD 7 HOURS FOR GMT

The Power of Nourishment

Cooking is a sacred act. You are taking the greatest gift of the Earth: nourishment, and you are transforming it with your being, your wit and desire—and a few other household ingredients—into food for you and your family and community. This is a holy act: nourishment makes a person *whole* and *hale*.

The act of cooking and food preparation has been trivialized by our society as "women's work." But Trivia was a goddess of the commonplace, the home—probably another name for Hecate, actually, the guardian goddess of these entire Mysteries. We know how powerful and holy she is! We are made holy by her presence in our kitchens. Hecate is the ultimate kitchen witch.

One of the other ways we can work on our connection to the world is by participating in communal celebration. Coming together to eat and honor the turning of the Wheel of the Year helps establish connections to each other and the rest of the planet. We express our gratitude for our plenty, we thank the Visibles and the Invisibles, and we eat together—sharing this bounty. We eat the same food, essentially, and are linked by it: it is a supremely intimate act. Celebrating in this way becomes a communal prayer to the forces of Nature, to the Divine.

© *excerpt from* The Salmon Mysteries: A Re-Imagining of the Demeter and Persephone Myth by *Kim Antieau 2002*

ħħħ   sábado

♑
≈

Saturday
3

☽☌♅   7:25 am   v/c
☽→≈   10:22 am
☽☌♂   8:44 pm

☉☉☉   domingo

≈

Sunday
4

♂☌♅   12:27 am
☽△♀   2:25 am
☿→♌   7:52 am
☽☌♆   10:15 am
☽✶♀   7:15 pm   v/c

July
juli

♒︎
♓︎

Monday
5

☽→♓︎ 11:26 am
☉⚹♃ 11:59 am
☽♂♅ 10:33 pm

♓︎

Tuesday
6

☽□♀ 5:15 am
☉⚻♆ 5:56 am
☽☍♃ 11:51 am
☉△☽ 1:21 pm
☽△♄ 4:03 pm
☽□♀ 10:30 pm v/c

♓︎
♈︎

Wednesday
7

☽→♈︎ 4:03 pm

♈︎

Thursday
8

☿⚻♅ 1:37 am
☽△☿ 4:22 am
☽△♂ 9:17 am
☉♂♄ 9:38 am
☽⚹♀ 12:30 pm
♄ApG 3:11 pm
♇PrG 4:15 pm
☽⚹♆ 7:25 pm
☽□♄ 11:34 pm

♈︎

Friday
9

☉□☽ 12:34 am
☽△♀ 5:52 am v/c
♃⚻♆ 2:10 pm

Waning Half Moon in ♈︎ Aries 12:34 am PDT

All aspects in Pacific Daylight Time; add 3 hours for EDT; add 7 hours for GMT

© Anna Oneglia 2001

Cancer

♈
♉

Saturday
10

☽→♉	12:51 am
☽⚹♅	1:31 pm
☿☌♂	4:50 pm
☽□♂	10:25 pm
☽□☿	10:55 pm

♉

Sunday
11

☽□♆	5:51 am	☿⚹♀	1:30 pm	
☽△♃	6:28 am	☉⚹☽	4:29 pm	v/c
☽⚹♄	10:59 am	☉⚻♀	8:53 pm	

July
Jawqay Ruski killa

――――))) Killachaw ――――――――――――――――――――

♉
♊   Monday
                           12

☽→♊ 12:45 pm

―――――――――――― ♂♂♂ Atichaw ―――――――――――――

♊   Tuesday
                           13

☽□♅ 1:42 am
☿☍♆ 4:31 am
☽✳♂ 2:21 pm
☽☌♀ 3:11 pm
☽△♆ 6:24 pm
☽□♃ 8:00 pm
☽✳♄ 8:26 pm

―――――――――― ☿☿☿ Quyllurchaw ――――――――――

♊   Wednesday
                           14

☽☍♀ 5:33 am   v/c
☽ApG 2:09 pm

―――――――――――― ♃♃♃ Illapachaw ―――――――――――

♊
♋   Thursday
                           15

☽→♋ 1:40 am
☉☍♇ 3:59 am
☽△♅ 2:28 pm

―――――――――――― ♀♀♀ Ch'askachaw ――――――――――

♋   Friday
                           16

☽✳♃ 9:36 am
♀✳♂ 9:47 am
☽☌♄ 1:46 pm
♂☍♆ 3:26 pm
♀△♆ 4:30 pm
☿△♀ 11:26 pm

―――――――――――――――――――――――――――――――――――――

ALL ASPECTS IN PACIFIC DAYLIGHT TIME; ADD 3 HOURS FOR EDT; ADD 7 HOURS FOR GMT

Ode to the Corporate You

Woman, the sun rises and sets on whether
        you feel the connection between your tears
      and the toxic rain the sky is crying.
The fate of the people
      of this lovely, lovely planet
        hinges on your womanhood.
Equality is about being
      as valuable as the plants
      as precious as the animals
      as creative as the force of reason
      a stone among diamonds
 a wave, curling, gathering, looming, crashing
as vital as any other.
      Equality is not about
        being equally destructive
        wasting your life, your gifts,
        throwing the stone into the waves.
You are the stone. You are the wave. Do you feel the power?
You the soul-ocean. Wade in.

Rain Deva in Contemplation
© *Baraka Robin Berger 2001*

excerpt ¤ Madeline Moss 2002

ᕼᕼᕼ K'uychichaw

♋
♌

Saturday

17

⊙☌☽   4:24 am   v/c
☽→♌   1:56 pm

New Moon in ♋ Cancer 4:24 am PDT

◦◦◦ Intichaw

♌

Sunday

18

☽☍♆   6:31 pm
☽⚹♀   8:59 pm
☽☌♂   9:24 pm

The Summer I Discovered Power

The summer I discovered power
the ink flowed dark and freely from my pen
like a river of moon's blood.
I discovered what was between my legs,
wore no undergarments
and made peace with chin hair.

The summer I discovered power
I only read books written by optimists,
only ate what came out of the ground,
spent enough time outside
to truly know my insides.

The summer I discovered power
I left the sunscreen
off
because I wanted the fiery lips of the sun
to seduce my skin into wearing Her erotic afterglow,
left the deodorant
off
because I wanted to breathe the sweet smell of
my body's own ripeness
rich like Sumatran coffee.

The summer I discovered power
I discovered strange and impossible
places
deep wells and live wires.
I went straight to the Source
and plugged in.

MOON VIII. CANCER/LEO

July 17–August 15

New Moon in ♋ Cancer July 17, Sun in ♌ Leo July 22, Full Moon in ♒ Aquarius July 31

Blue Plate Special
¤ *Robyn Waters 1995*

July
Juli

Monday
19

☽△♀   5:18 am
☿⊼♇   6:08 am
☽♂♅   11:50 am   v/c

Tuesday
20

☽→♍   12:44 am
♀□♃   1:57 am
☽☍♅   12:38 pm

Wednesday
21

☽♂♃   8:38 am
☽□♀   9:45 am
☽⚹♄   12:08 pm
☽□♇   2:48 pm   v/c

Thursday
22

☉→♌   4:50 am
☽→♎   9:39 am
☉⚹☽   10:02 am

Sun in Leo 4:50 am PDT

Friday
23

☽△♆   12:03 pm
☽□♄   8:09 pm
☽△♀   8:12 pm
☽⚹♂   8:37 pm
☽⚹♀   10:06 pm

ALL ASPECTS IN PACIFIC DAYLIGHT TIME; ADD 3 HOURS FOR EDT; ADD 7 HOURS FOR GMT

Year at a Glance for ♌ LEO (July 23-Aug. 23)

Leo took some bold steps forward late 2002–mid 2003, and the world applauded. The image for Leo 2004 is "a delighted child at an awards banquet playing with the plaques, arranging and rearranging them in formations." You are being influenced by two significant cycles: one of new talents and interests developing, the other of old business being completed, resolved and released. It's most important to close well and honorably with your past—this will impact future happiness. Do not perpetuate situations where you play to the expectations of others rather than being true to yourself. Make choices regarding what you want to keep in your life and what must be set aside to best improve your personal life. Simplify your commitments, value private time, make healthy choices.

Put your considerable presence on the line for the well being of the planet. Give time or contributions to institutions and organizations concerned with social issues. Follow untried paths to collaborate; transform habitual procedures in joint activities through new techniques. You inspire others to play with new principles of conduct. Yes Leo, love and passion are presently in your stars. The child-self Leo is revitalized and wants playmates. You have a very sweet and generous heart. Profound encounters with lovers, children or playful companions bring breakdowns/breakthroughs.

This is a test. You'd like to project divinity onto others and if you do it, don't be surprised if you're disappointed. Relationships where you are both equally committed to a common vision or devotion rather than falling into saving each other will be most successful.

by Gretchen Lawlor © Mother Tongue Ink 2003

© Nicole DiPierre 2000

♎
♏
Saturday
24

☽⚹♅ 2:54 pm v/c
☽→♏ 4:08 pm
☉□☽ 8:37 pm

Waxing Half Moon in ♏ Scorpio 8:37 pm PDT

♏
Sunday
25

☽△♅ 2:47 am   ♀☍♀ 8:00 am
♂△♀ 2:52 am   ☽□♆ 5:06 pm
☿→♍ 6:58 am   ☽⚹♃ 10:37 pm

July/August
julio/agosto

♏
♐

Monday
26

☽△♄ 1:22 am
☽□♂ 3:48 am v/c
☽→♐ 7:48 pm
☽□☿ 10:31 pm

♐

Tuesday
27

♀⚹♂ 1:29 am
☉△☽ 3:42 am
☽□♅ 5:46 am
☽⚹♆ 7:23 pm

♐
♑

Wednesday
28

☽□♃ 1:20 am
☽☌♀ 4:30 am
☽△♂ 7:53 am
☽☍♀ 8:06 am v/c
☉⚻♅ 10:07 am
☽→♑ 8:57 pm
♀⚻♇ 9:54 pm

♑

Thursday
29

☽△♅ 2:40 am
♂⚻♇ 4:52 am
☽⚹♅ 6:27 am
☽PrG 11:14 pm

♑
♒

Friday
30

☽△♃ 2:10 am
☽☍♄ 4:21 am v/c
☽→♒ 8:54 pm

Power Of—

Goddess Conference, Glastonbury, Lammas

of red, black and white
   silk, chiffon and cotton
of dancing a spiral
of weaving spider connections
of prayer flags and bread
of voices raised in discussion
     three hundred
of given wisdom and service
of ritual and image
of earth symbol on skin
   each body in beauty

of feather and incense and fire
of feet washed in spring water
     three hundred
of entering shadows
of the dark walk to the heart centre
of light guiding to love
of the Many Names and the One
Lady—of three hundred women
here in your precinct and temple
and the power of their single prayer.

© Rose Flint 2002

Summertime Dance

© Diane Rigoli 1996

ħħħ   sábado

♒

Saturday
31

ħ⊼♀   8:20 am
☉☌☽   11:05 am
☽☌♆   7:36 pm

Lunar Lammas
Full Moon in ♒ Aquarius 11:05 am PDT

☉☉☉   domingo

♒
♓

Sunday
1

August

☿☌♅   3:50 am
☽⚹♀   4:45 am
☽☍♂   12:35 pm
☽△♀   1:51 pm   v/c
☽→♓   9:34 pm

August
augustus

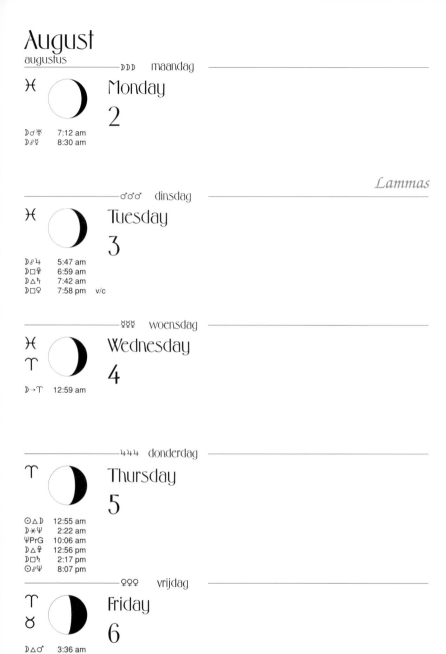

────── ☽☽☽ maandag ──────────────────

♓

Monday
2

☽♂♅ 7:12 am
☽☍♀ 8:30 am

Lammas

────── ♂♂♂ dinsdag ──────

♓

Tuesday
3

☽☍♃ 5:47 am
☽□♀ 6:59 am
☽△♄ 7:42 am
☽□♀ 7:58 pm   v/c

────── ☿☿☿ woensdag ──────

♓
♈

Wednesday
4

☽→♈ 12:59 am

────── ♃♃♃ donderdag ──────

♈

Thursday
5

☉△☽ 12:55 am
☽⚹♆ 2:22 am
♆PrG 10:06 am
☽△♀ 12:56 pm
☽□♄ 2:17 pm
☉☍♆ 8:07 pm

────── ♀♀♀ vrijdag ──────

♈
♉

Friday
6

☽△♂ 3:36 am
☽⚹♀ 6:59 am   v/c
☽→♉ 8:26 am
♃□♀ 2:31 pm
☽⚹♅ 7:15 pm

─────────────────────────────────────

ALL ASPECTS IN PACIFIC DAYLIGHT TIME; ADD 3 HOURS FOR EDT; ADD 7 HOURS FOR GMT

Expansion Through Nature
© *Marja de Vries 2001*

Lammas

Lammas is the cross-quarter day initiating the harvest season. Paradoxically a time of both riches and risks, we celebrate those efforts that have been fruitful and carefully tend those yet to bear. We revel in our luck while the moment is lucky, knowing nothing is certain.

Set an altar with fruit, every color and shape—this is our hard work and its results. Fill a chalice with honey, the sweetness of fortune, the blessing of grace without which nothing comes to fruition. Dress bold and beautiful, embodying the way of the lavish earth. Sing and dance the four directions, making ceremony into festival. Pass the chalice, pouring into its amber center those dear wishes yet ungranted: hearts, desires and hopes for ourselves, our world. Make a spiral dance, gaze meeting gaze, knowing that when each is empowered, cooperation replaces struggle. When the chalice is molten and glowing, begin the feast, dipping fruit into honey, taking in the riches and risks of the season. But no one feeds oneself; feed each other and experience the interdependence of the web. Life feeds on life and all are cared for—we do all we can, then let love do the rest. *by Jessica Montgomery © Mother Tongue Ink 2003*

Care of the Growing Crop

I am here to tell you
this night on the festival of Lughnasad
the time of ensuring the harvest
        your personal harvest   the village harvest
  and the safety of the good we are all growing in the world
I am here to tell you what the ancients know
that if you give up your crop along the way   out of carelessness
      or nobility   it doesn't matter
your spirit will be a hollow husk and no one not you not others
      will be fed

But if you tend your own patch to completion
      (no matter how insignificant it seems)
if you let yourself swell with joy with the rich nourishing
milk of fulfillment
      you will have raised a miracle
Your small garden of life, of art, of love, of work, of mothering
and building and being a wise woman
      whatever you have planted and tended and grown
will feed yourself   your village
there will be corn for feasting   for flour
      for popping over winter fires
      and enough to plant next year
There will be seeds that open spontaneously in the hearts
of other women
and wild possibilities will appear in dreams
on the other side of the world

excerpt ¤ Miriam Dyak 1995

Corn Maiden
© Diane Rigoli 1998

ħħħ zaterdag

♉

Saturday

7

☽△♀	12:47 am
♀→♋	4:02 am
☽□♇	11:33 am
☉□☽	3:01 pm
☽△♃	11:27 pm

Waning Half Moon in ♉ Taurus 3:01 pm PDT

☉☉☉ zondag

♉
♊

Sunday

♉

☽⚹♄	12:59 am	
☽□♂	5:46 pm	v/c
☽→♊	7:33 pm	

August
Chakraqunakuy Killa

¤ Gloria Kemper-O'Neil 2000

Goddess Hilaria

〗〗〗 Killachaw

♊

Monday
9

☽□♅	6:42 am
☽□☿	1:16 pm
☿R	5:33 pm
☽△♆	11:37 pm

♂♂♂ Atichaw

♊

Tuesday
10

♂→♍	3:14 am
☉✶☽	8:39 am
☽☍♀	11:20 am
☽□♃	12:59 pm v/c

☿☿☿ Quyllurchaw

♊
♋

Wednesday
11

☽ApG	2:32 am
☽→♋	8:20 am
☽✶♂	9:59 am
☽☌♀	4:29 pm
☉△♀	5:19 pm
☽△♅	7:19 pm

♄♄♄ Illapachaw

♋

Thursday
12

☽✶☿	1:35 am

♀♀♀ Ch'askachaw

♋
♌

Friday
13

☽✶♃	2:33 am
☽☌♄	3:17 am v/c
♀△♅	3:57 am
☉⚻♇	7:07 pm
☽→♌	8:30 pm

ALL ASPECTS IN PACIFIC DAYLIGHT TIME; ADD 3 HOURS FOR EDT; ADD 7 HOURS FOR GMT

Hidden Fruit

Seated across from me, a woman,

dark skin, straight bangs,

shiny leather jacket

and one banana

dangling from her fingers

like a purse.

Maybe big enough for a lipstick,

but not a hairbrush.

Maybe a comb.

I want to pull my persimmon out of my bag,

compare fruit.

Instead I ooze out through the train doors

with the rest of the people

who are keeping their produce

under wraps.

Kaminari
© Lynn Dewart 2001

¤ *Annie Kohut Frankel 2001*

ħħ K'uychichaw

♌ **Saturday**
14

☽☍♆ 11:28 pm

☉☉☉ Intichaw

♌ **Sunday**
15

ħ☍♂ 1:42 am
☿⚹♀ 7:10 am
☽△♀ 10:50 am
☉☌☽ 6:24 pm v/c
♃△♂ 8:59 pm

New Moon in ♌ Leo 6:24 pm PDT

Living Altar

My body is an altar in the temple that is Earth. I cast the circle inward, carry it as the sun arcs across the sky, lay it under the stars each night, dreaming the next world into being. I cast the circle inward: do it with me.

Rub palms together to make heat and bring them to rest on your deep belly, raising the power of earth. Call the ancestors, feeling the momentum of every act of kinship ever risked, every tribal bond. Know what the stones know, what the animals and green things know. Deepen your connection to the matrix. Bring groundedness into the bones of this temple.

Lay your hot hands on your solar plexus, raising the power of fire. Feel righteous desire leap like a flame being fed. Harvest purpose and beauty from the Life Tree in high summer. Make the world you need from rhythm and rage. Bring passion into the cells of this temple.

Lay your hot hands on your heart, raising the power of water. Flow easily, tumbling or lazy, across the landscape of longing: the ocean of love receives every stream. Quench thirst with the purest nectar, no matter what the cup. Bring devotion into the blood of this temple.

Lay your hot hands on your throat, raising the power of air. Know full force your imagination, your capacity to create and inform. Sing the song of the planet and her people, bright clear note of hope. Delight in renewal: ceaseless, ceaseless. Bring inspiration into the breath of this temple.

Lay your hot hands on your crown, raising the power of a spirit born directly from Earth. Offer thanks; offer yourself. Blessed be.

¤ *Jessica Montgomery 2002*

MOON IX. LEO/VIRGO
August 15–September 14
New Moon in ♌ Leo August 15, Sun in ♍ Virgo August 22, Full Moon in ♓ Pisces August 29

© Beth Budesheim 1995

August

August

───── ☽☽☽ Montag ─────────────────

 ♌
♍

Monday
16

☽→♍ 6:49 am
☽☌♂ 2:39 pm
☽☍♅ 4:48 pm
☽☌☿ 7:14 pm
☽⚹♀ 11:53 pm

───── ♂♂♂ Dienstag ─────────────────

 ♍

Tuesday
17

♃⚹♄ 9:33 am
☽□♀ 7:49 pm

───── ☿☿☿ Mittwoch ─────────────────

♍
♎

Wednesday
18

☽⚹♄ 12:09 am
☽☌♃ 12:15 am   v/c
♂☍♅ 7:14 am
☿☌♂ 12:47 pm
☽→♎ 3:09 pm
☿☍♅ 6:00 pm

───── ♃♃♃ Donnerstag ─────────────────

♎

Thursday
19

☽□♀ 12:03 pm
☽△♆ 4:07 pm

───── ♀♀♀ Freitag ─────────────────

♎
♏

Friday
20

☽⚹♀ 2:54 am
☽□♄ 7:35 am
☿PrG 10:40 am
☉⚹☽ 6:39 pm   v/c
☽→♏ 9:37 pm

───────────────────────────────────

ALL ASPECTS IN PACIFIC DAYLIGHT TIME; ADD 3 HOURS FOR EDT; ADD 7 HOURS FOR GMT

Year at a Glance for ♍ VIRGO (Aug. 23–Sept. 23)

You have a gift, a skill, tool or talent that you have been developing for years with devotion: you realize it's now as perfect as it will ever be. Virgo's image for 2004 is "you are given a key that returns a lost part unlocking immense new horizons." Celebrate your determination; celebrate the maturity, presence and authority you now possess. All this becomes the sturdy foundations for your next great Work. This is a good year to claim new long-range goals (especially in July). Don't limit yourself, you've got plenty of time.

Ready to engage with others at a new level, some friendships are complete and will fade. People show up in your life to shock you, wake you up, stretch you. They see you and celebrate you in a way that helps you to be as unique (or as odd) as you really are. Connect with those who match you at your deepest level of power. Get off your proverbial cell phone and show up in person. Aim high, you convey an upbeat, confident enthusiasm and those who get to know you now will always think of you imbued with the delightful energy you emanate now. You are searing away old emotional responses; what may seem to be small gestures towards your health and well-being are actually heroic victories crafting enduring self-determination out of bedrock. You need deep companionships to communicate and release what you are discovering—do not isolate yourself. You will need to experiment with ways of relating to your chosen intimates that provide lots of spaciousness, less traditional, more sparky, spontaneous adventures.

by Gretchen Lawlor © Mother Tongue Ink 2003

Healing Hand
© Eleanor Ruckman 2002

ᚻᚻᚻ Samstag

♏ **Saturday**
21

☽✶☿ 3:19 am
☽△♅ 6:37 am
☽✶♂ 10:20 am

♀⊼♅ 5:18 pm
☽□♆ 9:36 pm
☽△♀ 9:57 pm

⊙⊙⊙ Sonntag

♏ **Sunday**
22

⊙→♍ 11:53 am
☽△♄ 1:04 pm
☽✶♃ 1:54 pm v/c

♍

Sun in Virgo 11:53 am PDT

August
agosto

♏︎
♐︎

Monday
23

☽→♐︎	2:08 am
☉□☽	3:12 am
☽□♉︎	4:31 am
☽□♅	10:40 am
☉♂♉︎	1:50 pm
☽□♂	4:51 pm

Las Manos de Celia, Bolivia
© Elizabeth Staber 2001

Waxing Half Moon in ♐︎ Sagittarius 3:12 am PDT

♐︎

Tuesday
24

☽⚹♆	1:09 am
☽♂♀	11:20 am
☽□♃	5:42 pm
☿♌︎	6:33 pm

♐︎
♑︎

Wednesday
25

☽△☿	4:13 am	v/c
☽→♑︎	4:46 am	
☉△☽	9:24 am	
☽⚹♅	12:53 pm	
☽△♂	9:19 pm	

♑︎

Thursday
26

☽☍♀	10:59 am	
♅PrG	12:28 pm	
☽☍♄	6:30 pm	
☽△♃	7:58 pm	v/c
☽PrG	10:31 pm	

♑︎
♒︎

Friday
27

☽→♒︎	6:08 am
☉☍♅	11:41 am
♀⚻♀	3:58 pm

The Womyn of "La Vida Nueva"

I met Pastora, Violeta, their Grandmother, Mother and three sisters in November 2001 when we gathered in their dirt floored, thin bamboo-walled home, to introduce my travel group to the womyn's cooperative they had formed five years earlier. Living in a womyn only household, in the Zapotec community of Teotitlan del Valle, in Mexico's southern state of Oaxaca, is a radical act in itself. This indigenous community is ruled by tradition, strictly reinforced by male dominated authorities, who are given complete control.

La Vida Nueva is a weaving cooperative of womyn who have been singled out for ridicule, humiliation and personal violence because they have acted on their own collective strength and power. They are determined to stand on their own, to sell their rugs directly to the consumer, thereby avoiding the exploitation of the male storeowners.

As they displayed their 100% wool, handcrafted, beautiful "tapetes" (rugs), they shared how they begin by cleaning the wool of twigs, then taking it to the river to wash. In the mountains they collect herbs, bark and insects used to concoct the natural dyes. It is they who collect the firewood they need for their wood fires for cooking. It is they who sell gelatins, rice puddings, etc., at the market to earn the little money they need. It is they who maintain their "milpa" (corn patch), where they grow the food they need for the year. There was no holding back how PROUD they were to be living independently.

See page 139 ☐ *Juanita Rodriquez 2003*

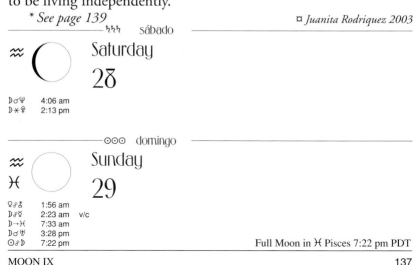

ጉጉጉ sábado

≈ Saturday
28

☽☌♆ 4:06 am
☽✶♀ 2:13 pm

☉☉☉ domingo

≈
♓ Sunday
29

♀☍♃ 1:56 am
☽☍♉ 2:23 am v/c
☽→♓ 7:33 am
☽☌♅ 3:28 pm
☉☍☽ 7:22 pm

Full Moon in ♓ Pisces 7:22 pm PDT

August/September

♓

Monday
30

☽☍♂	5:00 am
♀D	12:38 pm
☽□♀	4:36 pm
☽△♀	10:25 pm
☽△♄	11:09 pm

♂♂♂ dinsdag

♓
♈

Tuesday
31

☽☍♃	1:28 am v/c
♂⚹♆	2:47 am
♀♂♄	9:08 am
☽→♈	10:46 am

☿☿☿ woensdag

♈

Wednesday
1

☽⚹♆	10:28 am
☽△♀	9:50 pm

September

♃♃♃ donderdag

♈
♉

Thursday
2

♀⚹♃	12:15 am
☽□♄	5:16 am
☿D	6:09 am
☽□♀	8:46 am
☽△♉	9:17 am v/c
☽→♉	5:16 pm

♀♀♀ vrijdag

♉

Friday
3

☽⚹♅	1:52 am
☉△☽	3:37 pm
☽□♆	6:31 pm
☽△♂	11:28 pm

ALL ASPECTS IN PACIFIC DAYLIGHT TIME; ADD 3 HOURS FOR EDT; ADD 7 HOURS FOR GMT

"Diamonds and Rivets"

This intensely colorful and traditional Zapotec design is achieved through the use of the cochinilla insect carcass and lemon juice for dye. More lemon juice is added to get the orange and yellow colors. In the middle of each diamond shape is a butterfly, the symbol of power among the Zapotec. It is surrounded by many layers of color providing protection. The butterfly can represent new life in the family or community, the outer colors, relatives, or generations, that protect this new vulnerable life.

¤ *Juanita Rodriquez 2003*

¤ Rug by Violeta Vasquez Gutierrez, photo by Pastora Gutierrez 2003

ħħħ   zaterdag

♉

Saturday
4

☽✶♄	3:10 pm
☽△♃	6:50 pm
☽□♅	7:54 pm
☽✶♀	11:56 pm v/c

⊙⊙⊙   zondag

♉
♊

Sunday
5

☽→♊	3:24 am
⊙⽫♆	4:03 am
☽□♅	12:18 pm
♂ApG	12:24 pm

September
Chakrayapuy Killa

♌ Killachaw

♊

Monday
6

☽△♆ 5:50 am
☉□☽ 8:10 am
☽□♂ 2:29 pm
♀→♌ 3:16 pm
☽☍♀ 6:42 pm

♂♂♂ Atichaw

Waning Half Moon in ♊ Gemini 8:10 am PDT

♊
♋

Tuesday
7

☽□♃ 8:11 am
☽⚹☿ 11:08 am   v/c
☽→♋ 3:50 pm
☽ApG 7:34 pm

☿☿☿ Quyllurchaw

♋

Wednesday
8

☽△♅ 12:40 am

♃♃♃ Illapachaw

♋

Thursday
9

☉⚹☽ 2:12 am
☽⚹♂ 6:32 am
☽♂♄ 4:47 pm
♂□♀ 9:06 pm
☽⚹♃ 9:41 pm   v/c

♀♀♀ Ch'askachaw

♋
♌

Friday
10

☿→♍ 12:38 am
☽→♌ 4:06 am
☽♂♀ 12:22 pm
♀⚻♅ 1:52 pm

ALL ASPECTS IN PACIFIC DAYLIGHT TIME; ADD 3 HOURS FOR EDT; ADD 7 HOURS FOR GMT

Fighting Back

My daughter decked a kid at school the other day. He tried to snatch something that belonged to her, so she tackled him and he fell down.

Even though I am a person who believes in solving conflict with words instead of force, a woman who has never hit anyone, I found myself cheering my daughter's plucky response.

My reaction may have something to do with the fact that the disputed item was her Bugs Bunny pacifier, that Sasha is a petite eight-month-old just learning to stand, and that the boy she toppled is a sturdy one-year-old who already knows how to walk.

This happened the same day that hijackers steered American planes into the World Trade Center. As I listened to rhetoric of revenge on the news that night, I felt not proud, but sick.

The lives lost that day carve a trench in all our hearts; we understand fear and vulnerability in a sharp new way. I believe the yen for revenge comes from that grief, fragility and fear. We move toward action because action feels better than sitting still with our unspeakable pain.

But revenge is an old story. We could use this horror as the chance to write a new one—a story of feeling loss without lashing out, experiencing insult without needing to demonize or destroy. It is the lesson I want my daughter to learn. Even—perhaps especially—when the other kid decks her first.

© Anndee Hochman 2002

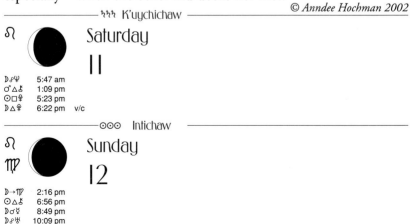

──────────── ↖↖↖ K'uychichaw ────────────

♌ Saturday

11

☽☍♆	5:47 am	
♂△♄	1:09 pm	
☉□♀	5:23 pm	
☽△♀	6:22 pm	v/c

──────── ⊙⊙⊙ Intichaw ────────

♌
♍ Sunday

12

☽→♍	2:16 pm	
☉△♄	6:56 pm	
☽☌♉	8:49 pm	
☽☍♅	10:09 pm	

She Is

Entertaining the brain-injured
Embracing special needs children
Grandmother, friend and
therapist to the neighborhood,
She is my Mother.

Midwifing the dying
Consoling the living
Serving up love in her
cornbread and collard greens,
She is my Colleague.

Taking in the displaced and injured
Be it four-legged or teenagers
Her heart and her hearth
know no limits,
She is my Refuge.

Building bonds from Colorado
To Bangladesh
Honoring two cultures,
matriarching her family,
She is my Example.

Identifying animal guides
Creating sacred space
Retrieving lost soul parts
for wholeness in community,
She is my Shaman.

Shooting mountain river rapids
Riding trail through the woods
Circled by turkey vultures
while she redefines disability,
She is my Compadre.

Communicating non-violence
Disaster planning in Nicaragua
Mediating conflict
between humans and horses,
She is my Friend.

Shapeshifter of occupations
Educator in all walks
Drawing back life
from the edge,
She is my Soul Sister.

Embodying wisdom and support
Wrapping all wounded in her arms
Piecing worlds together
when they splinter,
She is my Spiritual Counselor.

Studying ancient teachings
Of Mayan women weavers
Breaking worlds of stereotypes
to help our children,
She is my Neighbor.

Artfully brushing love
And diplomacy into all
She does and
everyone she touches,
She is my Reminder.

She feeds, She believes,
She attends, She teaches,
She listens, She remembers,
She shares, She loves,
She weaves, She dances,

She Is.

MOON X. VIRGO/LIBRA

September 14–October 13

New Moon in ♍ Virgo Sept. 14, Sun in ♎ Libra Sept. 22, Full Moon in ♈ Aries Sept. 28

Open Your Heart
¤ Robyn Waters 1998

September

September ——— ⊃⊃⊃ Montag ———

♍

Monday
13

☿ ♂ ♅ 8:54 am

Wild Woman Legend

© *Amarah K. Gabriel 1994*

——— ♂♂♂ Dienstag ———

♍
♎

Tuesday
14

☽□♀	2:53 am	
☉☌☽	7:29 am	
☽☌♂	8:05 am	
☽✶♄	12:20 pm	
☽☌♃	5:55 pm	v/c
☽→♎	9:54 pm	

——— ☿☿☿ Mittwoch ——— New Moon in ♍ Virgo 7:29 am PDT

♎

Wednesday
15

☉☌♂	5:55 am
☽✶♀	3:38 pm
☽△♆	9:17 pm

——— ♃♃♃ Donnerstag ———

♎

Thursday
16

| ☽✶♀ | 9:06 am | |
| ☽□♄ | 6:31 pm | v/c |

——— ♀♀♀ Freitag ———

♎
♏

Friday
17

☽→♏	3:25 am
☉✶♄	6:32 am
☽△♅	10:26 am
☽✶☿	11:17 pm

ALL ASPECTS IN PACIFIC DAYLIGHT TIME; ADD 3 HOURS FOR EDT; ADD 7 HOURS FOR GMT

Do Something

We can't just sit here and watch the wonderfully woven world unravel around us. I pledged myself to do something for the environmental good. Every morning I'd set off to the Dominican Castillo for two cafe con leche grandes to go, my own paper bag in hand. Each time I handed over my crumpled, much-folded bag along with my money, I would comment, "I'm recycling." Just how long would one bag last? How many bags make a tree? I used that same bag again and again, toting 20 ounces of liquid plus cups—almost one and a half pounds in weight—each time. I finally retired that bag into the re-cycling bin when it began to feel too flimsy after nine weeks of service. That's 63 bags worth. At that rate, a person would only need to use six bags a year, saving 359 bags in all. And that's just for coffee. Times how many people, how many meals? How many trees?

Very impressive. A perfect example that everything matters. Every single thing counts. We live in a participatory universe, and since everything is connected, there is no such thing as an outsider, a disinterested observer. According to quantum physics, observers, by the very fact of observation, affect events.

Our not doing is as potent as our action. By doing something positive, even just by thinking positive thoughts, negative trends are altered and transformed, as are we. Let us become aware, attentive, involved, evolved.

excerpt ¤ Donna Henes 2002

ħħħ   Samstag

♏︎ **Saturday**

18

☽□♀	1:16 am	☿⊼♆	9:15 pm
☽□♆	2:03 am	☽△ħ	11:07 pm
♀☍♆	10:50 am	☽⚹♂	11:37 pm
♂⚹ħ	11:32 am		

⊙⊙⊙   Sonntag

♏︎ ♐︎ **Sunday**

19

⊙⚹☽	1:55 am	
☽⚹♃	5:24 am	v/c
☽→♐︎	7:30 am	
☽□♅	2:14 pm	

September
septiembre

☽☽☽ lunes

♐

Monday 20

☽✶♆	5:35 am
☽△♀	9:20 am
☽□☿	10:14 am
☽☌♇	5:04 pm
♃ApG	7:34 pm

♂♂♂ martes

♐ ♑

Tuesday 21

☽□♂	5:16 am	
☉□☽	8:54 am	
☽□♃	9:19 am	v/c
☽→♑	10:35 am	
☉☌♃	4:47 pm	
☽✶♅	5:06 pm	

Waxing Half Moon in ♐ Sagittarius 8:54 am PDT

☿☿☿ miércoles

♑

Wednesday 22

☉→♎	9:30 am
☽PrG	1:53 pm
☿□♇	4:04 pm
☽△☿	8:21 pm

Equinox

Sun in Libra 9:30 am PDT

♃♃♃ jueves

♑ ♒

Thursday 23

☿△⚷	2:52 am	
☽☍♄	5:33 am	
☽△♂	10:16 am	
☽△♃	12:41 pm	v/c
☽→♒	1:10 pm	
☉△☽	3:12 pm	

♀♀♀ viernes

♒

Friday 24

☽☌♆	10:49 am	
♀△♇	11:07 am	
♃→♎	8:23 pm	
☽✶♇	10:27 pm	
☽☍♀	11:25 pm	v/c

Year at a Glance for ♎ LIBRA (Sept. 23–Oct. 23)

The image is "a hand appearing out of the mists helps you stand atop a large rock." A position of authority is at hand if you are willing to step up. Support for longstanding aspirations come from an unexpected quarter. Something to which you have been devoted for many years is coming to its culminating moment to be harvested this year. Be careful, you will need a critical sense of timing in order not to (1) get stuck tending an old flame, an old position past its brilliance, or (2) be seduced by a flashy new field where you have to start all over again. In your enthusiasm you could scatter your energies in a million directions.

There is an exquisite Libran tension to hold as you balance: the terrifying realization that your experience and knowledge makes you the authority AND a hunger to explore new ways of doing things. Stay committed to your longstanding field of expertise while using progressive ways of expressing it. At first innovation can feel awkward and tender. Stifle the urge to bag it all to go scuba diving with a beloved. Your stance will be challenged. Don't crumple and don't give yourself away to preserve the peace. The originality you bring to your field has merit—try it out first in small settings. By September you will be ready for bigger venues. Remember to accept help from that unexpected mentor and maintain your balance by playing in the restorative sanctuaries of nature, art and music. You continue to be a dreamer in love: someone new may flit across your screen.

by Gretchen Lawlor © Mother Tongue Ink 2003

Dear Sappho,
© Lorraine Inzalaco 2001

ᚻᚻᚻ sábado

≈ ♓ **Saturday**

25

♀⊼♄ 3:51 am
☽→♓ 3:55 pm
☽♂♅ 10:16 pm
☿⚹♄ 10:38 pm

⊙⊙⊙ domingo

♓ **Sunday**

26

♂→♎ 2:15 am
⊙⊼♅ 4:10 am
♇D 8:00 am
♂♂♃ 5:17 pm

This is How We are Called

In the hours before the birds
stream airborne
with chiming voice,
a silent breath rests in the pines,
and upholds the surface of the lake
as if it were a fragile bubble
in the very hand of God.

And I think,
this is how we are called.

To cup our hands and hold
this peace,
even when the sirens begin
even when sorrow cries old and gnarled
even when words grow fangs and rend.

Cupped hands,
gently open,
supporting peace
like the golden hollow of a singing bowl,
like the towering rim of mountains
cradling
this slumbering and mist-draped valley.

Power of Peace
© *Amarah K. Gabriel 2002*

Autumn Equinox

Day and night are once again equal and we glory in the light before it yields. Summer lingers but the scent of change rises from fields. Harvest hangs heavy, carrying within glistening seeds actual and potential interpenetrated. Equinox offers the power of balance. We assess our harvest, finding both reward and disappointment, praise and blame. Resisting the habit of polarity, we practice the art of equanimity. Celebrate Equinox with sacred dance, creating dynamic balance in motion. Begin in silence, resting on the earth, gradually building organic rhythm. Let sky lift you, suspended on gravity and bones. Dance your invocations, using incense, bells, candle flame, water, salt and other elements to sanctify the groove temple. Add music and percussion, building intensity within sacred space. Experiment with impulse but identify only with the still point around which incarnation spirals ceaselessly.

As the energy peaks send it outward where balance is needed. Instead of war, may there be union. Instead of sides, may there be center. Instead of them, may there be we. Close in silence, in balance, dark and light contained like flame and shadow in the burning heart of the world.   *by Jessica Montgomery © Mother Tongue Ink 2003*

□ *Gloria Kemper-O'Neil 2000*

Moon Dancer

ꝺꝺꝺ　maandag

♓
♈

Monday
27

☽□♀	1:57 am	
☽△♄	12:32 pm	
☽☌♅	6:12 pm	v/c
☽→♈	7:57 pm	
☽☍♃	9:06 pm	
☽☌♂	10:02 pm	

♂♂♂　dinsdag

♈

Tuesday
28

☉☍☽	6:09 am
☿→♎	7:13 am
☿☌♃	6:21 pm
☽⚹♆	6:48 pm

Full Moon in ♈ Aries 6:09 am PDT

☿☿☿　woensdag

♈

Wednesday
29

☽△♀	7:31 am	
☿☌♂	12:21 pm	
☽△♀	6:33 pm	
☽□♄	6:53 pm	v/c

♃♃♃　donderdag

♈
♉

Thursday
30

☽→♉	2:24 am
☿⚹♅	6:22 am
☽⚹♅	9:04 am

♀♀♀　vrijdag

♉

Friday
1

| ☽□♆ | 2:28 am |
| ♂⚹♅ | 1:21 pm |

October

ALL ASPECTS IN PACIFIC DAYLIGHT TIME; ADD 3 HOURS FOR EDT; ADD 7 HOURS FOR GMT

Harvest Full Moon

The days burn blue
over frosty morning
signaling the clans
for the long journey ou h
Flocks of nervous travelers
chatter in the treetops,
crows hold caucus in the o cha d
while hawks keen prophecy
from invisible minarets.
In the field the chopper scream ;
a relentless conclusion
to the generosity of corn.

This night the women settle
around the encouraging warmth
of the autumnal fire.
They take the smooth hard kernel
of the shadowy blue corn
appraising the harvest
of another season lived.

Under witness of the rising moon
feelings shed like snakeskin
exposing an older beauty
faces rendered
by the chisel of hard lessons,
the abrasive winds of loss.
The stony seeds
become prayer beads;
promissory notes for wisdom,
self-knowledge,
integrity.

Surrounded as these women are
this illumined night
by the settling of the frost,
the sleeping birds,
the moonlit skeletons of trees
who know the wealth of surrender
with every soft clatter
of a falling leaf

¤ *Jayn Avery 2001*

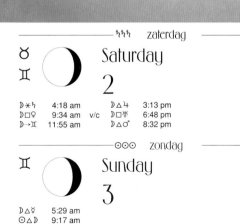

♄♄♄ — zaterdag

♉
♊

Saturday
2

☽⚹♄	4:18 am		☽△♃	3:13 pm
☽□♀	9:34 am	v/c	☽□♅	6:48 pm
☽→♊	11:55 am		☽△♂	8:32 pm

☉☉☉ — zondag

♊

Sunday
3

☽△♅	5:29 am
☉△☽	9:17 am
♀→♍	10:20 am
☽△♆	1:08 pm

October

Tarpuy killa

♊
♋

Monday

4

𝄐♂♀   3:28 am   v/c
𝄐→♋   11:54 pm

♋

Tuesday

5

𝄐⚹♀   3:59 am
𝄐□♃   4:24 am
𝄐△♅   6:50 am
☉△♆   7:59 am

☿△♆   9:30 am
☉♂♅   11:29 am
𝄐□♂   12:14 pm
𝄐ApG   3:18 pm

♋

Wednesday

6

☉□𝄐   3:12 am
𝄐□☿   4:22 am
♀♂♅   8:23 am

Waning Half Moon in ♋ Cancer 3:12 am PDT

♋
♌

Thursday

7

𝄐♂♄   5:13 am   v/c
𝄐→♌   12:23 pm
𝄐⚹♃   5:55 pm

♌

Friday

8

𝄐⚹♂   3:55 am
𝄐♂♆   1:29 pm
☉⚹𝄐   8:20 pm

ALL ASPECTS IN PACIFIC DAYLIGHT TIME; ADD 3 HOURS FOR EDT; ADD 7 HOURS FOR GMT

The Flavor of Yesterday

The particular flavor of yesterday
will not be tasted again
the melon sunrise will not be seen
and you and I will wander
into other arms
but always will be those first honeyed days
when love grew real
you arched your back
and in that moment
all became new
we were reborn in the grace of loving
days have passed . . . years
the memories distort
and in their place a calm acceptance grows
a delicious aftertaste
the bliss was real
can we ever stop loving those
who opened us to ourselves
can we ever express the depth of gratitude
in those precious hours
my heart exploded
and out walked someone new
she played upon the golden sunbeams
and sang rhapsodies
that will forever feed her days

© Cindy Ruda 2000

Emergence
© Katz Cowley 2002

ᕼᕼᕼ K'uychichaw

♌
♍

Saturday
9

☽⚹♉ 1:57 am
☽△♀ 3:42 am v/c
♉⚹♀ 2:49 pm
☽→♍ 11:00 pm
☿□♃ 11:59 pm

☉☉☉ Intichaw

♍

Sunday
10

♃⊼♅ 4:07 am
☽☍♅ 5:15 am
☽☌♀ 2:52 pm

Otter Woman

La mujera nutria en la noche estrellada
(The Otter Woman in the Star-studded Night)

Dryad, she rises from the river
Water sluicing from her hair and limbs,
She calls to the forest denizens,
The raven, the starling, the wolf, the bear,
Her soft bark echoing off the stands of alder.

Her narrow feet make sucking sounds
As she moves along the miry bank,
Breasts mirroring a luminous star band,
Her belly radiating power,
She glows in the shadow as phosphorescence,
Her way lighted as she steps.

Gazing at me with fathomless eyes,
Full of wise shamanic journeys,
Of ancient gris-gris,
Of fireside incantations,
This woman with whom I will tryst for long,
Who nuzzles against me in the charcoal dawn,
Who tells me to breathe as her hand slips inside me,
Who covers my mouth with her own
To receive my kiss.

¤ *Siobhán Houston 2001*

MOON XI. LIBRA/SCORPIO

October 13–November 12

New Moon in ♎ Libra Oct. 13, Sun in ♏ Scorpio Oct. 22, Full Moon in ♉ Taurus Oct. 27

Moonspell

October

Oktober

Lilith
© _Hrana Janto 1995_

ⅅⅅⅅ　Montag

♍

Monday
11

☽☐♀　12:24 pm

♂♂♂　Dienstag

♍
♎

Tuesday
12

☽⚹♄　12:32 am　v/c
☽→♎　6:32 am
☽☌♃　1:21 pm
☉⚹♀　6:10 pm

☿☿☿　Mittwoch

♎

Wednesday
13

☿ApG　12:03 am
☽☌♂　2:10 am
☽△♆　5:01 am
☉☐♅　9:48 am
☿☐♄　4:14 pm
☽⚹♀　6:00 pm
☉☌☽　7:48 pm

Partial Solar Eclipse* 6:53 pm PDT
New Moon in ♎ Libra 7:48 pm PDT

♃♃♃　Donnerstag

♎
♏

Thursday
14

♀⚹♆　5:07 am
☽☐♄　5:38 am
☽☌♅　7:22 am　v/c
☽→♏　11:10 am
☽△♅　4:38 pm

♀♀♀　Freitag

♏

Friday
15

☽☐♆　8:42 am
☽⚹♀　11:14 am
♂△♆　1:02 pm
☿→♏　3:57 pm

---

*Eclipse visible from Alaska, Japan, parts of China and Russia

Mother Snake

She teaches us to use indirect power
that's why we're experts at hiding ours

under doors, between blind slats,
we spit and slide through long grass.

Shed skin, combust commitment
into the dust of best left behind.

Or freeze, can't move, act like
we haven't changed one bit,

constrict love till it dies then swallow it.
Our tongues split truths in two,

we lose hands and feet to belly slide
up steep ravines, lie low, curled

in the roads deepest curves,
and when the time is right

strike with words.

¤ *Anne Bridgit Foye 2002*

ℏℏℏ   Samstag

♏︎
♐︎   **Saturday**
16

☽△♄	8:43 am	v/c
☽→♐︎	1:58 pm	
☽□♅	7:14 pm	
☽✶♃	9:52 pm	

☉☉☉   Sonntag

♐︎   **Sunday**
17

☽✶♆	11:04 am		☽PrG	5:00 pm
☽✶♂	1:17 pm		☽□♀	6:07 pm
☿△♅	2:30 pm		☽♂♀	11:40 pm

October
octubre

☽☽☽ lunes

Monday
18

♐ ♑

☉✶☽ 8:46 am v/c
☽→♑ 4:07 pm
☽✶♅ 9:18 pm

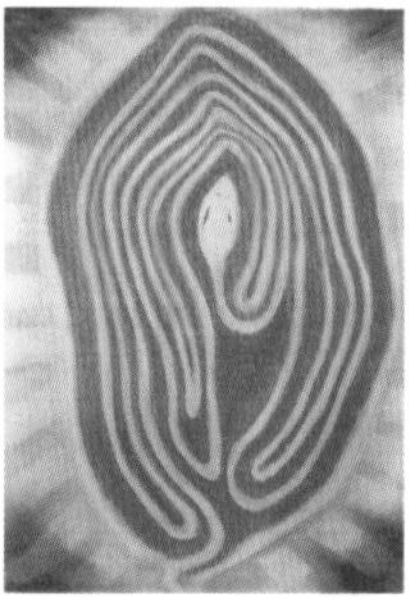

© Jill Smith 2002

Mystery of the Tor

♂♂♂ martes

Tuesday
19

♑

☽□♃ 12:45 am
☽✶☿ 1:12 am
☽□♂ 5:54 pm
☉□♄ 6:25 pm

☿☿☿ miércoles

Wednesday
20

♑ ♒

☽△♀ 12:57 am
☽☍♄ 1:35 pm
♀□♇ 2:28 pm
☉□☽ 2:59 pm v/c
☽→♒ 6:38 pm

Waxing Half Moon in ♑ Capricorn 2:59 pm PDT

♃♃♃ jueves

Thursday
21

♒

♀△⚷ 3:44 am
☽△♃ 4:10 am
☽□☿ 10:16 am
☽☌♆ 4:09 pm
☽△♂ 11:25 pm

♀♀♀ viernes

Friday
22

♒ ♓

☽✶♇ 5:20 am v/c
☉→♏ 6:49 pm
☽→♓ 10:13 pm
☉△☽ 10:29 pm

Sun in Scorpio 6:49 pm PDT

ALL ASPECTS IN PACIFIC DAYLIGHT TIME; ADD 3 HOURS FOR EDT; ADD 7 HOURS FOR GMT

Year at a Glance for ♏ SCORPIO (Oct. 23–Nov. 22)

2004's image for you is "small happy naked babies being catapulted into the air, arms wide, soaring into the distance." Scorpio is building towards a meaningful life peak in a couple of years. Now is a good time to anticipate and make plans for a better future. Claim dreams and ideas that need time to grow up. Name gifts or talents that you would like to bring out in a future job or integrate into your present one. A family tradition or themes/passions from another life may weave themselves into these dreams.

Current frustrations indicate a need to learn more about the rules of the game or you may need further training to help your credibility. Redefine your guiding principles whether they be political or spiritual and commit yourself to them—they will guide you well in times ahead. In a couple of years your confidence and ability to stand in your authority will be at a peak. Inspiration from peers or through group experiences will help you find the guts to stand out, to display yourself, to shine in ways you could not have crafted on your own. Volunteer time in situations that inspire you as it's both a chance to showcase yourself and to make good connections.

Love could be lively and unpredictable as you strut your stuff and people notice. If people fling themselves at you, kids rebel or family members act out—don't take it too seriously. Humor could change big dramas into high play. Let your own inner child fly now and then; simple, light frivolity is food for your soul.

by Gretchen Lawlor © Mother Tongue Ink 2003

Black Venus
© Sharon Virtue 1997

♄♄♄   sábado ---

♓ ☽

Saturday
23

☽☌♅   3:30 am
☿□♆   3:20 pm
☽△♅   9:00 pm

☉☉☉   domingo ---

♓ ☽

Sunday
24

♆D   4:56 am
☽□♀   10:04 am
☽☍♀   6:51 pm
☽△♄   10:17 pm   v/c

October
oktober

The Bone Fairy
¤ *Tatiana Makovkin 1998*

————— ☽☽☽　maandag —————

Monday
♓
♈

25

☽→♈　3:24 am
☽☌♃　3:14 pm
☉△♅　6:49 pm

————— ♂♂♂　dinsdag —————

Tuesday
♈

26

☽✶♆　2:20 am
♀✶♄　9:49 am
☽☍♂　3:48 pm
☽△♀　4:42 pm

————— ☿☿☿　woensdag —————

Wednesday
♈
♉

27

☽□♄　5:24 am　v/c
♂✶♀　10:17 am
☽→♉　10:37 am
☽✶♅　4:12 pm
☉☍☽　8:07 pm

Total Lunar Eclipse* 8:04 pm PDT (mag 1.313)
Full Moon in ♉ Taurus 8:07 pm PDT

————— ♃♃♃　donderdag —————

Thursday
♉

28

☽□♆　10:32 am
♂□♅　1:14 pm
♀→♎　5:39 pm

————— ♀♀♀　vrijdag —————

Friday
♉
♊

29

☽☍♅　2:28 am
☿✶♇　7:08 am
☽✶♄　2:50 pm　v/c
☽→♊　8:11 pm
☽△♀　11:05 pm

*ECLIPSE VISIBLE FROM WESTERN US, CANADA, HAWAII AND ALASKA
CENTRAL AND SOUTH AMERICA WILL SEE TOTAL PART BEFORE SUNRISE

Kali

Soul Journey
© *Maya Dobroth 1995*

Samhain

An ancient holy day with deep, strong roots, Samhain or Hallow'een is the shining portal to winter. As the energy of the green world withdraws into the earth, we also settle toward stillness. Nights lengthen, our center of gravity drops, barriers melt like leaves on damp soil, the veil between worlds is thin as a spider's web.

Dedicate Samhain to the root power of lineage. Deep in the belly bowl, find cellular memory of the line, knowledge of gifts we were born to carry forward. Whether our ancestors are biological, tribal or mythical, each of us is a child of dream and desire. Make an altar that honors ancestry, contributing offerings of color, scent, food and image vivid enough to tempt spirits earthward. Call yourself into circle by way of your line, however you perceive it: great aunt to Magdelene to Sappho and beyond. Name your inheritance and heirloom traits entrusted to you. Ask: what is the work of my people in this age? Use an oracle to answer this question or listen for quiet truth from within. From clarity, craft a vow—small or large, lofty or precise—committing to living this purpose. Leave a candle burning overnight infused with the light you carry. *by Jessica Montgomery © Mother Tongue Ink 2003*

on reading an account of Virginia Woolf's death

I'm thinking of a woMan who walked
into the waters of a river
with stones in her pockets

thinking of the waters
of the rivers of my life

thinking of the stones
in My pockets

woMen are born
with stones in their pockets

eMpty them   eMpty theM swiM

¤ *Karen Ethelsdatter 2002*

♄♄♄   zaterdag

♊ Saturday
30

☽□♅   1:57 am
☽△♃   10:57 am
☽△♆   9:05 pm

☉☉☉   zondag

♊ Sunday
31   *Samhain/Hallowmas*

♀⚻♅   2:44 am
☽☍♀   11:52 am
☽△♂   5:21 pm   v/c

Daylight Savings Time ends 2:00 am PDT

November
Pawqarwara killa

ⅮⅮⅮ Killachaw ─────────

We come from water.
The voice of all
the waters in the world
speaks of love.
excerpt © Sara Gama 2000

♊
♋

Monday
1

☽→♋	6:53 am
☽△♅	12:46 pm
☽□♀	4:39 pm
☽□♃	11:04 pm

───────── ♂♂♂ Atichaw ─────────

♋

Tuesday
2

☉△☽	3:54 am
☿△♄	10:01 am
☽ApG	10:13 am

───────── ☿☿☿ Quyllurchaw ─────────

♋
♌

Wednesday
3

☽□♂	9:31 am	
☽♂♄	2:08 pm	
☽△☿	6:00 pm	v/c
☽→♌	7:32 pm	

───────── ♃♃♃ Illapachaw ─────────

♌

Thursday
4

☿→♐	6:40 am
☉□♆	9:34 am
☽✳♀	12:07 pm
☽✳♃	12:38 pm
♀♂♃	6:11 pm
☽☍♆	8:52 pm
☉□☽	9:53 pm

Waning Half Moon in ♌ Leo 9:53 pm PST

───────── ♀♀♀ Ch'askachaw ─────────

♌

Friday
5

☽△♀	12:49 pm

─────────────────────────────

ALL ASPECTS IN PACIFIC STANDARD TIME; ADD 3 HOURS FOR EST; ADD 8 HOURS FOR GMT

Current Events

A small splash of news from the air waves.
I flood with the Absurd. Let me tell you:
In Bolivia, these days, it is illegal for people to catch rainwater.
Centuries of rainwater falling from roofs into barrels and tubs,
buckets of life from the sky for crops and herds, baths and drink.
It is illegal to catch raindrops. Corporations bought the water.
In South Asia, corporations copyright pollen.
Seeds that make plants that make seed become contraband.
Generations of botanical care wiped out by company patent.
Perhaps soon they will sell bottles of sunshine.
Clouds will wear brand names, and if you do not have
the price of air, you will not breathe.
Greed clutches the planet, sucks her juices,
gorges on the fat of the land,
will bloat/will choke/ will strangle
on the ferment of stolen harvest,
on the rising tide of earthwise peoples
catchers of rain, savers of seed, planters of hope.
Let me hope. Let me hope.

Epilogue: In Bolivia, these more recent days,
raincatchers rose up like a boiling flood
and swept the absurd corporations
our of their watershed, out of their country.
Like I told you.

ᖽᖽᖽ K'uychichaw

♌
♍

Saturday
6

☽✶♂	12:45 am	v/c	
☽→♍	7:00 am		
♅□♅	7:18 am		

☽☍♅	12:34 pm
☽□♅	1:15 pm
♂□♄	9:03 pm

☉☉☉ Intichaw

♍

Sunday
7

☉✶☽	1:10 pm
☽□♀	10:26 pm
♄R	10:54 pm

Flight

I will fly
I know barbed wire, thumbtacks, bare halls,
I've seen the white walls of slavery,
        and I can transform them.
Each thing, examined, regains beauty.

I will fly into color itself:
        red as the fiery robes of a huge woman
        blue as the veins in her breasts
        green as her hair trailing on the sea
        purple as her most secret self

I will fly like a plant flies:
invisibly in small seed-pods,
bourne on the friendly goddess-wind,
touching endless possibilities,
someday deciding where to land
        where to sprout
knowing: I'll fly again.

I'll fly rich, weighted by
        a hundred flying women.
Gold flashes from their earrings
as they fly by my window,
wearing images of the goddess
next to their skin.

I'll fly in a rising mist of desire,
I'll touch the smoke,
        taste the wet air,
        fly above, fly below,
        infinite acrobatics.

MOON XII. SCORPIO/SAGITTARIUS

November 12–December 11

New Moon in ♏ Scorpio Nov. 12, Sun in ♐ Sagittarius Nov. 21, Full Moon in ♊ Gemini Nov. 26

Women Help Each Other to Fly
© *Pamela Maresten 1996*

I will fly.
Fly in dreams, fly working,
break out of the shadows flying,
sky-write letters and invocations,
fly lonely as a purple dipping sun,
or fly in crowds of beautiful women,
or drift clinging to the long dress
      of the Mother herself.
I'll see as I fly: my eyes will fly.
I am simple and splendid in flight
like all natural things: a simple miracle:
a woman in flight.   ¤ *Jenny Yates 1994*

November

November

the compelling call
of the coy little cleavage
of a Scorpio new moon
golden and grinning
who walked me
all the way home

excerpt © Lila Kealoha 2000

DDD   Montag

♍ ♎

Monday

8

♀△♆   2:58 am
☽✶♄   10:32 am   v/c
☽ᐧ♎   3:23 pm

♂♂♂   Dienstag

♎

Tuesday

9

☽✶☿   3:44 am
☽♂♃   8:22 am
☽△♆   2:05 pm
☽♂♀   5:32 pm

☿☿☿   Mittwoch

♎ ♏

Wednesday

10

☽✶♀   4:21 am
☽□♄   3:32 pm
☽♂♂   8:02 pm   v/c
☽ᐧ♏   8:05 pm
♂ᐧ♏   9:11 pm

♃♃♃   Donnerstag

♏

Thursday

11

☽△♅   12:58 am
☿✶♃   8:31 am
♅D   11:11 am
☽□♆   5:28 pm

♀♀♀   Freitag

♏ ♐

Friday

12

☉♂☽   6:27 am
☽△♄   5:34 pm   v/c
☽→♐   9:56 pm

Lunar Samhain
New Moon in ♏ Scorpio 6:27 am PST

ALL ASPECTS IN PACIFIC STANDARD TIME; ADD 3 HOURS FOR EST; ADD 8 HOURS FOR GMT

¤ Robyn Waters 1992

Rethinking Red Riding Hood

♐

Saturday
13

☽□♅	2:37 am		☉⚹♆	3:40 pm
☿⚹♆	1:19 pm		☽⚹♆	6:37 pm
☽⚹♃	2:37 pm		☽☌☿	7:06 pm

♐
♑

Sunday
14

☽PrG	5:57 am	
☽⚹♀	6:43 am	
☽☌♀	7:58 am	v/c
♀⚹♀	10:11 pm	
☽→♑	10:33 pm	

November
noviembre

I choose freedom in falling
and learn to fly
like a peach with wings.
excerpt © Catherine Wilcox 2002

☽☽☽ lunes

♑

Monday
15

☽✶♂ 3:08 am
☽✶♅ 3:13 am
♂△♅ 4:58 am
☽□♃ 3:49 pm
♀□⚷ 6:59 pm

♂♂♂ martes

♑
♒

Tuesday
16

☽□♀ 11:57 am
☉✶☽ 3:17 pm
☽☍♄ 7:07 pm v/c
☽→♒ 11:39 pm

☿☿☿ miércoles

♒

Wednesday
17

☽□♂ 6:45 am
☽△♃ 6:06 pm
☽☌♆ 9:04 pm

♃♃♃ jueves

♒

Thursday
18

☽✶☿ 6:47 am
☽✶♇ 11:18 am
☽△♀ 7:18 pm
☉△♄ 9:33 pm
☉□☽ 9:50 pm v/c

Waxing Half Moon in ♒ Aquarius 9:50 pm PST

♀♀♀ viernes

♒
♓

Friday
19

☽→♓ 2:38 am
☽☌♅ 7:41 am
☽△♂ 12:42 pm
♀□♄ 11:12 pm

All aspects in Pacific Standard Time; add 3 hours for EST; add 8 hours for GMT

Year at a Glance for ♐ SAGITTARIUS (Nov. 22–Dec. 21)

Pluto, planet of crisis and transformation has been plowing through Sagittarius since 1995. The demands of the journey seem never ending, though, take heart, you are definitely in the rebirth canal. Sagittarius' image for 2004 is "a heavily dressed being shedding layers of clothing, which lie like rubble at their feet."

"I've been doing this for years already," wails Sagittarius. Longing for fresh pastures arises, a relocation at some point helps or has helped the clearing process. More than you consciously realize is being accomplished purely through your willingness to let go of the past. Hold strong to some act of will that symbolizes your capacity to change your destiny. Eliminate a bad habit, say no, give away objects evocative of an old life, do therapy, take up health building regimes (though your body gives you signs not to overdo it). Focusing your considerable will and truly confronting your own demons will produce an up swell of energy, more courage, more daring, which in turn catalyzes even more good changes. Parts of you that have been unavailable since childhood take up residence in your spacious new self.

Influential people recognize you as a kindred spirit. Your incurable optimism, wise perspective and imaginative, evocative ways of communicating captivate others. People feel more hopeful just being around you and you see your new self emerging, reflected in their eyes. In love, respect the very different values of your intimate companions and weave them into a mutual game plan that provides both time for deep communion and time alone. Your own inner work is rich and must not be neglected.

by Gretchen Lawlor © Mother Tongue Ink 2003

♓ **Saturday**

20

☽□♅	3:57 pm
☽□♀	4:12 pm
♅♂♀	7:23 pm

Firebird
© Deborah Koff-Chapin1994

⊙⊙⊙ domingo

♓ **Sunday**
♈

21

☽△♄	3:02 am	
⊙△☽	7:35 am	v/c
☽→♈	8:11 am	
⊙→♐	3:22 pm	

Sun in Sagittarius 3:22 pm PST

November

november ──── ⊅⊅⊅ maandag ────────────

♈ Monday

22

♀→♏ 5:31 am
☽☌♃ 6:00 am
☽⚹♆ 7:55 am
☽△♀ 11:44 pm

¤ *Cynthia Camille Brannan 1994*

──────── ♂♂♂ dinsdag ────────────

♈
♉ Tuesday

23

☽△☿ 3:43 am
☽□♄ 10:47 am v/c
☽→♉ 4:16 pm
☽☌♀ 8:03 pm
☽⚹♅ 9:52 pm

──────── ☿☿☿ woensdag ────────────

♉ Wednesday

24

☽☌♂ 9:33 am
☉□♅ 1:19 pm
♀△♅ 2:46 pm
☽□♆ 5:01 pm

──────── ♃♃♃ donderdag ────────────

♉ Thursday

25

☽⚹♄ 8:37 pm v/c

──────── ♀♀♀ vrijdag ────────────

♉
♊ Friday

26

☽→♊ 2:25 am
☽□♅ 8:16 am
☉☌☽ 12:07 pm

Full Moon in ♊ Gemini 12:07 pm PST

ALL ASPECTS IN PACIFIC STANDARD TIME; ADD 3 HOURS FOR EST; ADD 8 HOURS FOR GMT

Powah

The powah in the noise of the trees
The powah in the voice of the breeze
The powah in the whisper of the leaves
The powah in the wisdom of the seas
The powah in the orchestra of she . . .

© Sioux Patullo 2002

Autumn on Earth   ¤ *Janice Iliffe-Lewis 1985*

♄♄♄ zaterdag

♊ ◯ Saturday
27

☽△♃ 3:28 am
☽△♆ 4:01 am
☽☌♀ 9:02 pm

☉☉☉ zondag

♊ ◑ Sunday
♋ 28

☽☌♅ 7:04 am v/c
☽→♋ 2:10 pm
☽△♅ 8:13 pm

November/December
Pawqarwara killa/Ayamarq'ay killa

© Paula Mariedaughter 1999

Catherine Makes Fire

─────))) Killachaw ─────

♋ ## Monday
29

♃△Ψ	12:26 am
))△♀	7:53 am
))△♂	3:29 pm
))□♃	4:34 pm

───── ♂♂♂ Atichaw ─────

♋ ## Tuesday
30

))ApG	3:23 am
☿R	4:17 am
♂□Ψ	7:25 am
))♂♄	8:28 pm v/c

───── ☿☿☿ Quyllurchaw ─────

♋
♌ ## Wednesday
1

))→♌	2:50 am

December

───── ♃♃♃ Illapachaw ─────

♌ ## Thursday
2

☉△))	12:00 am
))□♀	3:38 am
))☊Ψ	5:08 am
))✶♃	6:03 am
))□♂	7:47 am
♀□Ψ	6:22 pm
))△♀	10:25 pm

───── ♀♀♀ Ch'askachaw ─────

♌
♍ ## Friday
3

))△☿	6:52 am v/c
))→♍	3:00 pm
))☊♅	9:05 pm

The Art of Making Fire

The art of making fire. An ancient skill once taught to the young. A woman near the eve of the 21st century. A fire-making class in the Ozark Mountains—a place she lived as a child. Women teaching wilderness skills, the art of the past conveyed through their hands. Sticks. A knife. Lengths of grass.

We'll begin by constructing a bow drill—a primitive tool for creating fire. As a girl in these southern forests, I felt that sticks were gifts from the trees. *Use the knife to carve the hand hold.* I've never handled a knife this large. *Hold the knife like this.* I can't do this. I'm not that strong. *Carve a point on the spindle, a corresponding hole in the fire board. Find a curved stick for the bow.* I've never encountered my body's power. *Twine the grass into cordage. Attach the cord to the bow.*

Frustration kindles my anger. Anger ignites my strength.

Loop the cord around the spindle. Balance the tip in the fire board's hollow. Draw the bow with the strength of your arm. Quickly. Back and forth. The spindle whirls in the fire board. Friction. Heat. Coal. *Transfer the coal to the kindling.*

The power of breath creates flame.

© *Catherine Alaria Vitale 2000*

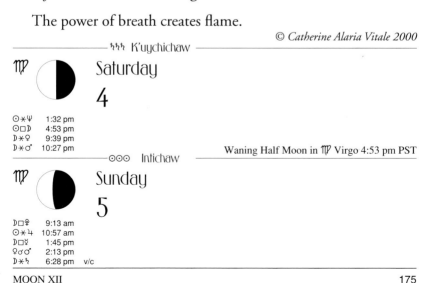

♄♄♄ K'uychichaw

♍ Saturday 4

☉⚹♆ 1:32 pm
☉□☽ 4:53 pm
☽⚹♀ 9:39 pm
☽⚹♂ 10:27 pm

Waning Half Moon in ♍ Virgo 4:53 pm PST

☉☉☉ Intichaw

♍ Sunday 5

☽□♇ 9:13 am
☉⚹♃ 10:57 am
☽□☿ 1:45 pm
♀☌♂ 2:13 pm
☽⚹♄ 6:28 pm v/c

December
Dezember

—————))) Montag —————

♍︎
♎︎

 Monday

6

☽→♎︎ 12:46 am

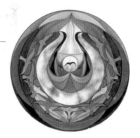

Turning Light into Dark
© Pamela Maresten 1980

————— ♂♂♂ Dienstag —————

♎︎

Tuesday

7

☽△♆ 12:55 am
☽♂♃ 2:54 am
☉⚹☽ 5:42 am
☿♂♀ 3:03 pm
☽⚹♅ 4:19 pm
☽⚹♀ 4:26 pm

————— ☿☿☿ Mittwoch —————

♎︎
♏︎

Wednesday

8

☽□♄ 12:41 am   v/c
☽→♏︎ 6:43 am
☽△♅ 12:13 pm

————— ♃♃♃ Donnerstag —————

♏︎

Thursday

9

☽□♆ 5:12 am
☽♂♂ 3:22 pm
☽♂♀ 7:31 pm
☿PrG 11:40 pm

————— ♀♀♀ Freitag —————

♏︎
♐︎

Friday

10

☉♂☿ 12:21 am
☽△♄ 3:03 am   v/c
☽→♐︎ 8:54 am
☽□♅ 2:08 pm

ALL ASPECTS IN PACIFIC STANDARD TIME; ADD 3 HOURS FOR EST; ADD 8 HOURS FOR GMT

I am Alive

I have been living my whole
Life in a wheelchair,
Hardly able to communicate
For I have no voice.
I communicate by touching
Letters on a board, but most
People have a hard time understanding.
I am alive, finally taking part
In my own life.
I have found my spirit and live
There more and more.
Owning it, like I never have before.
I can sing and dance without
Moving a muscle.
Yet now I dance for me and
Love it.
I used to feel sorry for myself,
Thinking I had been punished.
Now I laugh because I created it!
My life, my condition, to learn from.
Now I laugh all the time even when
Nothing is funny.
I laugh, because I am alive.

¤ *Kirsteen Main 2002*

ħħħ Samstag

♐

Saturday
11

☽⚹♆	6:11 am	☽☌♅	11:32 am		
☽⚹♃	8:45 am	☉☌☽	5:29 pm		
♀⚹⚷	10:59 am	☽☌♀	8:03 pm	v/c	

⊙⊙⊙ Sonntag

New Moon in ♐ Sagittarius 5:29 pm PST

♐
♑

Sunday
12

☽→♑	8:42 am
☽PrG	1:39 pm
☽⚹♅	1:52 pm
☿⚹♃	4:46 pm

Becoming a Lesbian

It was midnight in suburbia,
And there were dragons in the street

As I sat brooding by the window,
Flicking my fingers through a candle
Meditating on abstract theories,
I heard a roar bite through the night.

And peering past glass,
I saw the shine of her,
The dancing fire and carving scales,
Of my own child-known dragon,
My steamy mountain,
My nest of fire.

The window fought me
With its glass and sticking wood.
The walls themselves tightened
With stony sighs and old harangues.
But I watched my hands fight,
Watched them bleed, saw them win,
I leaned into that calling midnight
Heard my lungs gasp air like song.

Saw my feet like running water,
Felt my arms wrap dragon-neck,
And its tongue, that fork of fire,
Licked me gentle as a cat.

I leaped upward,
Filling my arms with snaky neck.
And its hot body burned my feet,
And my fingers shot magic fire.

The moon poured a milky glow,
And my hollow bones licked it up
And I called myself the name I feared.

And now astride, I run the streets,
And stir the pale air with my true name,
And dash the city with this hurricane
Of high-rearing dragon-wing.

Ah, I know this spiraling wind,
This dragon and I, we've flown before.
The earth has fallen away before,
And I've touched and gathered sky.

I've touched cool moonskin before,
My dreams have always insisted it,
And my knowing turns within me,
A lode-stone, rune-etched, charged,

Pointing to that clear remembered time,
When the dragons spotted the sky like stars,
And the mountain-egg sprouted rays,
Jagged and strong as dawn,
And I knew myself open.

¤ Jenny Yates 1984

MOON XIII. SAGITTARIUS/CAPRICORN

December 11–January 9

New Moon in ♐ Sagittarius Dec. 11, Sun in ♑ Capricorn Dec. 21, Full Moon in ♋ Cancer Dec. 26

Harnessing the Power

© *Wendy Page 2002*

December
diciembre

——————DDD lunes ——————————

♑

Monday
13

♀△♄ 8:26 am
☽□♃ 8:33 am
☉♂♀ 9:04 am
☽⚹♂ 7:38 pm

——————♂♂♂ martes ——————————

♑
♒

Tuesday
14

☽☍♄ 2:03 am
☽⚹♀ 3:43 am v/c
☿⚹♆ 5:46 am
☽→♒ 8:10 am
♀ApG 12:11 pm

——————☿☿☿ miércoles ——————————

♒

Wednesday
15

☽⚹♅ 4:17 am
☽♂♆ 5:45 am
☽△♃ 9:08 am
☽⚹♀ 8:13 pm
☽□♂ 10:38 pm

——————♃♃♃ jueves ——————————

♒
♓

Thursday
16

☉⚹☽ 12:33 am v/c
♀→♐ 9:10 am
☽→♓ 9:24 am
☽□♀ 9:25 am
☽♂♅ 3:09 am

——————♀♀♀ viernes ——————————

♓

Friday
17

♂⚹♆ 12:05 am
☽□♅ 4:24 am
☉⚼♄ 5:50 am
☽□♀ 11:54 pm

Mother Union

The stones are
the deep deep bones,
of the Earthmother,
Holding the Wisdom
of the Ages,
and the Ancient Ones.
The Crystals,
are the brain cells,
of the Starmothers,
Holding cosmic knowledge,
and cerebral Sparks
of Light.

¤ *Lorye Keats Hopper 2001*

Carmelita: Andean Wool Spinner, Peru
© *Elizabeth Staber 2001*

ħħħ   sábado

♓   **Saturday**
♈   **18**

☽△♂	5:06 am
☽△ħ	6:30 am
☉□☽	8:40 am v/c
☽→♈	1:52 pm
☽△♀	7:22 pm

Waxing Half Moon in ♓ Pisces 8:40 am PST

☉☉☉   domingo

♈   **Sunday**
19

♀□♅	3:53 am	☽⚹♆	2:37 pm
♂△ħ	6:10 am	☽☍♃	7:18 pm
☽△☿	9:03 am	☿D	10:29 pm

December
december

----------- ☽☽☽ maandag ------------------------------

♈
♉
Monday
20

☽△♀ 7:12 am
☽□♄ 1:45 pm
☉△☽ 9:16 pm v/c
☽→♉ 9:52 pm

----------- ♂♂♂ dinsdag ------------------------------

♉
Tuesday
21

☽✶♅ 4:40 am
☉→♑ 4:42 am

Solstice

♑

----------- ☿☿☿ woensdag ------------------------------

Sun in Capricorn 4:42 am PST

♉
Wednesday
22

☽□♆ 12:06 am
☽✶♄ 11:47 pm

----------- ♃♃♃ donderdag ------------------------------

♉
♊
Thursday
23

☽☍♂ 5:41 am v/c
☽→♊ 8:32 am
☽□♅ 3:44 pm

----------- ♀♀♀ vrijdag ------------------------------

♊
Friday
24

☽☍♀ 3:54 am
☽☍♃ 8:10 am
☽△♆ 11:42 am
☽△♃ 5:37 pm
☉✶♅ 6:50 pm

ALL ASPECTS IN PACIFIC STANDARD TIME; ADD 3 HOURS FOR EST; ADD 8 HOURS FOR GMT

Year at a Glance for ♑ CAPRICORN (Dec. 21–Jan. 20)

The image for Capricorn 2004 is "a figure holding something precious behind their back." Concerns over partnerships and intimate associations dominate your time and attention this year. Someone is holding something back from you, or conversely, you may have hidden issues that you have not yet revealed. It's a good time to lay everything out on the table, there's more to the situation that needs revealing. Be clear about agendas. Be honest. Having done this, negotiate agreements that suit the current circumstances of both parties. A burdensome relationship, or one in which honesty is not possible, will probably end. A good relationship will become richer and more supportive.

Finally people are beginning to sit up and listen when you speak. What you've been learning about yourself and about life seems helpful for others. Influential people respond well to your confident manner and quick mind. You have a charismatic manner and fresh perspectives. Follow up on ideas and connections that come in casual conversations. Trust your genius. You have a way of framing things in a different way with an immediate comprehension of problems and highly original solutions. This could lead to new work, if you're looking, by the end of the year.

This is an exceptionally good time to pursue advanced education or to travel. You hunger for variety in your day to day life and fresh intellectual stimulation. Exposure to a new daily world, a new community and progressive edges of science or technology will radically alter your whole way of thinking. From this, new avenues for the future will lay out before you.

by Gretchen Lawlor © Mother Tongue Ink 2003

Lunar Eclipse at Ale Stones (Sweden)
© Monica Sjöö 1995

♄♄♄   zaterdag

♊
♋

Saturday
25

☽☌♀   5:30 am   v/c
♂→♐   8:04 am
☽→♋   8:38 pm

☉☉☉   zondag

♋

Sunday
26

☽△♅   4:06 am
☉☍☽   7:06 am
☿⚹♆   9:35 pm

Full Moon in ♋ Cancer 7:06 am PST

Solstice

And I thought of Persephone, Queen of the Underworld,
six months beneath the snows, six in the sun,
her mother Demeter spreading wild fecundity in summer heat.
Persephone, who ate pomegranate seeds,
the blood on her hands
condemning her to winter darkness.
I know better now.
I know better, because beneath the snow
our compost is steaming.
There's churning life burning up those dead leaves,
a bacchanalia turning moldy rinds to soil.
There's Persephone's sticky heat
sweet with pomegranate juice,
her belly holding hot promise of spring.
She's not dead. She's got work to do.   *excerpt ¤ Elissa Malcohn 1997*

Winter Solstice

The longest night pulls us down into the resting season. Quiet land teaches by example: that which rises must also sleep; that which sings is silent too or the rhythm of life is lost. Give Solstice to the power of the dream. Like ancient priestesses in the Hypogeum practicing dream ritual for the tribe, become a vessel for magic.

Dream incubation—seeding imagination with sacred intention —is done through ceremony, divination or any potent creative practice. Begin with a ritual bath to calm the nervous system and empty the mind. Create a dream cave with cushions and darkness. Solo or with others, imagine … Imagine you had been raised to honor and enact the mysteries of birth, death and rebirth. Imagine through song, story and sacred rite, you were fed on the undiluted nectar of the goddess and so were made of her, by her, inseparable. Imagine details of daily life infused with evidence of her power, embodied by her children. How would life have been different? How would the world be changed? Then ask: what would it take to live now as if the dream were true? Plant seeds of your dream world deep, knowing the wheel turns, the light returns, the dreamer wakes and the world rises renewed.   *by Jessica Montgomery © Mother Tongue Ink 2003*

December/January

Dezember/Januar —♌♌♌ Killachaw —

♋

Monday

27

☽□♃	6:39 am	
♀⚹♆	8:32 am	
☽ApG	11:12 am	
♄⚹♇	9:32 pm	
☽♂♄	11:34 pm	v/c

—♂♂♂ Atichaw —

♋
♌

Tuesday

28

☽→♌	9:14 am	
☿♂♀	10:25 am	
☽△♂	1:43 pm	

—☿☿☿ Quyllurchaw —

♌

Wednesday

29

☽☍♆	1:02 pm	
☽△♅	6:14 pm	
☽△♀	7:01 pm	
☽⚹♃	7:44 pm	

—♃♃♃ Illapachaw —

♌
♍

Thursday

30

♀⚹♃	2:19 am	
☽△♀	6:54 am	v/c
☿⚹♃	1:07 pm	
☽→♍	9:33 pm	
♂□♅	11:49 pm	

—♀♀♀ Ch'askachaw —

♍

Friday

31

☽☍♅	5:18 am	
☽□♂	5:37 am	
☉△☽	6:57 pm	

© *Marja de Vries 1998*

One day I shall say to myself,
This is the way of being
you have shaped,
and the vastness of the view
was worth
the climb.

excerpt ¤ Veronica M. Murphy 1982

───────────────── ꙮꙮꙮ K'uychichaw ─────────────────

♍ Saturday

1

January 2005

☽□♅	11:42 am
☽□♀	1:26 pm
☽□♇	6:23 pm
☽⚹♄	10:23 pm v/c

───────────────── ☉☉☉ Intichaw ─────────────────

♍ Sunday
♎

2

☽→♎	8:19 am
☽⚹♂	7:25 pm

January

Qhapaqintiraymi killa ☽☽☽ Montag

Monday
3

♎

☉□☽ 9:46 am
☽△♆ 10:39 am
♀☌♇ 3:33 pm
☽☌♃ 5:23 pm

The Power of Life
¤ *Musawa 1999*

Waning Half Moon in ♎ Libra 9:46 am PST

♂♂♂ Dienstag

Tuesday
4

♎ ♏

☽⚹☿ 2:22 am
☽⚹♇ 3:04 am
☽⚹♀ 4:15 am
☽□♄ 6:20 am v/c
☿☌♇ 9:58 am
☽→♏ 4:00 pm
☽△♅ 11:16 pm

☿☿☿ Mittwoch

Wednesday
5

♏

♀⚻♄ 1:06 am
☽□♆ 4:39 pm
☿⚻♄ 5:30 pm
☉⚹☽ 7:57 pm

♃♃♃ Donnerstag

Thursday
6

♏ ♐

☽△♄ 10:29 am v/c
☽→♐ 7:44 pm

♀♀♀ Freitag

Friday
7

♐

☽□♅ 2:39 am
☽☌♂ 10:36 am
☉□♃ 6:12 pm
☽⚹♆ 6:48 pm

All aspects in Pacific Standard Time; add 3 hours for EST; add 8 hours for GMT

Building Peace

Many people were transformed by the events of 9/11, and in response to all the energies being focused on retaliation and war, I helped plan and priestess a community ritual dedicated to peace.

Many people came from diverse walks of life. We circled in front of the federal building in the center of town. Together we built a cairn—a pile of stones erected as a memorial or marker.

We had previously gathered river rocks and painted positive symbols on them. After creating sacred space, we passed them around; each person chose a stone. Closing our eyes, we drew the strength of the Earth up thru our feet as we inhaled, then as we exhaled we let that energy pour out of our hearts into the stone. We each thought about what strengths we had that could be used to help build our collective movement and acknowledged that every person had something special to share.

We sang and walked, spiraling into the center. One by one, stacking the stones on top of each other, we built a symbolic marker on the path to peace and justice, and a memorial to victims of terror worldwide. We knew then, that feeling power with others rather than using power over them is what brings true understanding. We raised energy and charged our cairn—inspiring each other to continue to think positive and move forward, sending power to peaceful people everywhere!

¤ *Diana Gardener 2002*

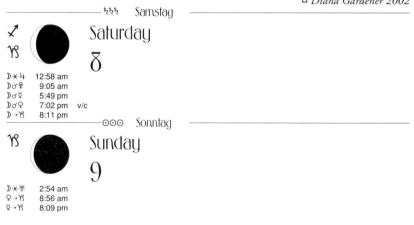

ħħħ   Samstag

♐
♑

Saturday
8

☽⚹♃	12:58 am	
☽☌♀	9:05 am	
☽☌♉	5:49 pm	
☽☌♀	7:02 pm	v/c
☽→♑	8:11 pm	

☉☉☉   Sonntag

♑

Sunday
9

☽⚹♅	2:54 am
♀→♑	8:56 am
☿→♑	8:09 pm

Moon Daughters

Moon-daughters, celebrate the power of your feet:
Earth-roots, journey-walkers,
> upholders of your growing and reaching,

Strong in the dance, the hike, the labor, the leaping and loving.
> Daughters of the moon, celebrate your strong feet.

Moon-daughters, celebrate the power of your hands:
Sky-fingers, dream-graspers, cradles of your burning hopes,
> Palms cupping life-water, friendship's clasp,
> raising up those behind and below,

Fingers reaching hammer, calculator, stethoscope,
keyboard, pen—Tools of self-making and world-protecting.
> Daughters of the moon, celebrate your strong hands.

Moon-daughters, celebrate the power of your minds:
Chalice of the Heavens and the Earth
> Your minds are wings, bright, eager, all-encompassing,
> as unfettered as the sun.

And celebrate the power of your hearts:
Fierce and tender, steel and softness, bone and blessing—
They kindle the flame of justice and uncage the dove of mercy.
> Daughters of the moon, celebrate your keen minds
> and wild hearts.

Moon-daughters, celebrate the power of your wombs:
Inner oceans of creativity, ferocious green-spark of vitality,
> For some, mind-children:

Buildings and bridges, calculus and costumes, science and songs,
> For others, body-children:

The blossoms of tomorrow watered by loving streams of now.
> Daughters of the moon, celebrate the ever-renewing
> chalice of the womb.

Daughters of the moon, celebrate the power that is all of you.

¤ *Margaret Hammitt-McDonald 2002*

Stream of Compassion
© *Mara Zareen Friedman 2002*

WE'MOON ANCESTORS PAGE

We honor we'moon who have gone between the worlds of life and death recently, beloved contributors to we'moon culture who continue to bless us from the other side. We appreciate receiving notice of their passing.

Jean Hardy (April 28, 1942–Nov. 9, 2002) **We'Moon** contributor (2002), died at her home surrounded by her family. She was a columnist for a variety of publications including *Crone Chronicles, Utne Reader* and *The Chronicle* as well as two self-published journals: *The Spotted Chicken Report* and *Birdy's Circle*.

June Jordan (July 9, 1936–June 14, 2002), extraordinary author of over 2 dozen books of non-fiction, poetry, fiction, drama and children's writing, she was a cultural and political activist. Most recently, she was African-American studies professor at University of California, Berkeley. For Toni Morrison, June Jordan was: "Forty years of tireless activism coupled with and fueled by flawless art."

Kay Gardner (Feb. 8, 1940–Aug. 28, 2002) A prolific composer, gifted musician, author, priestess and teacher died at her home in Maine. Her music and her dedication to her spiritual path and service to the Goddess empowered and inspired countless women worldwide.

Martingale (Marti) Bridget Mudgedell Napanangka (circa 1935–March 10, 2002) was a pillar of Aboriginal women's Law in the community of Balgo/Wirrimanu in Australia. Marti was a significant and prolific artist. She devoted her immense energy and enthusiasm to maintaining her Culture. Her passing is a great loss, not only to her family but to all who value the breadth and depth of her traditional knowledge.

Monique Wittig (July 13, 1935–Jan. 3, 2003), an exceptional writer, poet and social theorist. Born and schooled in France, her ideas and writings heavily influenced the fields of women's and gender studies. She taught women's studies and French at the University of Arizona. Her books include *Les Guérillères, The Lesbian Body, The Straight Mind and Other Essays*.

Tony (1987–2003) literary cat, with a generous purr and bright, big love; wishes for the sweetest of cat naps.

© Copyrights ¤ and Contacting Contributors

Copyrights of individual works in **We'Moon '04** belong to each contributor. Please honor the copyrights: © means do not reproduce without the express permission of the artist or author. Some we'moon prefer to free the copyright on their work. ¤ means this work may be passed on among women who wish to reprint it "in the spirit of **We'Moon**," with credit given (to them and **We'Moon**) and a copy sent to the author/artist. Contributors can be contacted directly when their addresses are given in the bylines, or by sending us a letter with an envelope with sufficient postage plus $1 handling fee for each contributor to be contacted.

Contributor Bylines and Index

Abby Wentworth (Seward, AK) lives in Alaska where she paints and plays and works only as much as necessary. p. 105

Amarah K. Gabriel (Salt Spring Island, BC, Canada), the environmental spirit of her paintings has put her in the spotlight of international arts activism. As CEO of Green Goddess Productions, her use of tree free paper is a powerful message for eco-consciousness. Lives on Salt Spring Is., gardens and raises Peace Doves. pp. 2, 43, 114, 144, 149

Anna Oneglia (Santa Cruz, CA) is a painter who lives by the sea in California. pp. 109, 117

Annalisa Cunningham (Gualala, CA) is a yoga teacher, writer, artist who takes people on journeys to the Yucatan every winter. She is author of *Stretch & Surrender*, and *Yoga Vacations: A Guide to International Yoga Retreats*. Email her at RioAnalisa@aol.com. p. 40

Anndee Hochman (Philidelphia, PA) is the author of *Anatomies: A Novella and Stories* (Picador USA, 2000) and *Everyday Acts & Small Subversions: Women Reinventing Family, Community and Home* (The Eighth Mountain Press, 1994). p. 141

Anne Bridgit Foye (Nantucket, MA) is a poet dedicated to facilitating poetry circles of healing words. She is the author of two chap books and can be reached at: annefoye@mediaone.net. p.157

Annie Kohut Frankel (Berkeley, CA) lives with her beautiful husband and two wild Hawaiian cats. p. 131

Ba'ella Bo Conlan (Crescent Valley, BC, Canada): I'm a lover of beauty, have been a professional musician for 20 years and have discovered how much I love to paint. p. 31

Baraka Robin Berger (Gloucester, MA), BFA painter/printmaker, lives with her daughter. She believes that beauty is essential to our well-being. The intention behind her artwork is to bring beauty into life as a healing force. p. 119

Beate Metz (Berlin, Germany) is an astrologer, translator and author, inspired by being in nature where everything returns to its real relativity . . . For further information: www.pallas-athena.de. p. 204

Becki Hoffman (St. Augustine, FL) is an artist, massage therapist, yogini and lover of life. She sees so much healing POWER! in nature— her biggest inspiration. Learn more about Becki and her mission at www.hoffmans.net/becki. p. 113

Beth Budesheim (Kansas City, MO), may you feel, know and experience the light & love that you are! To see more or to order prints and greeting cards, please enjoy a visit to www.paintedjourneys.com. Namaste. p. 133

Bethroot Gwynn (Myrtle Creek, OR) has been living on wimmin's land for 28 years, growing food, art, ritual. Loves working with **We'Moon**! FFI about spiritual gatherings, working visits or possible residency on the land, send SASE to Fly Away Home, PO Box 593, Myrtle Creek, OR 97457. pp. 32, 165

Carol Wylie (Biggar, SK, Canada): I am a visual artist/actor/singer living in the amazing prairies of Western Canada. I continue to seek joy, independence, love and sisterhood through my life and my work and wish the same for all. p. 65

Carolyn Lee Boyd (Concord, MA) is a gardener of stories about Goddess for our new generation of women. She lives a quiet life where she is a freelance writer and editor. She first became chums with the Goddess in Manhattan's East Village, which is why she can be reached at GoddessAveA@aol.com. p. 69

Catherine Alaria Vitale (Madison, WI): A writer and artist, my work is inspired by nature, dreams and the ancient past. Currently creating a performance piece about the return of the 13–Year Cicadas to my childhood home near the Ozark Mountains. p. 175

Catherine Holmes (Rock Hill, SC) is a self-taught artist. Catherine specializes in 2-D & 3-D collage using old books, magazines and photographs. All of her work reflects her personal spiritual journey, a process she describes as watching a dream emerge while she is awake. p. 61

Catherine Wilcox (Victoria, BC, Canada), devoted poetic and musical channel of the Big Mama and practitioner of Deep Joy, Big Love and Wild Hope. Direct your inspiration and inquiries to cwilcox71@hotmail.com. Bright and Beautiful Blessings! pp. 120, 170

Celestína Pearl (San Francisco, CA) is a Chicana femme dyke, performance artist, poet, Bruja. She's performed with the fierce Pussy Posse, Liquid Fire, Debauchery, at Lunasea Women's Theatre and in *Please Don't Stop and Voluptuous Vixens*, two movies celebrating the erotic lives of lesbians of color. p. 70

Cindy Ruda (Sedona, AZ) is an intuitive artist and writer whose personal journeying began with letters to herself. Her aim is to reap the fullness of who she is. She opens to creativity and watches as her art invents itself. p. 153

Colette Gardiner (Portland, OR) is an herbalist and plant lover. She offers herbal programs and classes in Portland, Oregon. She can be reached at gcoletteg@aol.com p. 24

Corey Alicks (Cottage Grove, OR) is a photographer, writer, homebirth midwife and mother of five young children. She is currently working on the publication of her first book. p. 48

Cosima Hewes (Buckland, MA): I recently moved to the Pioneer Valley in Massachusettes. My work over the years has mostly revolved around my contemplation of relationships and pregnancy, the joy and beauty of childhood and personal reflection on the birth process. p. 94

Cynthia Camille Brannan (Irving, TX): What the mother is, the daughter is becoming. Blessed be. p. 172

Cynthia Ré Robbins (Eureka Springs, AR): Art Power! Creating art clears my mind, brings me joy and increases my energy. I am sharing my visions through publications, websites, galleries, cafes and street fairs. May the power travel far and wide. www.art4spirit.com front cover

Deborah Jones (Trumansburg, NY): Thirty years later I still live and work in the home I created. Through the colossal building task maybe, Hestia, Goddess of the hearth, was the sole-guide who helped and encouraged me to stay with it. artemisdj@hotmail.com p. 95

Deborah Koff-Chapin (Langley, WA), her evocative images are created through the simple yet profound process she calls Touch Drawing. Deborah is creator of *SoulCards 1 & 2* and author of *Drawing Out Your Soul*. She teaches internationally and is founding director of The Center for Touch Drawing. www.touchdrawing.com pp. 4, 37, 171

Debráe FireHawk (Eugene, OR): I am a channel, a minister and a dancer. Those are the things that fill me with that feeling of complete joy and rightness . . . This, and loving great people, which is my favorite pastime! p. 46

Diana Gardener (Eugene, OR) encourages everyone to take action to help create a better world. Magical activism is her current passion. When she isn't helping plan or priestess rituals, she connects with spirit thru nature, art, gardening, drumming, dancing and sacred sex. Correspond at priestessdivine@yahoo.com p. 189

Diane Porter Goff (Blacksburg, VA) is an artist and healer who lives and works in the mountains of VA. She belongs to the "Hotchas," Hot Chocolate Amazons, Goddess group. She has taught Sacred Art on Lesbos for Ariadne Institute. p. 55

Diane Rigoli (San Francisco, CA) weaves together the visible and invisible worlds with her art. She works as an artist, illustrator, graphic and web designer. Contact her at PO Box 330157, San Francisco, CA 94133 or rigoliarts@earthlink.net. pp. 125, 129

Diane M. Bergstrom (Louisville, CO): Unfolding what grows corn for me; continually circling back to my art, writing, holding space for the death process—be it in a garden or at a bedside, finding healing in Nature for myself and others and dancing this all together. p. 142

Donna Henes (Brooklyn, NY), Urban Shaman, is the author of *Moon Watcher's Companion, Celestially Auspicious Occasions* and *Dressing Our*

Wounds in Warm Clothes, as well as the highly acclaimed quarterly journal, *Always in Season*.   pp. 56, 145

Durga Bernhard (Phoenicia, NY), painter, printmaker, illustrator for more than 15 children's books, teacher of West African dance/drum and mother of two children. She's inspired by ancient and tribal cultures from all over the world. durga@netstep.net   p. 51

EagleHawk (Tesuque, NM): I love taking photos of our Mother Earth in all Her elements—earth, water, fire and air. I'm praying for balance in my life and on our planet. Every moment is precious.   p. 38

Eleanor Ruckman (San Francisco, CA): My work is spiritual, hopeful, feminist and environmental. I believe that art transforms and empowers, both through the process of making and through the process of looking. I have a BA in fine art and a master's degree in art therapy.   p. 135

Elissa Malcohn (Cambridge, MA): I live with an extraordinary woman and two wise, elderly cats. The Goddess blesses us with words, visions, humor, song, and the power of Nature slowly overcoming asphalt. Writer, artist, musician, teacher, perpetual student. http://www.home.earthlink.net/emalcohn/index.html.   p. 184

Elizabeth Roberts (Nyack, NY), a witchy revolutionary, does anti-racist and anti-imperialist education and organizing with Resistance in Brooklyn and The Brecht Forum. She takes leadership from her cats, Mali and Kito. Her chapbook, *Brave as Planets*, is available at lizard@mail.tco.com   pp. 83, 100

Elizabeth Staber (New York, NY): Currently, I am in the process of getting a Masters in Education. I love taking photographs of inspirational women of the world—may we live and carry peace within our hearts.   pp. 136, 181

Ellen S. Jaffe (Hamilton, ON, Canada) is a writer, therapist and student of shamanism, originally from New York, now living in Canada. Mother, gardener and involved in Poets for Peace.   p. 103

Elsie Williams (Birmingham, AL) is a poet, artist, editor, healer who deals every day with her sun and four planets in Gemini as she seeks the Oneness. Loving energy welcomed.   p. 74

Gloria Kemper-O'Neil (Louisville, KY): I am a fiber artist. I create contemporary quilt art. Inspiration for my designs comes to me in dreams and features Goddess figures. They exemplify my soul's expression of the Sacred in Female form.   p. 130

Gretchen Lawlor (Seattle, WA): Passionate astrologer for over 30 years. I teach, write and do astrological consultations with We'Mooners all around the world. light@whidbey.com or 206-391-8681.   pp. 25, 27, 28, Moons II–XIII

Heather Roan Robbins (New York, NY) is an astrologer from NM and NYC who is fascinated by how astrology maps relationship strengths and challenges within a natal chart: partnership, family, work situation or cultural. You can reach her at RoanRobbins@aol.com. www.roanrobbins.com or 914-375-9598.   pp. 12, 15, 28

Helen Rowan (Whitley Bay, Tyne and Wear, UK) is deeply interested in women's spirituality and the ancient female mysteries and their relevance today.   p. 54

Holli Zollinger (Tremonton, UT) p. 56

Hrana Janto (Tillson, NY) is an artist long inspired by mythology, history, fantasy and the sacred. Works include *The Goddess Oracle* (HarperCollins) and many Llewellyn book covers and calendars, children's book art and more. For info: www.hranajanto.org PO Box 18, Tillson, NY 12486 pp. 28, 41, 71, 156, 161, back cover

J. Davis Wilson (Eugene, OR): I find freedom and joy in painting, dancing, practicing handstands, teaching toddlers and watching myself shift the many-seated teetertotter of this weird, beautiful life. I am just myself again. Say hi to me at: www.justdavis.net. Also visit: www.stand.org. pp. 57, 62

Jackie Joice (Long Beach, CA) resides in Long Beach, CA. Jackie writes, empowers, plays Flamenco guitar and enjoys eating early breakfast. pp. 67, 113

Jan Salerno (Durango, CO): Ever incarnating, lover, empath, healer, mother of goddess ananda, spatial magician transforming the mundane to the sublime . . . passionately drumming my selves awake in gratitude of life. Published in 14 countries. jancis_salerno@hotmail.com p. 15

Janice Iliffe-Lewis (Launceston, Cornwall, UK): Whilst I am on this Earth I aim to bring to others an awareness at nature and her wonderful creative possibilities. I do this by song, dance, art and craft, and revealing more of myself everyday. Nam myoho renge kyo. p.173

Jayn Avery (Floyd, VA) lives a mile off the Blue Ridge Pkwy in a rural county of Virginia. A potter and homesteader, her writing reflects a deep connection to the natural world and her place in its cycles. p. 151

Jenny Yates (Abascal, Quito, Ecuador) works as an astrologer, mostly via e-mail from Quito. She travels in the summer giving workshops at women's events & writes a column for lesbian.com. Write her at jenny_yates@yahoo.com. pp. 90, 167, 178

Jessica Montgomery (Portland, OR) is a ceremonialist and therapist deeply devoted to the dignity of earth and soul. Drawing from the world's mystical traditions, she specializes in bringing individuals and groups into direct contact with the wild divine. Pilgrim at heart, she travels and teaches internationally. blessica@msn.com. pp. 55, 74, 91, 111, 127, 132, 149, 162, 184

Jill Smith (Glastonbury, UK), artist, writer, performer, inspired by myth of ancient sites and sacred landscapes. Originals, cards, prints, books, CD available: 20 Monington Rd, Glastonbury BA6 8HE UK. airghid@hotmail.com www.jill-smith.co.uk p. 158

Juanita Rodriguez (Corvallis, OR) calls herself a "Freelance Community Catalyst." She volunteers her time to actively support the Zapotec women from La Vida Nueva weaving cooperative. For rug orders or information, contact her at juanitar@proaxis.com. pp. 137, 139

K. Marie Bender (Vancouver, WA), vintage 1960, wise woman, wife, friend, sister, daughter, step mom, wild woman, runner, vegetable and weed grower, storyteller, motorcycle tamer, earth lover & finder of lost rocks. p. 77

Kami McBride (Vacaville, CA), creator *of Cultivating the Herbal Medicine*

Woman Within, an Experiential Earth Awareness and Herbal Studies program for Women. Her workshops create a sanctuary for women to remember their heritage as healers and herbalists. www.livingawareness.com.   pp. 24, 112

Karen Ethelsdattar (Jersey City, NJ) is a poet & liturgist who has published two chapbooks, *Woman Artists & Woman as Art* and *The Cat Poems*. Her most recent full-length book is *Earthwalking & other poems*, c2001 (Xlibris). Her poems have appeared in a number of periodicals & anthologies.   pp. 60, 81, 163

Katey Branch (S. Paris, ME) lives in Maine with her twin nine-year old daughters and partner. She loves to sing, dance, write and create art. She facilitates seasonal celebrations and Opening to the Divine Feminine creativity workshops. Check out her website at www.wildworksunlimited.com.   p. 84

Katheryn M. Trenshaw (Totnes, Devon, UK) is an artist & workshop facilitator integrating creativity, transformation & magic. She is committed to working with bringing the sacred back into the mundane & living until we die. She is currently completing her book, *Breaking the Silence*. Originals & reproductions available. www.ktrenshaw.com   p. 101

Katz Cowley (Auckland, New Zealand) trained as an illustrator in the UK & is currently living in New Zealand. Her powerful, mystical and spirited images are created spontaneously and herein lies their power, carrying the essence of life & bridging inner and outer worlds.   p. 153

Kim Antieau (Stevenson, WA) is an eco-artist and writer. Her latest novel is *Coyote Cowgirl*.   p. 115

Kim Sahana Beyer-Nelson (Lincoln, NE) holds a master's degree in comparative religion and a graduate degree in holistic health care. She teaches yoga, meditation and introductory health classes in the Lincoln, Nebraska area. Her new book, *A Little Book of Wholeness and Prayer: An Eight-Week Meditation Guide*, will be published in October, 2002 by Skinner Horse Press.   p. 148

Kirsteen Main (Vancouver, BC, Canada): I write poetry using an alphabet board. I have been doing this since elementary school. I am now 23 years old, a young women with cerebral palsy. Most of my poems have been serious up to now, but I would like to be more humorous.   p. 177

Krista Lynn Brown (Sebastopol, CA): Mate, mother, painter of visions, budding shamaness weaving intuitive magic, deep dreamer, earth devotee, daughter of water and believer in the healing power of invocative art. See my mythic visionary art at www.devaluna.com.   pp. 63, 155

Lila Kealoha (Durham, NC): Sprouted in Honolulu, weathered in Indiana, now blooming in the South, a well-mulched modern anchorite. Grateful my art often surprises me. Needing for now only to have more life to dance about.   p. 168

Lilian de Mello (Kapaa, HI), mostly passionate about B&W, infrared, transfers, collages, intending to develop "soul healing imagery"—looking for emotions & goddess aspect of women & nature. Multi-layered images searching for feelings and soul. LDMPHOTO@GTE.NET www.liliandemello.com.   p. 39

Linda Ann Brunner (Stockton, MO) currently resides in rural Missouri.   p. 98

Linda Chido (Rego Park, NY) is self-taught in her chosen medium of oils, a figurative artist who uses traditional techniques of the Old Master's to create her visionary images. Exhibited internationally, her art has been seen in publications worldwide. She lives and paints in Queens, NY with her husband Ron Gross. To learn more: www.lindachido.com. p. 97

Linda Kerby-Spiral Crone (Leawood, KS) is an hereditary witch and Reiki Master Teacher and practitioner. p. 106

Lorena Babcock Moore (Corona De Tucson, AZ): I am a geologist, an artist in hand-ground mineral pigments and a blacksmith specializing in iron jewelry and shaman's bells. p. 50

Lorraine Inzalaco (Tucson, AZ): I painted for many years with constant awareness of my formal training. Since my recovery from illness several years ago, I now paint healing images based on intuitive inner images. My studio is a happier and healthy support for me to play, create and heal. p. 147

Lorraine Schein (Sunnyside, NY) is a New York poet and writer whose work has appeared in *FemSpec, The Beltane Papers, Strange Horizons*, and the story anthology *Mondo Alice*. p. 64

Lorye Keats Hopper (Somerset, UK) works with Creative Healing Arts. She has been helping women & young people to heal from wounds of abuse and empowering creativity. Her passion is to write poetry, create ceremony and to dance on the Earth. p. 181

Louise Chambers AKA Phrag-Hag/weezul (Denver, CO): I thank Goddess for Coven With No Name, Moonday Circle, my power animals, HotGoddess and all my wonderful friends! E-mail to: mooncrone13@aol.com. p. 3

Lynn Dewart (San Diego, CA): Artist, teacher, costumer honoring the cycles, rhythms and stories of the inner and outer worlds and the human experience. My sculptures serve as icon, avenue, totem, fetish, trophy, mirror and vessel. Artwork and workshops for adults and children at www.lynndewart.com. pp. 73, 131

Madeline Moss (Friday Harbor, WA), author of *Gaia Smiles,* is an ecofeminist and pagan living in the San Juan Islands. p. 119

Mara Zareen Friedman (Lorane, OR): Changes, waves of emotion, uncertainty . . . remember to focus on the Love Light Within. Painting the Sacred Feminine and connecting with the land are my ways of remembrance and prayer. For a free catalog: PO Box 23, Lorane, OR 97451, mara@newmoonvisions.com. p. 191

Margaret Hammitt-McDonald (Portland, OR) is a naturopathic medical student, organic gardener, science fiction writer, outdoorswemon, ecofeminist and devotee of the Goddess Oyá and the Monty Python Pantheon. pp. 93, 190

Margot Foxfire (Deming, WA): I am a becoming-elder living in community at River Farm. I feel art is a form of prayer—a bridge between the seen and unseen, the known and unknown. p. 12

Marion Cloaninger (Vilas, NC): I am a self-taught artist and find the figure exciting to draw/paint. Currently, I am working on a goddess series. p. 8

Marja de Vries (Oldenzaal, The Netherlands): As an artist, dream worker and light worker, I make wall-hangings and paintings mainly in commission using psychic reading to get to see the images. For more information www.marjadevries.nl; phone +31(0) 541-533593. pp. 127, 187

Marleen Grommers (Culemborg, The Netherlands), artist and nature photographer, whose challenge it is to show the Beauty and Uniqueness of living on Mother Earth. pp. 38, 39

Marna (Portland, OR) thanks Earth daily for this benevolent, spacious, wondrous life. Goddess Astologist-PO Box 14194, Portland, OR 97293. p. 111

Mary Mackey (Sacramento, CA) is the author of 11 novels including *The Year The Horses Came* (based on the work of Marija Gimbutas). She has also published four collections of poetry, some of which is on her web page at www.csus.edu/indiv/m/mackeym. p. 36

Maya Dobroth (Fort Collins, CO) lives with her family in Colorado. She spends her days teaching, creating, exploring, gardening and "doing Cat time" with her cat Krishna. pp. 102, 162

Megan Myfanwy Harris (Waterville, VT) lives in the northern hills of VT. with her spicy daughter Ella, two more women, two more kids, two more goats and two more cats—beauty all around and within. p. 140

Miriam Dyak (Seattle, WA) lives, teaches, writes, gardens, celebrates on Puget Sound. She is a Voice Dialogue facilitator and the author of three books of poetry. mdyak@life-energy.net p. 128

Molly Sullivan (San Diego, CA), this busy 32-year old artist-entrepreneur sponsors a schedule of classes at her store, Starcrafts in Ocean Beach, and a web site, www.starcraftsob.com. pp. 35, 49

Monica Sjöö (Bristol, UK): I am Swedish artist & writer, but live in Britain since many years. I have exhibited many years. Co authored *The Great Cosmic Mother*, author of *Return of the Dark/Light Mother or New Age Armageddon* & *The Norse Goddess*. I travel widely & do slide shows of my work. p. 183

Musawa (Estacada, OR/Tesuque, NM): I am a Capricorn turning 60 this year. Having co-founded We'Moon Land and the **We'Moon** in my thirties, I have now spent half my life creating wemoon land, community, culture—a baby Crone, ripening. pp. 6, 9, 20, 32, 188

Myra Dutton (Idyllwild, CA): *Healing Ground*, a collaboration of my poetry with nature photography by Trish Tuley, will be published by Celestial Arts in May, 2003. Our hope is that you will always find healing ground in your lives. p. 76

Nicole Di Pierre (Monte Rio, CA): PO Box 863, Monte Rio, CA 95462. "*It doesn't interest me where or what or with whom you have studied. I want to know what sustains you from the inside when all else falls away.*" Oriah Mountain Dreamer p. 123

nicole lori mamann (San Juan Bautista, CA): My journey towards knowing Life Art and Spirituality are one, is apparent in my being, from crystals as earrings to making my own clothes. Photography, collage, jewelry, music and herbs are among the many things that encompass my expression. p. 89

Nola Ann Conn (Anahola, HI): Island dreamer, healer, actor, partner, friend. Birds, ocean and breezes are my soul music; every breath a prayer of gratitude to this Goddess, Earth.   pp. 42, 47

Pamela Ewasiuk (Masset, BC, Canada): Saree dancin mama on Haida Gwaii. Creativity flowing through me, reflecting in all aspects of my life—my relationship with my daughter, myself, my community, our Mother Earth and our spirit companions. Opening Artistic Expression, Spiritual Ressurection!   p. 95

Pamela Maresten (Lopez Island, WA) is a grandmother enjoying life as art in a quiet rural island in the Pacific Northwest.   pp. 167, 176

Parimal Danielle Tonossi (Victoria, BC, Canada) lives on Vancouver Island. Author of several books in French about Crystals, Reiki, Meditation. For many years she has shared her intuitive feminine "wise" leadership in her holistic center: www.crystalgardenspirit.com. She is an Aura-Soma® Colour Therapy Teacher.   p. 45

Patricia Mary Brown (Ithaca, NY) creates mixed media sculptures, paintings and beaded jewelry. In her figurative images, Brown incorporates ancient symbols which express timeless and contemporary concerns of the feminine, spirit, ritual and nature.   pp. 85, 99, 185

Paula E. Mariedaughter (St. Paul, AR)   p.174

Robyn Waters (Portland, OR) lives in Portland with high hopes of spiritual enlightenment and semi-low hopes of amazing wealth, fame and grandeur. She is confident these hopes will all eventually materialize. Peace and blessings of balance to us all!   pp. 32, 75, 121, 143, 169

Rose Flint (Bath, Somerset, UK): Poet, artist, teacher, art therapist, Priestess of Avalon, I celebrate and serve the goddess through the wheel of the year at her Temple in Glastonbury and bring sacred poetry to the goddess conference there, every Lammas.   p. 125

Sandra Pastorius (Medford, OR): I am a crone-wise, heavenly body on a mission for 24 years as an Astrologer and writer. My birthchart readings and transit updates are lovingly offered by phone or in person. You can contact me at (541) 734-8835 or Laughinggiraffe2001@yahoo.com. Peace Be.   p. 26

Sandra Stanton (Farmington, ME), devoted to the Goddess & Her myths for 2 decades, Sandra's paintings express her great love of Mother Earth & all Her creatures. Her work can be seen online at www.goddessmyths.com.   pp. 107, 110

Sara Gama (Reston, VA): I am a university student and student of the mysteries. I am exploring the many ways I can express myself and communicate with others.   p. 164

Sarah Teofanov (Farmington, NM): I am a myth maker, peace activist, community organizer. My creativity creates links between the worlds and to local/global communities. I am here to en-vision the new and mid wife it into existence.   p. 6

Sharon Virtue AKA Sistar Skyclad (San Francisco, CA): As a mystical activist my vision is to spread love, peace and joy in the world. My next project is to build an art school in Africa—free art education is the answer if you would like to help contact virtuevision@earthlink.net. pp. 79, 80, 159

Shoshana Rothaizer (Flushing, NY) is a Native New Yorker who has sojourned and traveled in various parts of North America and Europe. She enjoys connecting with the spirits of nature in both city and country. Many of Shoshana's best-known images were taken on lesbian land. For info on photo postcards, please send a SASE to 147-44 69th Rd, Flushing, NY 11367. p. 92

Siobhán Houston (Lafayette, CO) is a writer and mother who facilitates women's circles and is a doctoral student in religious studies. She lives with her spouse, Rae and their many deities of Kali Ma. www.spiritualpassages.com alexandria@post.harvard.edu p. 154

Sioux Patullo (Drysdale, Victoria, Australia): Growing in Australia. Discovering the settled part of a restless soul. Studying again. Designing second skins. Teaching at a Sleina school. Love. Color. Crayons. pp. 59, 96, 173

Soma AKA Jeanne-Marie de Moissac (Biggar, SK, Canada) sends blessings from the hills. Her book, *Second Skin*, published by Coteau Books is available in bookstores. p. 88

Sue Silvermarie (Ontario, WI): I channel Spirit into poetry and children's stories. My second Saturn Return in 2003 brought me to Croning. I now turn myself over to my largest art, least visible and most crucial, the creation of harmony in my life and life partnership. ssilvermarie@yahoo.com p. 68

Suraj Holzwarth (Anchorage, AK) is an internationally known spiritual leader, healer, teacher and drum maker/musician. She has traveled the world for over 20 years leading women's spiritual journeys, rites of passage, traditional healing practices, ritual arts and initiation ceremonies in the women's mysteries. rainbowdream@chugach.net p. 53

Susan Levitt (San Francisco, CA) is a witch and author of Taoist Astrology, Taoist Feng Shui, Teen Feng Shui and Introduction to Tarot. Susan maintains a web site at www.susanlevitt.com and her phone number is 415-842-8019. pp. 18, 19, 31

Tanya Pergola (Arusha, Tanzania, East Africa and Seattle, WA) is as an environmental sociologist and social change agent. She is founding Co-Director of Terrawater— www.terrawater.org. Tanya lives in both the northern and southern hemispheres and practices yoga, writing and dancing that bridge indigenous and modern worlds. p. 45

Tatiana Makovkin (Redwood Valley, CA) lives with her partner and child in and around the golden hills of California. They go to the ocean at low tide, dig roots in the fall and seek wild mushrooms beneath deep moist canopy of conifer forest. p. 160

Toni Truesdale (Pecos, NM) has been in many group shows both Nationally and Internationally. She is also a mural artist, often working with youth crews; she is just starting her 14th mural in the Santa Fe area this summer. Toni presently teaches at the Santo Domingo Middle School. pp. 52, 87

Trenah (St. Peter, MN): I am a socially-conscious mother of three, creatively inspired by environmentally friendly, re-usable and recycled materials. Through

this I design and create many things in my studio—including clothing. A portion of all my products go to Save the Earth! Namaste—Trenah, Flutter-By Studio.
p. 67

Veronica M. Murphy (Toledo, OH): Starting my 3rd Saturn and 5th Jupiter cycles. Lawyer, teacher, writer, performing poet. A woman journeying toward wholeness, a woman who wants to heal.
p. 187

Vicki Noble (Freedom, CA) is co-creator of Motherpeace Tarot (with Karen Vogel) and the author of seven books, including *The Double Goddess: Women Sharing Power* (Inner Traditions, July 2003). Website: www.motherpeace.com. Email: vicki@motherpeace.com.
pp. 22, 90

Wendy Page (Victoria, BC, Canada): I try to reflect in my work what I see and believe of the world, "Our Connectedness," a vital unit, where each entity survives with the love and assistance of the next.
p. 179

See page 240 for: HOW TO BECOME A CONTRIBUTOR

ACKNOWLEDGEMENTS

In a year of ongoing change and challenges for **We'Moon** (We'Moon Land community and Mother Tongue Ink, our cottage industry), everyone involved in producing **We'Moon '04** has done an outstanding job.

Big bouquets go to the whole fabulous **We'Moon** staff (from left to right, starting with the front row, in staff photo above): Meghan, Amy, Musawa, Cherie/Gwen, Eagle, Mountain. I also want to thank everyone in the wide network of We'moon involved in its creation: contributors of art and writing from all over the world (including our fine feature writers who had to meet especially early deadlines), the many womyn in surrounding communities who review it initially in Weaving Circles, the Creatrix (Bethroot, Meghan, Musawa, with Gwen joining in) who meet in intensive marathons to select and craft the final product, extra proofers (NiAodagain and Lori), and Labyrinth Verlag (Gisela, Rosemarie, Beate) who translate the German edition. Great blessings to all the empowered womyn who have made this edition of **We'Moon** so power-full!

Musawa

Asteroids, an Impetus for a New Cooperation

The small planets, formerly known as asteroids, enable us to realize their special qualities and let us name them as urgently needed strength. These qualities have not yet been fully appreciated—not even within astrology. If we use the small planets in chart-reading, we can recognize, appreciate and integrate numerous abilities which have been defined as purely female for far too long and therefore been devalued up to now.

The once supposed gap between Mars and Jupiter turned out to be an error two hundreds years ago. Since 1801, thousands of small celestial bodies have been discovered there. Ceres, Pallas, Juno and Vesta, the biggest of them, were discovered between 1801 and 1807. In terms of time, they form a bridge between Uranus (discovered in 1781) and Neptune (1846). Moreover, they are a bridge in terms of space, too; they link the inner, personal planets (Sun to Mars) with the social and collective planets (Jupiter to Pluto). They function as trainers for a new vocabulary, encouraging us to learn a new language within astrology and to accept the split between matter and mind no longer. They support us in bringing heaven and the divine down to earth at long last, to overcome the separation between above and below and to reconcile body and mind.

Ceres symbolizes our ability to nourish ourselves and others in a substantial and metaphoric way. She helps us to learn to let go and to die, just like in the Greek myth of Demeter and Persephone. In chart-reading Ceres helps us to realize problems between parent and child and especially between mother and daughter or problems with our own concrete nourishment.

Juno shows us, which kind of committed partnership we long for. Juno wants fair partnerships with equal rights and responsibilities and she wants partners to be team-workers. She also tells us something about our individual way to create fulfilled personal as well as professional partnerships.

Pallas is a symbol for our creative intelligence. She mostly focuses on conflicts between father and daughter. Often enough she hints at the sacrifice of women's own creativity or the lack of respect for it. Pallas symbolizes the difficulties to link head, heart and womb.

Vesta, last but not at all least, can be our anchor in the storms of everyday live. She shows us where and how we can regenerate. She reminds us that in the first place we belong to ourselves and that we are allowed to do so! Vesta symbolizes where we activate our greatest, most energetic and concentrated devotion without becoming workaholics. Vesta shows the place and the way we carefully watch over our inner fire.

Ceres, Pallas, Juno and Vesta are facets of the Great Goddess who is reawakening in our consciousness now. With the small planets as symbols for diversity we deepen our power of discernment in chart-reading. We may strengthen the so-called female signs in astrology, especially the sign of Virgo. Without a wise and decent use of the qualities of Virgo there is no real balance with the sign of Pisces and this is a problem for stepping into the Age of Aquarius.

In the course of the coming years the importance of groups, with like-minded and other-minded people, networks and therefore all kinds of relationships with highly different individuals will increase. In chart-reading, the small planets Ceres, Pallas, Juno and Vesta help us to recognize and respect special facets of our nature which should become more essential. For example, the "female" activities to lavish care and attention on something and somebody, to create, to accompany, to plant, to nourish, to feed, to give shelter, to support, to encourage and to sustain . . . these are the abilities we urgently need if we want to solve our numerous personal, social, ecological and political problems. Everyone is able to change the relationship to oneself in every single moment. The more we learn about ourselves and the deeper we integrate this knowledge into our everyday life, the more loving we may form our relationships with other individuals. We then may develop new role models that give us more freedom for creating fair balance and true harmony.

Ceres, Pallas, Juno and Vesta can be path-breaking signposts!

2004 Asteroid Ephemeris

Date 2004	Ceres 1	Pallas 2	Juno 3	Vesta 4
Jan 1	20♋R37.9	11♈50.7	22♐21.4	06♑14.7
11	18♋17.8	14 02.9	25 47.8	11 37.0
21	15 58.8	16 48.5	29 11.0	16 57.5
31	13 58.7	20 03.2	02♑29.7	22 15.5
Feb 10	12 31.4	23 43.0	05 42.4	27 30.3
20	11 44.5	27 44.6	08 47.7	02♒41.2
Mar 1	11D41.1	02♉05.5	11 43.8	07 47.4
11	12 19.5	06 42.9	14 28.6	12 48.0
21	13 35.9	11 35.1	17 00.1	17 42.2
31	15 26.1	16 40.4	19 15.5	22 28.9
Apr 10	17 44.9	21 56.8	21 12.1	27 06.9
20	20 28.0	27 23.2	22 46.8	01♓35.1
30	23 31.7	02♊58.3	23 55.8	05 51.6
May 10	26 52.5	08 40.4	24 35.9	09 55.0
20	00♌27.6	14 28.5	24R43.6	13 42.9
30	04 14.7	20 21.3	24 16.6	17 12.8
Jun 9	08 11.8	26 17.4	23 14.5	20 21.6
19	12 17.4	02♋15.7	21 39.6	23 05.6
29	16 30.0	08 14.9	19 38.1	25 20.5
Jul 9	20 48.4	14 13.7	17 20.6	27 01.8
19	25 11.7	20 11.0	14 59.9	28 04.1
29	29 39.0	26 05.7	12 50.5	28R22.8
Aug 8	04♍09.4	01♌56.6	11 04.5	27 55.3
18	08 42.4	07 43.0	09 50.6	26 41.6
28	13 17.1	13 23.6	09 13.9	24 47.5
Sep 7	17 52.9	18 57.6	09D15.1	22 25.5
17	22 29.3	24 24.2	09 53.1	19 53.1
27	27 05.4	29 42.2	11 05.2	17 31.1
Oct 7	01♎40.6	04♍50.9	12 47.7	15 36.9
17	06 14.1	09 49.1	14 57.4	14 22.5
27	10 45.1	14 35.4	17 30.9	13 53.7
Nov 6	15 12.6	19 08.6	20 25.1	14D10.3
16	19 35.7	23 26.8	23 37.5	15 09.2
26	23 52.9	27 27.7	27 05.6	16 45.7
Dec 6	28 03.1	01♎09.0	00♒47.4	18 54.3
16	02♏04.8	04 27.4	04 41.4	21 30.0
26	05 55.8	07 18.7	08 45.8	24 28.5
Jan 5	09♏34.3	09♎38.8	12♒59.4	27♓45.5

Date 2004	Psyche 16	Eros 433	Lilith 1181	Toro 1685
Jan 1	00♒59.7	14♈29.0	20♒47.2	05♐00.1
11	04 53.2	20 29.0	25 09.4	10 00.5
21	08 46.0	26 26.9	29 40.2	14 59.5
31	12 37.0	02♉23.0	04♓18.5	19 56.8
Feb 10	16 24.9	08 17.3	09 03.1	24 52.6
20	20 08.9	14 10.5	13 53.2	29 47.2
Mar 1	23 47.5	20 02.7	18 47.9	04♑40.4
11	27 19.3	25 54.1	23 46.5	09 32.6
21	00♓42.8	01♊45.3	28 48.2	14 24.5
31	03 56.2	07 36.6	03♈52.5	19 16.3
Apr 10	06 57.5	13 28.2	08 58.6	24 09.2
20	09 44.4	19 21.0	14 06.1	29 04.9
30	12 14.1	25 15.1	19 14.4	04♒05.1
May 10	14 23.6	01♋11.2	24 22.7	09 13.8
20	16 09.5	07 10.1	29 30.7	14 36.5
30	17 28.0	13 12.3	04♉37.5	20 21.9
Jun 9	18 15.5	19 18.6	09 42.5	26 45.8
19	18R28.7	25 30.0	14 45.0	04♓14.4
29	18 05.6	01♌47.2	19 44.0	13 33.5
Jul 9	17 06.8	08 11.3	24 38.4	26 06.0
19	15 36.0	14 43.7	29 27.3	13♈53.3
29	13 41.8	21 25.1	04♊08.8	08♉03.1
Aug 8	11 36.6	28 17.2	08 41.6	04♊32.4
18	09 35.0	05♍21.3	13 03.6	26 31.0
28	07 51.6	12 38.5	17 12.0	12♋35.4
Sep 7	06 37.6	20 10.4	21 04.1	24 50.0
17	06 00.0	27 58.3	24 36.3	05♌06.6
27	06D01.8	06♎02.5	27 44.0	14 27.0
Oct 7	06 42.4	14 24.2	00♋22.4	23 19.4
17	07 59.2	23 02.7	02 25.5	01♍50.8
27	09 48.8	01♏56.5	03 47.3	09 58.8
Nov 6	12 07.2	11 03.9	04 22.4	17 40.0
16	14 50.5	20 20.6	04R06.8	24 51.2
26	17 55.5	29 41.3	03 01.6	01♎29.6
Dec 6	21 18.7	09♐00.7	01 14.2	07 34.1
16	24 57.6	18 10.8	28♊59.4	13 02.9
26	28 49.7	27 03.3	26 39.0	17 53.0
Jan 5	02♈52.9	05♑30.8	24♊35.3	22♎01.0

Date 2004	Sappho 80	Amor 1221	Pandora 55	Icarus 1566
Jan 1	16♈59.7	12♒00.1	10♐27.5	05♒46.0
11	22 42.9	22 38.4	14 08.6	11 47.0
21	28 31.4	03♓54.5	17 45.1	18 34.8
31	04♉24.3	15 36.3	21 15.4	26 26.1
Feb 10	10 21.1	27 27.4	24 37.9	05♓52.5
20	16 21.3	09♈08.0	27 51.0	11R47.7
Mar 1	22 24.2	20 18.8	00♑52.3	01 19.7
11	28 29.0	00♉45.9	03 39.7	20 00.4
21	04♊35.2	10 20.3	06 10.5	18D39.7
31	10 42.1	18 56.0	08 21.5	19 18.2
Apr 10	16 48.7	26 30.9	10 09.4	20 22.9
20	22 54.6	03♊03.0	11 30.4	21 17.8
30	28 58.6	08 29.1	12 20.7	21 40.7
May 10	04♋59.9	12 46.1	12R37.0	21R13.8
20	10 57.6	15 48.3	12 16.8	19 37.7
30	16 50.5	17 28.5	11 19.8	16 30.8
Jun 9	22 37.5	17R40.9	09 49.4	11 34.5
19	28 17.2	16 22.5	07 52.8	04 42.5
29	03♌48.0	13 40.0	05 41.8	26♓19.6
Jul 9	09 08.3	09 55.8	03 31.0	17 30.2
19	14 16.1	05 45.3	01 34.9	09 31.2
29	19 08.6	01 49.9	00 06.0	03 16.0
Aug 8	23 43.3	28♉41.8	29♐12.3	28♐58.1
18	27 56.6	26 36.7	28D57.4	26 25.9
28	01♍43.9	25 37.4	29 21.8	25 20.3
Sep 7	05 00.6	25D37.6	00♑23.1	25D22.1
17	07 40.5	26 27.8	01 58.1	26 16.2
27	09 36.5	27 59.3	04 03.1	27 51.5
Oct 7	10 42.2	00♊03.5	06 34.3	29 59.0
17	10R51.3	02 33.8	09 28.4	02♑33.1
27	10 01.5	05 25.1	12 42.2	05 29.5
Nov 6	08 17.3	08 32.9	16 12.9	08 44.9
16	05 51.8	11 54.0	19 58.4	12 17.5
26	03 08.1	15 25.6	23 56.5	16 05.9
Dec 6	00 33.0	19 05.5	28 05.3	20 09.4
16	28♌30.2	22 52.2	02♒23.5	24 28.5
26	27 15.5	26 44.0	06 49.5	29 03.6
Jan 5	26♌D54.1	00♋39.5	11♒22.1	03♒56.3

Date 2004	Diana 78	Hidalgo 944	Urania 30	Chiron 2060
Jan 1	14♐59.3	29♒25.4	20♒02.1	18♑28.3
11	18 53.6	02♓03.5	25 03.6	19 25.0
21	22 40.5	04 53.0	00♓11.8	20 21.4
31	26 18.3	07 52.2	05 25.8	21 16.5
Feb 10	29 45.7	10 59.4	10 44.5	22 09.4
20	03♑01.1	14 13.3	16 07.1	22 59.1
Mar 1	06 02.3	17 32.5	21 32.8	23 44.6
11	08 47.3	20 56.0	27 00.9	24 25.0
21	11 13.5	24 22.8	02♈30.8	24 59.6
31	13 17.9	27 51.9	08 01.9	25 27.7
Apr 10	14 57.5	01♈22.3	13 33.5	25 48.7
20	16 09.1	04 53.5	19 05.2	26 02.1
30	16 49.3	08 24.3	24 36.4	26 07.8
May 10	16R55.5	11 54.0	00♉06.4	26R05.7
20	16 26.1	15 21.8	05 34.9	25 56.0
30	15 21.4	18 46.6	11 01.1	25 39.2
Jun 9	13 45.3	22 07.4	16 24.6	25 16.1
19	11 44.8	25 22.9	21 44.6	24 47.7
29	09 30.7	28 31.5	27 00.4	24 15.2
Jul 9	07 15.9	01♉31.6	02♊11.2	23 40.2
19	05 13.1	04 20.8	07 16.1	23 04.3
29	03 33.1	06 56.3	12 13.8	22 29.0
Aug 8	02 23.2	09 14.9	17 03.1	21 56.0
18	01 46.7	11 12.1	21 42.4	21 26.8
28	01D44.4	12 42.6	26 09.6	21 02.8
Sep 7	02 14.5	13 40.6	00♋22.6	20 44.8
17	03 14.3	13R58.7	04 18.6	20 33.7
27	04 40.7	13 29.9	07 53.8	20D30.2
Oct 7	06 30.2	12 09.2	11 04.3	20 34.2
17	08 39.8	09 55.4	13 45.1	20 45.9
27	11 06.7	06 56.8	15 50.3	21 05.0
Nov 6	13 48.0	03 32.2	17 50.2	21 31.1
16	16 41.9	00 09.5	17R34.4	22 03.6
26	19 46.1	27♈19.8	16 26.5	22 41.7
Dec 6	22 58.9	25 27.0	14 32.2	23 24.8
16	26 18.9	24 44.4	12 06.0	24 11.8
26	29 44.4	25D15.7	10 06.0	25 01.8
Jan 5	03♒14.2	26♈57.3	09♋29.2	25♑53.9

Giving the positions of asteroids every
ten days in LONGITUDE at 00:00 GMT

Noon Planetary Ephemeris: GMT*

LONGITUDE — JANUARY 2004

Day	Sid.Time	☉	0 hr ☽	Noon ☽	True ☊	☿	♀	♂	♃	♄	♅	♆	♇
1 Th	18 41 57	10♑24 2	27♈29 17	3♉27 10	19♉17.5	28♐22.2	13♒49.8	9♈28.2	18♍53.6	9♋42.6	0♓ 5.2	11♒42.2	20♐30.9
2 F	18 45 54	11 25 10	9♉22 57	15 17 14	19R 18.5	27R 36.6	15 3.5	10 4.6	18 54.0	9R 37.7	0 7.7	11 44.2	20 33.0
3 Sa	18 49 50	12 26 19	21 10 39	27 3 43	19 18.2	27 1.3	16 17.1	10 41.2	18R 54.2	9 32.7	0 10.3	11 46.3	20 35.2
4 Su	18 53 47	13 27 28	2♊56 58	8♊50 52	19 15.9	26 36.3	17 30.7	11 17.8	18 54.2	9 27.8	0 12.9	11 48.3	20 37.3
5 M	18 57 43	14 28 36	14 45 50	20 42 14	19 11.2	26 21.5	18 44.2	11 54.6	18 54.0	9 22.9	0 15.5	11 50.4	20 39.5
6 Tu	19 1 40	15 29 44	26 40 23	2♋40 32	19 3.9	26D 16.2	19 57.8	12 31.3	18 53.6	9 18.0	0 18.2	11 52.5	20 41.6
7 W	19 5 36	16 30 52	8♋42 55	14 47 41	18 54.3	26 19.9	21 11.2	13 8.2	18 53.0	9 13.1	0 20.9	11 54.6	20 43.7
8 Th	19 9 33	17 32 0	20 54 57	27 4 51	18 43.2	26 32.0	22 24.6	13 45.1	18 52.3	9 8.2	0 23.6	11 56.7	20 45.8
9 F	19 13 30	18 33 8	3♌17 24	9♌32 40	18 31.5	26 51.7	23 38.0	14 22.1	18 51.3	9 3.3	0 26.4	11 58.8	20 47.9
10 Sa	19 17 26	19 34 16	15 50 41	22 11 30	18 20.3	27 18.4	24 51.3	14 59.1	18 50.1	8 58.5	0 29.2	12 0.9	20 49.9
11 Su	19 21 23	20 35 23	28 35 8	5♍ 1 39	18 10.6	27 51.4	26 4.5	15 36.2	18 48.8	8 53.7	0 32.0	12 3.1	20 52.0
12 M	19 25 19	21 36 30	11♍31 7	18 3 39	18 3.3	28 30.0	27 17.7	16 13.4	18 47.2	8 48.9	0 34.8	12 5.2	20 54.0
13 Tu	19 29 16	22 37 38	24 39 21	1♎18 23	17 58.7	29 13.7	28 30.8	16 50.6	18 45.5	8 44.2	0 37.7	12 7.4	20 56.0
14 W	19 33 12	23 38 45	8♎ 0 54	14 47 5	17 56.6	0♑ 2.0	29 43.9	17 27.8	18 43.6	8 39.4	0 40.6	12 9.6	20 58.0
15 Th	19 37 9	24 39 52	21 37 7	28 31 7	17D 56.3	0 54.4	0♓57.0	18 5.2	18 41.5	8 34.8	0 43.5	12 11.8	21 0.0
16 F	19 41 5	25 40 59	5♏29 13	12♏31 28	17R 56.7	1 50.4	2 9.9	18 42.5	18 39.2	8 30.1	0 46.5	12 14.0	21 2.0
17 Sa	19 45 2	26 42 6	19 37 51	26 48 14	17 56.5	2 49.8	3 22.8	19 20.0	18 36.7	8 25.6	0 49.5	12 16.2	21 3.9
18 Su	19 48 59	27 43 13	4♐ 2 23	11♐19 52	17 54.5	3 52.1	4 35.7	19 57.5	18 34.0	8 21.0	0 52.5	12 18.4	21 5.9
19 M	19 52 55	28 44 19	18 40 12	26 2 41	17 49.8	4 57.1	5 48.5	20 35.0	18 31.1	8 16.5	0 55.5	12 20.6	21 7.8
20 Tu	19 56 52	29 45 26	3♑26 30	10♑50 44	17 42.3	6 4.5	7 1.2	21 12.6	18 28.1	8 12.1	0 58.6	12 22.8	21 9.7
21 W	20 0 48	0♒46 31	18 14 21	25 36 18	17 32.2	7 14.1	8 13.9	21 50.2	18 24.8	8 7.7	1 1.7	12 25.1	21 11.6
22 Th	20 4 45	1 47 36	2♒55 33	10♒11 5	17 20.5	8 25.7	9 26.5	22 27.9	18 21.4	8 3.4	1 4.8	12 27.3	21 13.4
23 F	20 8 41	2 48 40	17 22 0	24 27 32	17 8.5	9 39.1	10 39.0	23 5.6	18 17.8	7 59.1	1 7.9	12 29.6	21 15.2
24 Sa	20 12 38	3 49 44	1♓27 4	8♓20 9	16 57.5	10 54.1	11 51.4	23 43.4	18 14.0	7 54.9	1 11.1	12 31.8	21 17.1
25 Su	20 16 35	4 50 46	15 6 33	21 46 11	16 48.6	12 10.7	13 3.8	24 21.2	18 10.0	7 50.7	1 14.2	12 34.1	21 18.8
26 M	20 20 31	5 51 47	28 19 9	4♈45 40	16 42.4	13 28.7	14 16.1	24 59.1	18 5.9	7 46.7	1 17.4	12 36.4	21 20.6
27 Tu	20 24 28	6 52 47	11♈ 6 8	17 20 59	16 38.8	14 47.9	15 28.3	25 37.0	18 1.6	7 42.6	1 20.6	12 38.6	21 22.3
28 W	20 28 24	7 53 47	23 30 49	29 36 14	16 37.4	16 8.4	16 40.4	26 14.9	17 57.1	7 38.7	1 23.9	12 40.9	21 24.1
29 Th	20 32 21	8 54 44	5♉37 54	11♉36 31	16 37.2	17 30.1	17 52.4	26 52.8	17 52.5	7 34.8	1 27.1	12 43.2	21 25.8
30 F	20 36 17	9 55 41	17 32 47	23 27 26	16 37.1	18 52.8	19 4.3	27 30.8	17 47.7	7 31.1	1 30.4	12 45.5	21 27.4
31 Sa	20 40 14	10 56 37	29 21 8	5♊14 34	16 36.0	20 16.6	20 16.2	28 8.8	17 42.7	7 27.3	1 33.7	12 47.7	21 29.1

LONGITUDE — FEBRUARY 2004

Day	Sid.Time	☉	0 hr ☽	Noon ☽	True ☊	☿	♀	♂	♃	♄	♅	♆	♇
1 Su	20 44 10	11♒57 31	11♊ 8 23	17♊ 3 11	16♉32.8	21♑41.4	21♓27.9	28♈46.9	17♍37.6	7♋23.7	1♓37.0	12♒50.0	21♐30.7
2 M	20 48 7	12 58 24	22 59 32	28 57 55	16R 26.9	23 7.1	22 39.5	29 24.9	17R 32.4	7R 20.2	1 40.3	12 52.3	21 32.3
3 Tu	20 52 4	13 59 16	4♋58 46	11♋ 2 29	16 18.0	24 33.7	23 51.1	0♉ 3.0	17 27.0	7 16.7	1 43.6	12 54.6	21 33.9
4 W	20 56 0	15 0 7	17 9 22	23 19 38	16 6.6	26 1.2	25 2.5	0 41.1	17 21.4	7 13.3	1 46.9	12 56.9	21 35.5
5 Th	20 59 57	16 0 56	29 33 26	5♌50 52	15 53.3	27 29.5	26 13.8	1 19.3	17 15.7	7 10.0	1 50.3	12 59.1	21 37.0
6 F	21 3 53	17 1 44	12♌11 55	18 36 34	15 39.2	28 58.7	27 25.0	1 57.4	17 9.9	7 6.8	1 53.7	13 1.4	21 38.5
7 Sa	21 7 50	18 2 31	25 4 41	1♍36 7	15 25.6	0♒28.8	28 36.1	2 35.6	17 3.9	7 3.7	1 57.0	13 3.7	21 40.0
8 Su	21 11 46	19 3 17	8♍10 41	14 48 13	15 13.7	1 59.7	29 47.1	3 13.8	16 57.8	7 0.6	2 0.4	13 6.0	21 41.4
9 M	21 15 43	20 4 2	21 28 28	28 11 17	15 4.5	3 31.4	0♈58.0	3 52.0	16 51.5	6 57.7	2 3.8	13 8.2	21 42.8
10 Tu	21 19 39	21 4 45	4♎56 30	11♎43 57	14 58.4	5 3.9	2 8.7	4 30.2	16 45.2	6 54.8	2 7.2	13 10.5	21 44.2
11 W	21 23 36	22 5 28	18 33 32	25 25 12	14 55.1	6 37.3	3 19.4	5 8.5	16 38.7	6 52.1	2 10.6	13 12.7	21 45.6
12 Th	21 27 33	23 6 9	2♏18 55	9♏14 39	14D 54.1	8 11.5	4 29.9	5 46.7	16 32.1	6 49.4	2 14.0	13 15.0	21 46.9
13 F	21 31 29	24 6 49	16 12 25	23 12 14	14R 54.1	9 46.5	5 40.2	6 25.0	16 25.4	6 46.8	2 17.5	13 17.3	21 48.2
14 Sa	21 35 26	25 7 29	0♐14 3	7♐17 50	14 53.7	11 22.4	6 50.5	7 3.3	16 18.6	6 44.4	2 20.9	13 19.5	21 49.5
15 Su	21 39 22	26 8 7	14 23 29	21 30 48	14 51.7	12 59.1	8 0.6	7 41.6	16 11.6	6 42.0	2 24.3	13 21.7	21 50.7
16 M	21 43 19	27 8 44	28 39 32	5♑49 20	14 47.1	14 36.7	9 10.6	8 20.0	16 4.6	6 39.8	2 27.8	13 24.0	21 52.0
17 Tu	21 47 15	28 9 20	12♑59 45	20 10 13	14 39.6	16 15.1	10 20.4	8 58.3	15 57.5	6 37.6	2 31.2	13 26.2	21 53.2
18 W	21 51 12	29 9 55	27 20 9	4♒28 51	14 29.6	17 54.4	11 30.2	9 36.7	15 50.3	6 35.6	2 34.7	13 28.4	21 54.3
19 Th	21 55 8	0♓10 28	11♒35 36	18 39 41	14 17.9	19 34.7	12 39.7	10 15.0	15 43.0	6 33.6	2 38.2	13 30.6	21 55.5
20 F	21 59 5	1 11 0	25 40 25	2♓37 10	14 5.8	21 15.8	13 49.1	10 53.4	15 35.7	6 31.8	2 41.6	13 32.8	21 56.6
21 Sa	22 3 2	2 11 30	9♓29 22	16 16 34	13 54.5	22 57.9	14 58.4	11 31.8	15 28.2	6 30.0	2 45.1	13 35.0	21 57.6
22 Su	22 6 58	3 11 58	22 58 28	29 34 50	13 45.1	24 40.9	16 7.5	12 10.3	15 20.7	6 28.4	2 48.5	13 37.2	21 58.7
23 M	22 10 55	4 12 24	6♈ 5 39	12♈30 56	13 38.4	26 24.8	17 16.5	12 48.7	15 13.2	6 26.9	2 52.0	13 39.4	21 59.7
24 Tu	22 14 51	5 12 49	18 50 55	25 5 52	13 34.3	28 9.7	18 25.3	13 27.1	15 5.6	6 25.5	2 55.4	13 41.5	22 0.7
25 W	22 18 48	6 13 12	1♉16 12	7♉22 23	13 32.6	29 55.6	19 33.9	14 5.5	14 57.9	6 24.2	2 58.9	13 43.7	22 1.6
26 Th	22 22 44	7 13 33	13 24 57	19 24 31	13D 32.6	1♓42.5	20 42.3	14 44.0	14 50.2	6 23.0	3 2.3	13 45.8	22 2.5
27 F	22 26 41	8 13 52	25 21 43	1♊17 13	13 33.1	3 30.4	21 50.5	15 22.4	14 42.5	6 21.9	3 5.8	13 47.9	22 3.4
28 Sa	22 30 37	9 14 9	7♊11 43	13 5 52	13R 33.2	5 19.2	22 58.6	16 0.9	14 34.7	6 20.9	3 9.2	13 50.1	22 4.2
29 Su	22 34 34	10 14 24	19 0 24	24 55 57	13 31.9	7 9.1	24 6.5	16 39.4	14 26.9	6 20.0	3 12.7	13 52.2	22 5.1

Astro Data Dy Hr Mn	Planet Ingress Dy Hr Mn	Last Aspect Dy Hr Mn	☽ Ingress Dy Hr Mn	Last Aspect Dy Hr Mn	☽ Ingress Dy Hr Mn	☽ Phases & Eclipses Dy Hr Mn
♃ R 3 23:58	☿ ♑ 14 11:03	1 2:28 ☿ △	♉ 1 5:03	2 12:57 ♂ ⚹	♋ 2 14:04	7 15:41 ○ 16♋40
☿ D 6 13:45	♀ ♓ 14 17:17	2 19:22 ♃ △	♊ 3 17:59	4 17:54 ☿ ☍	♌ 5 0:51	15 4:47 ☾ 24♎21
☽0S 13 23:18	☉ ♒ 20 17:43	5 23:15 ☿ ☍	♋ 6 6:40	6 17:39 ♇ △	♍ 7 9:04	21 21:06 ● 1♒10
☽0N 26 16:59		7 20:01 ♃ ⚹	♌ 8 17:39	9 0:24 ♇ □	♎ 9 15:14	29 6:04 ☽ 8♉40
	♂ ♉ 3 10:05	10 22:01 ☿ △	♍ 11 2:39	11 5:43 ☉ □	♏ 11 19:59	
♀0N 9 14:46	☿ ♒ 7 4:21	13 8:02 ☿ □	♎ 13 9:39	13 13:41 ☉ □	♐ 13 23:36	6 8:48 ○ 16♌54
☽0S 10 3:54	♀ ♈ 8 16:22	15 4:47 ☉ □	♏ 15 14:34	15 20:21 ☉ ⚹	♑ 16 2:15	13 13:41 ☾ 24♏11
☽0N 23 1:40	☉ ♓ 19 7:51	17 11:49 ☉ ⚹	♐ 17 17:19	17 5:01 ♃ △	♒ 18 4:28	20 9:19 ● 1♓04
	☿ ♓ 25 12:59	19 3:59 ♇ ☌	♑ 19 18:25	19 17:35 ♇ ⚹	♓ 20 7:28	28 3:25 ☽ 8♊53
		21 5:35 ♂ □	♒ 21 19:12	21 22:11 ♇ □	♈ 22 12:46	
		23 9:34 ♂ ⚹	♓ 23 21:30	24 18:56 ☿ ⚹	♉ 24 21:31	
		25 11:10 ♇ □	♈ 26 3:07	26 2:56 ♃ △	♊ 27 9:23	
		28 5:01 ♂ ☌	♉ 28 12:47	29 10:09 ♀ ⚹	♋ 29 22:13	
		30 2:05 ♀ ⚹	♊ 31 1:19			

Astro Data

1 JANUARY 2004
Julian Day # 37986
Galactic Ctr 26♐54.3
SVP 05♓12'26"
Obliquity 23°26'25"
⚷ Chiron 18♑31.2
☽ Mean ☊ 17♉40.5

1 FEBRUARY 2004
Julian Day # 38017
Galactic Ctr 26♐54.4
SVP 05♓12'21"
Obliquity 23°26'26"
⚷ Chiron 21♑24.7
☽ Mean ☊ 16♉02.0

*Giving the positions of planets daily at noon, in LONGITUDE Greenwich Mean Time (UT)

Each planet's retrograde period is shaded gray.

Noon Planetary Ephemeris: GMT*

MARCH 2004

LONGITUDE

Day	Sid.Time	☉	0 hr ☽	Noon ☽	True ☊	☿	♀	♂	♃	♄	♅	♆	♇
1 M	22 38 31	11♓14 37	0♋53 11	6♋52 41	13♉28.5	8♓59.9	25♈14.1	17♉17.8	14♍19.1	6♋19.3	3♓16.1	13♒54.2	22♐ 5.9
2 Tu	22 42 27	12 14 48	12 55 3	19 0 47	13R 22.7	10 51.7	26 21.6	17 56.3	14R 11.2	6R 18.7	3 19.5	13 56.3	22 6.6
3 W	22 46 24	13 14 57	25 10 18	1♌24 0	13 14.7	12 44.4	27 28.9	18 34.8	14 3.4	6 18.1	3 23.0	13 58.4	22 7.3
4 Th	22 50 20	14 15 4	7♌42 9	14 4 57	13 4.9	14 38.1	28 35.9	19 13.2	13 55.6	6 17.7	3 26.4	14 0.4	22 8.0
5 F	22 54 17	15 15 9	20 32 30	27 4 47	12 54.4	16 32.6	29 42.7	19 51.7	13 47.7	6 17.4	3 29.8	14 2.4	22 8.7
6 Sa	22 58 13	16 15 12	3♍41 43	10♍23 5	12 44.2	18 27.9	0♉49.3	20 30.2	13 39.9	6 17.2	3 33.2	14 4.4	22 9.3
7 Su	23 2 10	17 15 13	17 8 37	23 57 59	12 35.3	20 24.0	1 55.7	21 8.6	13 32.0	6D 17.2	3 36.6	14 6.4	22 9.9
8 M	23 6 6	18 15 13	0♎50 47	7♎46 33	12 28.5	22 20.7	3 1.8	21 47.1	13 24.2	6 17.2	3 39.9	14 8.4	22 10.4
9 Tu	23 10 3	19 15 10	14 44 51	21 45 13	12 24.2	24 17.9	4 7.7	22 25.5	13 16.5	6 17.3	3 43.3	14 10.4	22 11.0
10 W	23 13 59	20 15 6	28 47 14	5♏50 27	12D 22.4	26 15.5	5 13.3	23 4.0	13 8.7	6 17.6	3 46.7	14 12.3	22 11.4
11 Th	23 17 56	21 15 0	12♏54 33	19 59 11	12 22.4	28 13.2	6 18.6	23 42.4	13 1.0	6 18.0	3 50.0	14 14.2	22 11.9
12 F	23 21 53	22 14 52	27 4 4	4♐ 9 0	12 23.4	0♈11.0	7 23.8	24 20.9	12 53.3	6 18.5	3 53.3	14 16.1	22 12.3
13 Sa	23 25 49	23 14 43	11♐13 46	18 18 11	12R 24.2	2 8.5	8 28.6	24 59.3	12 45.7	6 19.1	3 56.6	14 18.0	22 12.7
14 Su	23 29 46	24 14 32	25 22 6	2♑25 23	12 24.0	4 5.5	9 33.2	25 37.8	12 38.1	6 19.8	3 60.0	14 19.9	22 13.1
15 M	23 33 42	25 14 20	9♑27 49	16 29 16	12 22.0	6 1.6	10 37.5	26 16.2	12 30.5	6 20.6	4 3.2	14 21.7	22 13.4
16 Tu	23 37 39	26 14 6	23 29 29	0♒28 14	12 18.0	7 56.5	11 41.5	26 54.7	12 23.1	6 21.5	4 6.5	14 23.5	22 13.7
17 W	23 41 35	27 13 50	7♒25 14	14 20 13	12 12.1	9 49.9	12 45.2	27 33.1	12 15.7	6 22.5	4 9.8	14 25.3	22 14.0
18 Th	23 45 32	28 13 32	21 12 50	28 2 46	12 4.9	11 41.3	13 48.6	28 11.6	12 8.3	6 23.7	4 13.0	14 27.1	22 14.2
19 F	23 49 28	29 13 13	4♓49 41	11♓33 16	11 57.3	13 30.3	14 51.7	28 50.0	12 1.1	6 25.0	4 16.2	14 28.9	22 14.4
20 Sa	23 53 25	0♈12 51	18 13 15	24 49 23	11 50.3	15 16.4	15 54.5	29 28.5	11 53.9	6 26.3	4 19.4	14 30.6	22 14.5
21 Su	23 57 22	1 12 27	1♈21 30	7♈49 27	11 44.4	16 59.2	16 57.0	0♊ 6.9	11 46.8	6 27.8	4 22.6	14 32.3	22 14.6
22 M	0 1 18	2 12 2	14 13 12	20 32 46	11 40.4	18 38.3	17 59.1	0 45.4	11 39.8	6 29.4	4 25.8	14 34.0	22 14.7
23 Tu	0 5 15	3 11 34	26 48 16	2♉59 51	11 38.3	20 13.1	19 0.8	1 23.8	11 32.9	6 31.1	4 28.9	14 35.7	22 14.8
24 W	0 9 11	4 11 4	9♉ 7 48	15 12 25	11D 38.0	21 43.3	20 2.2	2 2.2	11 26.2	6 32.9	4 32.0	14 37.3	22R 14.8
25 Th	0 13 8	5 10 32	21 14 6	27 13 17	11 38.9	23 8.4	21 3.2	2 40.7	11 19.5	6 34.8	4 35.1	14 39.0	22 14.8
26 F	0 17 4	6 9 58	3♊10 27	9♊ 6 9	11 40.6	24 28.1	22 3.8	3 19.1	11 12.9	6 36.9	4 38.2	14 40.6	22 14.7
27 Sa	0 21 1	7 9 21	15 0 58	20 55 28	11 42.3	25 42.1	23 4.0	3 57.5	11 6.4	6 39.0	4 41.3	14 42.1	22 14.7
28 Su	0 24 57	8 8 42	26 50 17	2♋46 3	11 43.4	26 49.9	24 3.8	4 35.9	11 0.1	6 41.2	4 44.3	14 43.7	22 14.6
29 M	0 28 54	9 8 1	8♋43 25	14 43 0	11R 43.4	27 51.4	25 3.2	5 14.3	10 53.9	6 43.6	4 47.3	14 45.2	22 14.4
30 Tu	0 32 51	10 7 18	20 45 25	26 51 16	11 42.0	28 46.2	26 2.1	5 52.7	10 47.8	6 46.0	4 50.3	14 46.7	22 14.2
31 W	0 36 47	11 6 32	3♌ 1 5	9♌15 22	11 39.3	29 34.3	27 0.6	6 31.1	10 41.9	6 48.6	4 53.2	14 48.2	22 14.0

APRIL 2004

LONGITUDE

Day	Sid.Time	☉	0 hr ☽	Noon ☽	True ☊	☿	♀	♂	♃	♄	♅	♆	♇
1 Th	0 40 44	12♈ 5 44	15♌34 34	21♌59 1	11♉35.4	0♉15.5	27♉58.6	7♊ 9.5	10♍36.0	6♋51.2	4♓56.2	14♒49.6	22♐13.8
2 F	0 44 40	13 4 54	28 29 1	5♍ 4 43	11R 31.0	0 49.6	28 56.0	7 47.8	10R 30.3	6 54.0	4 59.1	14 51.0	22R 13.5
3 Sa	0 48 37	14 4 1	11♍46 11	18 33 20	11 26.6	1 16.6	29 53.0	8 26.2	10 24.8	6 56.8	5 1.9	14 52.4	22 13.2
4 Su	0 52 33	15 3 6	25 25 59	2♎23 50	11 22.8	1 36.5	0♊49.4	9 4.5	10 19.4	6 59.8	5 4.8	14 53.8	22 12.9
5 M	0 56 30	16 2 9	9♎26 27	16 33 17	11 20.0	1 49.3	1 45.3	9 42.9	10 14.1	7 2.8	5 7.6	14 55.1	22 12.5
6 Tu	1 0 26	17 1 10	23 43 45	0♏57 8	11 18.5	1R 55.1	2 40.6	10 21.2	10 9.0	7 5.9	5 10.4	14 56.4	22 12.1
7 W	1 4 23	18 0 9	8♏12 43	15 29 45	11D 18.2	1 54.1	3 35.4	10 59.5	10 4.1	7 9.2	5 13.1	14 57.7	22 11.7
8 Th	1 8 20	18 59 7	22 47 29	0♐ 5 13	11 18.9	1 46.6	4 29.5	11 37.8	9 59.3	7 12.5	5 15.9	14 58.9	22 11.2
9 F	1 12 16	19 58 2	7♐22 16	14 38 2	11 20.2	1 32.8	5 23.1	12 16.1	9 54.6	7 16.0	5 18.6	15 0.2	22 10.7
10 Sa	1 16 13	20 56 56	21 52 0	29 3 42	11 21.6	1 13.2	6 15.9	12 54.4	9 50.2	7 19.5	5 21.2	15 1.4	22 10.2
11 Su	1 20 9	21 55 48	6♑12 45	13♑18 51	11 22.4	0 48.2	7 8.2	13 32.7	9 45.8	7 23.1	5 23.9	15 2.5	22 9.7
12 M	1 24 6	22 54 39	20 21 47	27 21 22	11R 22.6	0 18.5	7 59.7	14 10.9	9 41.7	7 26.9	5 26.5	15 3.7	22 9.1
13 Tu	1 28 2	23 53 27	4♒17 29	11♒10 3	11 21.9	29♈44.6	8 50.5	14 49.2	9 37.7	7 30.7	5 29.1	15 4.8	22 8.5
14 W	1 31 59	24 52 14	17 59 2	24 44 26	11 20.4	29 7.2	9 40.6	15 27.5	9 33.9	7 34.6	5 31.6	15 5.9	22 7.8
15 Th	1 35 55	25 50 59	1♓26 13	8♓ 4 26	11 18.4	28 27.1	10 30.0	16 5.7	9 30.2	7 38.6	5 34.1	15 6.9	22 7.1
16 F	1 39 52	26 49 43	14 39 6	21 10 15	11 16.3	27 45.2	11 18.5	16 44.0	9 26.7	7 42.6	5 36.6	15 7.9	22 6.4
17 Sa	1 43 49	27 48 24	27 37 56	4♈ 2 12	11 14.4	27 2.1	12 6.3	17 22.2	9 23.4	7 46.8	5 39.0	15 8.9	22 5.7
18 Su	1 47 45	28 47 4	10♈23 8	16 40 48	11 12.9	26 18.8	12 53.2	18 0.4	9 20.3	7 51.1	5 41.4	15 9.9	22 5.0
19 M	1 51 42	29 45 42	22 55 19	29 6 47	11 12.0	25 36.0	13 39.2	18 38.7	9 17.3	7 55.4	5 43.8	15 10.8	22 4.2
20 Tu	1 55 38	0♉44 18	5♉15 22	11♉21 14	11D 11.7	24 54.5	14 24.3	19 16.9	9 14.6	7 59.9	5 46.1	15 11.7	22 3.4
21 W	1 59 35	1 42 52	17 24 35	23 25 40	11 11.9	24 15.0	15 8.4	19 55.1	9 12.0	8 4.4	5 48.4	15 12.5	22 2.5
22 Th	2 3 31	2 41 24	29 24 45	5♊22 9	11 12.6	23 38.1	15 51.6	20 33.3	9 9.6	8 9.0	5 50.6	15 13.4	22 1.7
23 F	2 7 28	3 39 54	11♊18 13	17 13 20	11 13.4	23 4.4	16 33.7	21 11.5	9 7.3	8 13.7	5 52.8	15 14.2	22 0.8
24 Sa	2 11 24	4 38 22	23 7 55	29 2 26	11 14.2	22 34.3	17 14.8	21 49.7	9 5.3	8 18.4	5 55.0	15 14.9	21 59.8
25 Su	2 15 21	5 36 48	4♋57 21	10♋53 11	11 14.8	22 8.3	17 54.8	22 27.9	9 3.4	8 23.3	5 57.2	15 15.7	21 58.9
26 M	2 19 18	6 35 11	16 50 29	22 49 48	11 15.2	21 46.6	18 33.5	23 6.0	9 1.7	8 28.2	5 59.3	15 16.4	21 57.9
27 Tu	2 23 14	7 33 33	28 51 42	4♌56 44	11R 15.3	21 29.5	19 11.1	23 44.2	9 0.2	8 33.2	6 1.3	15 17.0	21 56.9
28 W	2 27 11	8 31 53	11♌ 5 30	17 18 31	11 15.3	21 17.2	19 47.5	24 22.3	8 58.9	8 38.3	6 3.3	15 17.7	21 55.9
29 Th	2 31 7	9 30 10	23 36 19	29 59 24	11 15.1	21 9.6	20 22.5	25 0.5	8 57.8	8 43.4	6 5.3	15 18.3	21 54.9
30 F	2 35 4	10 28 26	6♍28 10	13♍ 2 58	11 15.0	21D 7.0	20 56.2	25 38.6	8 56.9	8 48.7	6 7.3	15 18.9	21 53.8

Astro Data	Dy Hr Mn
♃⊼♆	4 0:13
♄ D	7 16:52
☽0S	8 10:27
☿0N	13 3:14
☽0N	21 10:11
♇ R	24 15:10
☽0S	4 19:38
☿ R	6 20:28
☽0N	17 17:23
☿ D	30 13:06

Planet Ingress	Dy Hr Mn
♀ ♉	5 18:13
☿ ♈	12 9:45
☉ ♈	20 6:50
♂ ♊	21 7:40
☿ ♉	1 2:29
♀ ♊	3 14:58
☿ ♈	13 1:24
☉ ♉	19 17:51

Last Aspect Dy Hr Mn		☽ Ingress Dy Hr Mn
3 3:43	♀ □	♌ 3 9:19
5 17:14	♀ △	♍ 5 17:19
7 8:50	♇ □	♎ 7 22:32
9 12:44	♇ ⚹	♏ 10 2:04
12 4:12	☿ △	♐ 12 4:58
13 21:02	☉ □	♑ 14 7:53
16 5:35	♂ △	♒ 16 11:11
18 12:16	♂ □	♓ 18 15:27
20 20:58	♂ ⚹	♈ 20 21:30
22 15:15	♇ △	♉ 23 6:11
24 22:30	♀ ☌	♊ 25 17:36
27 22:45	☿ ⚹	♋ 28 6:24
30 16:01	☿ □	♌ 30 18:08

Last Aspect Dy Hr Mn		☽ Ingress Dy Hr Mn
1 23:57	♀ □	♍ 2 2:46
3 18:25	♇ □	♎ 4 7:53
5 21:28	♇ ⚹	♏ 6 10:25
7 11:07	♆ □	♐ 8 11:51
10 0:31	♇ ☌	♑ 10 13:34
12 3:47	☉ □	♒ 12 16:34
14 19:28	☿ ⚹	♓ 14 21:25
16 13:44	♇ □	♈ 17 4:25
19 13:22	☉ ☌	♉ 19 13:44
20 19:37	♆ □	♊ 22 1:11
23 23:23	☿ ⚹	♋ 24 13:57
26 9:57	☿ □	♌ 27 2:15
29 2:09	♂ ⚹	♍ 29 12:01

☽ Phases & Eclipses Dy Hr Mn	
6 23:15	○ 16♍43
13 21:02	☾ 23♐37
20 22:42	● 0♈39
28 23:49	☽ 8♋38
5 11:04	○ 15♎60
12 3:47	☾ 22♑35
19 13:22	● 29♈49
19 13:35:06	• P 0.737
27 17:34	☽ 7♌47

Astro Data

1 MARCH 2004
Julian Day # 38046
Galactic Ctr 26♐54.5
SVP 05♓12'17"
Obliquity 23°26'26"
⚷ Chiron 23♑46.7
☽ Mean ☊ 14♉29.9

1 APRIL 2004
Julian Day # 38077
Galactic Ctr 26♐54.5
SVP 05♓12'13"
Obliquity 23°26'27"
⚷ Chiron 25♑31.3
☽ Mean ☊ 12♉51.3

*Giving the positions of planets daily at noon, in LONGITUDE Greenwich Mean Time (UT)

NOON PLANETARY EPHEMERIS: GMT*

LONGITUDE — MAY 2004

Day	Sid.Time	☉	0 hr ☽	Noon ☽	True ☊	☿	♀	♂	♃	♄	♅	♆	♇
1 Sa	2 39 0	11♉26 39	19♍44 5	26♍31 38	11♉15.0	21♈ 9.2	21♊28.5	26♊16.7	8♍56.1	8♋54.0	6♓ 9.1	15♒19.4	21♐52.7
2 Su	2 42 57	12 24 50	3♎25 41	10♎26 6	11D 15.1	21 16.2	21 59.3	26 54.8	8R 55.5	8 59.3	6 11.0	15 19.9	21R 51.6
3 M	2 46 53	13 23 0	17 32 37	24 44 50	11 15.2	21 27.9	22 28.6	27 32.9	8 55.1	9 4.8	6 12.8	15 20.4	21 50.5
4 Tu	2 50 50	14 21 7	2♏ 2 11	9♏23 57	11R 15.3	21 44.3	22 56.3	28 10.9	8 54.9	9 10.3	6 14.6	15 20.8	21 49.3
5 W	2 54 47	15 19 13	16 49 18	24 17 15	11 15.2	22 5.2	23 22.4	28 49.0	8D 54.9	9 15.9	6 16.3	15 21.2	21 48.1
6 Th	2 58 43	16 17 18	1♐46 50	9♐16 57	11 14.9	22 30.5	23 46.8	29 27.1	8 55.1	9 21.5	6 18.0	15 21.6	21 46.9
7 F	3 2 40	17 15 21	16 46 33	24 14 38	11 14.4	22 60.0	24 9.5	0♋ 5.1	8 55.4	9 27.3	6 19.6	15 22.0	21 45.7
8 Sa	3 6 36	18 13 22	1♑40 14	9♑ 2 32	11 13.6	23 33.6	24 30.4	0 43.1	8 55.9	9 33.1	6 21.2	15 22.3	21 44.5
9 Su	3 10 33	19 11 22	16 20 48	23 34 27	11 12.9	24 11.2	24 49.4	1 21.2	8 56.6	9 38.9	6 22.8	15 22.6	21 43.2
10 M	3 14 29	20 9 21	0♒43 3	7♒46 19	11 12.4	24 52.5	25 6.5	1 59.2	8 57.5	9 44.8	6 24.3	15 22.8	21 42.0
11 Tu	3 18 26	21 7 19	14 44 5	21 36 19	11D 12.2	25 37.6	25 21.7	2 37.2	8 58.6	9 50.8	6 25.8	15 23.0	21 40.7
12 W	3 22 22	22 5 15	28 23 3	5♓ 4 28	11 12.4	26 26.1	25 34.8	3 15.2	8 59.8	9 56.8	6 27.2	15 23.2	21 39.3
13 Th	3 26 19	23 3 10	11♓40 45	18 12 11	11 13.1	27 18.1	25 45.8	3 53.2	9 1.2	10 2.9	6 28.5	15 23.4	21 38.0
14 F	3 30 16	24 1 3	24 39 4	1♈ 1 42	11 14.2	28 13.3	25 54.7	4 31.2	9 2.8	10 9.1	6 29.9	15 23.5	21 36.7
15 Sa	3 34 12	24 58 55	7♈20 27	13 35 37	11 15.3	29 11.8	26 1.4	5 9.2	9 4.6	10 15.3	6 31.2	15 23.5	21 35.3
16 Su	3 38 9	25 56 46	19 47 32	25 56 31	11 16.3	0♉13.3	26 5.9	5 47.2	9 6.6	10 21.6	6 32.4	15 23.6	21 33.9
17 M	3 42 5	26 54 36	2♉ 2 52	8♉ 6 52	11R 16.8	1 17.7	26R 8.1	6 25.2	9 8.7	10 27.9	6 33.6	15R 23.6	21 32.5
18 Tu	3 46 2	27 52 25	14 8 49	20 8 57	11 16.6	2 25.1	26 7.9	7 3.1	9 11.0	10 34.3	6 34.7	15 23.6	21 31.1
19 W	3 49 58	28 50 12	26 7 31	2♊ 4 48	11 15.6	3 35.2	26 5.4	7 41.1	9 13.5	10 40.8	6 35.8	15 23.5	21 29.7
20 Th	3 53 55	29 47 57	8♊ 1 2	13 56 27	11 13.6	4 48.1	26 0.5	8 19.1	9 16.2	10 47.3	6 36.9	15 23.5	21 28.2
21 F	3 57 51	0♊45 42	19 51 20	25 45 57	11 10.9	6 3.7	25 53.2	8 57.0	9 19.0	10 53.8	6 37.9	15 23.4	21 26.8
22 Sa	4 1 48	1 43 25	1♋40 36	7♋35 35	11 7.6	7 21.8	25 43.4	9 35.0	9 22.0	11 0.4	6 38.8	15 23.2	21 25.3
23 Su	4 5 45	2 41 6	13 31 14	19 27 55	11 4.2	8 42.6	25 31.3	10 12.9	9 25.2	11 7.1	6 39.7	15 23.0	21 23.9
24 M	4 9 41	3 38 46	25 26 2	1♌25 59	11 1.1	10 5.9	25 16.7	10 50.8	9 28.5	11 13.8	6 40.6	15 22.8	21 22.4
25 Tu	4 13 38	4 36 25	7♌28 13	13 33 12	10 58.7	11 31.7	24 59.7	11 28.8	9 32.1	11 20.5	6 41.4	15 22.6	21 20.9
26 W	4 17 34	5 34 2	19 41 25	25 53 22	10 57.2	12 60.0	24 40.4	12 6.7	9 35.7	11 27.3	6 42.2	15 22.3	21 19.4
27 Th	4 21 31	6 31 37	2♍ 9 34	8♍30 30	10D 56.9	14 30.7	24 18.8	12 44.6	9 39.6	11 34.2	6 42.9	15 22.0	21 17.8
28 F	4 25 27	7 29 11	14 56 39	21 28 28	10 57.5	16 3.9	23 54.9	13 22.5	9 43.6	11 41.1	6 43.5	15 21.7	21 16.3
29 Sa	4 29 24	8 26 44	28 6 22	4♎50 41	10 58.8	17 39.5	23 29.0	14 0.4	9 47.7	11 48.0	6 44.1	15 21.3	21 14.8
30 Su	4 33 20	9 24 15	11♎41 38	18 39 22	11 0.3	19 17.5	23 1.1	14 38.2	9 52.1	11 55.0	6 44.7	15 20.9	21 13.2
31 M	4 37 17	10 21 45	25 43 51	2♏54 55	11 1.4	20 58.0	22 31.3	15 16.1	9 56.5	12 2.0	6 45.2	15 20.5	21 11.7

LONGITUDE — JUNE 2004

Day	Sid.Time	☉	0 hr ☽	Noon ☽	True ☊	☿	♀	♂	♃	♄	♅	♆	♇
1 Tu	4 41 14	11♊19 14	10♏12 15	17♏35 17	11♉ 1.4	22♉40.9	21♊59.8	15♋54.0	10♍ 1.2	12♋ 9.0	6♓45.7	15♒20.0	21♐10.1
2 W	4 45 10	12 16 41	25 3 18	2♐35 25	11R 0.1	24 26.1	21R 26.8	16 31.8	10 6.0	12 16.1	6 46.1	15R 19.5	21R 8.6
3 Th	4 49 7	13 14 8	10♐10 32	17 47 29	10 57.3	26 13.8	20 52.4	17 9.7	10 10.9	12 23.2	6 46.5	15 19.0	21 7.0
4 F	4 53 3	14 11 34	25 24 59	3♑ 1 44	10 53.3	28 3.8	20 16.9	17 47.5	10 16.0	12 30.4	6 46.8	15 18.4	21 5.4
5 Sa	4 57 0	15 8 59	10♑36 26	18 7 53	10 48.5	29 56.2	19 40.5	18 25.4	10 21.3	12 37.6	6 47.1	15 17.9	21 3.9
6 Su	5 0 56	16 6 23	25 35 1	2♒56 55	10 43.8	1♊50.8	19 3.4	19 3.2	10 26.7	12 44.8	6 47.3	15 17.3	21 2.3
7 M	5 4 53	17 3 46	10♒12 52	17 22 19	10 39.8	3 47.8	18 25.9	19 41.1	10 32.2	12 52.1	6 47.5	15 16.6	21 0.7
8 Tu	5 8 49	18 1 9	24 24 58	1♓20 39	10 37.1	5 46.9	17 48.2	20 18.9	10 37.9	12 59.4	6 47.6	15 16.0	20 59.1
9 W	5 12 46	18 58 31	8♓ 9 26	14 51 28	10D 35.9	7 48.0	17 10.6	20 56.7	10 43.7	13 6.7	6 47.7	15 15.3	20 57.5
10 Th	5 16 43	19 55 53	21 27 4	27 56 36	10 36.0	9 51.2	16 33.2	21 34.5	10 49.7	13 14.1	6R 47.8	15 14.5	20 55.9
11 F	5 20 39	20 53 14	4♈20 32	10♈39 21	10 37.2	11 56.1	15 56.4	22 12.3	10 55.8	13 21.5	6 47.7	15 13.8	20 54.3
12 Sa	5 24 36	21 50 35	16 53 36	23 3 48	10 38.7	14 2.8	15 20.4	22 50.2	11 2.1	13 28.9	6 47.7	15 13.0	20 52.7
13 Su	5 28 32	22 47 55	29 10 28	5♉14 9	10R 39.8	16 10.9	14 45.4	23 28.0	11 8.5	13 36.4	6 47.6	15 12.2	20 51.1
14 M	5 32 29	23 45 15	11♉15 18	17 14 24	10 39.7	18 20.3	14 11.5	24 5.8	11 15.0	13 43.8	6 47.4	15 11.3	20 49.6
15 Tu	5 36 25	24 42 34	23 11 51	29 8 5	10 37.8	20 30.6	13 39.1	24 43.6	11 21.7	13 51.3	6 47.2	15 10.5	20 48.0
16 W	5 40 22	25 39 53	5♊ 3 25	10♊58 12	10 34.0	22 41.8	13 8.2	25 21.4	11 28.5	13 58.9	6 46.9	15 9.6	20 46.4
17 Th	5 44 18	26 37 11	16 52 42	22 47 13	10 28.1	24 53.4	12 39.0	25 59.2	11 35.5	14 6.4	6 46.6	15 8.7	20 44.8
18 F	5 48 15	27 34 29	28 41 58	4♋37 11	10 20.4	27 5.2	12 11.8	26 37.0	11 42.5	14 14.0	6 46.3	15 7.7	20 43.2
19 Sa	5 52 12	28 31 47	10♋33 4	16 29 52	10 11.6	29 17.0	11 46.4	27 14.8	11 49.7	14 21.6	6 45.9	15 6.8	20 41.6
20 Su	5 56 8	29 29 4	22 27 46	28 27 0	10 2.4	1♋28.4	11 23.2	27 52.6	11 57.1	14 29.2	6 45.4	15 5.8	20 40.1
21 M	6 0 5	0♋26 20	4♌27 49	10♌30 28	9 53.7	3 39.3	11 2.2	28 30.4	12 4.5	14 36.8	6 44.9	15 4.7	20 38.5
22 Tu	6 4 1	1 23 35	16 35 14	22 42 26	9 46.4	5 49.2	10 43.4	29 8.3	12 12.1	14 44.5	6 44.4	15 3.7	20 37.0
23 W	6 7 58	2 20 50	28 52 24	5♍ 5 31	9 40.9	7 58.2	10 27.0	29 46.0	12 19.8	14 52.1	6 43.8	15 2.6	20 35.4
24 Th	6 11 54	3 18 5	11♍22 11	17 42 47	9 37.6	10 5.8	10 12.8	0♌23.8	12 27.6	14 59.8	6 43.2	15 1.5	20 33.9
25 F	6 15 51	4 15 18	24 7 47	0♎37 36	9D 36.4	12 12.0	10 1.1	1 1.6	12 35.6	15 7.5	6 42.5	15 0.4	20 32.3
26 Sa	6 19 48	5 12 31	7♎12 40	13 53 21	9 36.6	14 16.7	9 51.7	1 39.4	12 43.7	15 15.2	6 41.8	14 59.3	20 30.8
27 Su	6 23 44	6 9 44	20 40 1	27 32 56	9 37.4	16 19.7	9 44.7	2 17.2	12 51.8	15 22.9	6 41.0	14 58.1	20 29.3
28 M	6 27 41	7 6 56	4♏32 16	11♏38 5	9R 37.7	18 20.8	9 40.1	2 55.0	13 0.1	15 30.7	6 40.2	14 56.9	20 27.8
29 Tu	6 31 37	8 4 8	18 50 16	26 8 32	9 36.7	20 20.1	9D 37.8	3 32.8	13 8.5	15 38.4	6 39.3	14 55.7	20 26.3
30 W	6 35 34	9 1 19	3♐32 24	11♐ 1 13	9 33.5	22 17.5	9 37.9	4 10.6	13 17.0	15 46.2	6 38.4	14 54.5	20 24.8

Astro Data	Planet Ingress	Last Aspect	☽ Ingress	Last Aspect	☽ Ingress	☽ Phases & Eclipses	Astro Data
Dy Hr Mn	Dy Hr Mn	Dy Hr Mn	Dy Hr Mn	Dy Hr Mn	Dy Hr Mn	Dy Hr Mn	1 MAY 2004
♃✶♄ 1 20:32	♂ ♋ 7 8:47	1 11:32 ♂ □	♎ 1 18:04	1 21:17 ☿ ☍	♐ 2 7:53	4 20:34 ○ 14♏42	Julian Day # 38107
☽0S 2 6:00	☿ ♉ 16 6:55	3 16:50 ♂ △	♏ 3 20:40	3 17:13 ♇ ☌	♑ 4 7:13	4 20:31 • T 1.303	Galactic Ctr 26♐54.6
♃ D 5 3:08	☉ ♊ 20 17:00	4 21:38 ♆ □	♐ 5 21:09	5 12:29 ♂ ☍	♒ 6 7:11	11 11:05 ☾ 21♒05	SVP 05♓12'10"
☽0N 14 23:10		7 11:52 ♀ ☍	♑ 7 21:18	7 18:10 ♇ ✶	♓ 8 9:39	19 4:53 ● 28♉33	Obliquity 23°26'26"
♀ R 17 22:29	☿ ♊ 5 12:49	9 13:04 ☿ □	♒ 9 22:47	9 23:38 ♂ △	♈ 10 15:50	27 7:58 ☽ 6♍22	⚷ Chiron 26♑07.9
♆ R 17 12:14	☿ ♋ 19 19:51	11 19:32 ☿ ✶	♓ 12 2:53	12 11:32 ♂ □	♉ 13 1:38		☽ Mean ☊ 11♉16.0
☽0S 29 15:28	☉ ♋ 21 0:58	14 2:15 ♀ □	♈ 14 10:03	15 2:35 ♂ ✶	♊ 15 13:45	3 4:21 ○ 12♐56	
	♂ ♌ 23 20:52	16 12:18 ♀ ✶	♉ 16 19:58	17 20:28 ☉ ☌	♋ 18 2:38	9 20:03 ☾ 19♓18	1 JUNE 2004
♅ R 10 15:48		19 4:53 ☉ ☌	♊ 19 7:48	20 10:47 ♂ ☌	♌ 20 15:06	17 20:28 ● 26♊57	Julian Day # 38138
☽0N 11 4:29		21 12:15 ♀ ☌	♋ 21 20:36	22 7:55 ♇ △	♍ 23 2:11	25 19:09 ☽ 4♎32	Galactic Ctr 26♐54.7
♄⊼♆ 24 16:41		22 18:59 ♄ ☌	♌ 24 9:08	24 17:20 ♇ □	♎ 25 10:51		SVP 05♓12'05"
☽0S 25 22:40		26 9:43 ♀ ✶	♍ 26 19:53	26 23:42 ♇ ✶	♏ 27 16:14		Obliquity 23°26'26"
♀ D 29 23:16		28 16:18 ♀ □	♎ 29 3:24	29 0:58 ☿ △	♐ 29 18:17		⚷ Chiron 25♑33.9R
		30 19:10 ♀ △	♏ 31 7:09				☽ Mean ☊ 9♉37.5

*Giving the positions of planets daily at noon,
in LONGITUDE Greenwich Mean Time (UT)

Noon Planetary Ephemeris: GMT*

JULY 2004 — LONGITUDE

Day	Sid.Time	☉	0 hr ☽	Noon☽	True☊	☿	♀	♂	♃	♄	♅	♆	♇
1 Th	6 39 30	9♋58 30	18♐34 4	26♐ 9 54	9♉27.9	24♋12.9	9♊40.2	4♌48.3	13♍25.7	15♋53.9	6♓37.5	14♒53.3	20♐23.3
2 F	6 43 27	10 55 41	3♑47 30	11♑25 30	9R 20.3	26 6.3	9 44.9	5 26.1	13 34.4	16 1.7	6R 36.5	14R 52.0	20R 21.8
3 Sa	6 47 23	11 52 52	19 2 34	26 37 18	9 11.4	27 57.7	9 51.7	6 3.9	13 43.3	16 9.5	6 35.4	14 50.7	20 20.4
4 Su	6 51 20	12 50 3	4♒ 8 25	11♒34 46	9 2.3	29 47.0	10 0.7	6 41.7	13 52.2	16 17.2	6 34.4	14 49.4	20 18.9
5 M	6 55 17	13 47 14	18 55 23	26 9 28	8 54.2	1♌34.3	10 11.9	7 19.5	14 1.2	16 25.0	6 33.2	14 48.1	20 17.5
6 Tu	6 59 13	14 44 25	3♓16 30	10♓16 8	8 47.8	3 19.5	10 25.0	7 57.3	14 10.4	16 32.8	6 32.1	14 46.7	20 16.1
7 W	7 3 10	15 41 37	17 8 17	23 53 1	8 43.7	5 2.7	10 40.2	8 35.0	14 19.6	16 40.6	6 30.9	14 45.4	20 14.7
8 Th	7 7 6	16 38 48	0♈30 34	7♈ 1 19	8 41.7	6 43.8	10 57.3	9 12.8	14 29.0	16 48.4	6 29.6	14 44.0	20 13.3
9 F	7 11 3	17 36 1	13 25 44	19 44 23	8D 41.3	8 22.9	11 16.3	9 50.6	14 38.4	16 56.2	6 28.3	14 42.6	20 11.9
10 Sa	7 14 59	18 33 13	25 57 51	2♉ 6 47	8 41.6	9 59.9	11 37.1	10 28.4	14 48.0	17 3.9	6 27.0	14 41.2	20 10.6
11 Su	7 18 56	19 30 26	8♉11 49	14 13 36	8R 41.6	11 34.9	11 59.7	11 6.2	14 57.6	17 11.7	6 25.6	14 39.8	20 9.2
12 M	7 22 52	20 27 40	20 12 44	26 9 50	8 40.2	13 7.8	12 23.9	11 44.0	15 7.3	17 19.5	6 24.2	14 38.3	20 7.9
13 Tu	7 26 49	21 24 54	2♊ 5 28	8♊ 0 8	8 36.7	14 38.6	12 49.8	12 21.8	15 17.2	17 27.3	6 22.8	14 36.9	20 6.6
14 W	7 30 46	22 22 9	13 54 18	19 48 26	8 30.5	16 7.3	13 17.3	12 59.7	15 27.1	17 35.1	6 21.3	14 35.4	20 5.3
15 Th	7 34 42	23 19 24	25 42 53	1♋37 59	8 21.6	17 34.0	13 46.2	13 37.5	15 37.1	17 42.9	6 19.8	14 33.9	20 4.1
16 F	7 38 39	24 16 40	7♋34 3	13 31 17	8 10.4	18 58.4	14 16.6	14 15.3	15 47.2	17 50.6	6 18.2	14 32.4	20 2.8
17 Sa	7 42 35	25 13 56	19 29 56	25 30 9	7 57.6	20 20.7	14 48.4	14 53.1	15 57.4	17 58.4	6 16.6	14 30.9	20 1.6
18 Su	7 46 32	26 11 12	1♌32 6	7♌35 54	7 44.3	21 40.8	15 21.6	15 31.0	16 7.6	18 6.1	6 15.0	14 29.4	20 0.4
19 M	7 50 28	27 8 29	13 41 42	19 49 35	7 31.6	22 58.6	15 56.0	16 8.8	16 18.0	18 13.9	6 13.4	14 27.9	19 59.2
20 Tu	7 54 25	28 5 46	25 59 43	2♍12 14	7 20.5	24 14.2	16 31.7	16 46.7	16 28.4	18 21.6	6 11.7	14 26.3	19 58.0
21 W	7 58 21	29 3 3	8♍27 17	14 45 6	7 11.9	25 27.3	17 8.5	17 24.5	16 38.9	18 29.3	6 9.9	14 24.8	19 56.9
22 Th	8 2 18	0♌ 0 21	21 5 52	27 29 52	7 6.1	26 38.1	17 46.6	18 2.4	16 49.5	18 37.0	6 8.2	14 23.2	19 55.8
23 F	8 6 15	0 57 39	3♎57 22	10♎28 41	7 2.9	27 46.3	18 25.7	18 40.2	17 0.2	18 44.7	6 6.4	14 21.6	19 54.7
24 Sa	8 10 11	1 54 57	17 4 7	23 44 1	7 1.8	28 51.9	19 5.9	19 18.1	17 10.9	18 52.4	6 4.5	14 20.0	19 53.6
25 Su	8 14 8	2 52 16	0♏28 39	7♏18 20	7 1.7	29 54.9	19 47.1	19 56.0	17 21.8	19 0.0	6 2.7	14 18.5	19 52.5
26 M	8 18 4	3 49 35	14 13 15	21 13 33	7 1.4	0♍55.1	20 29.4	20 33.8	17 32.6	19 7.6	6 0.8	14 16.9	19 51.5
27 Tu	8 22 1	4 46 55	28 19 17	5♐30 20	6 59.6	1 52.4	21 12.5	21 11.7	17 43.6	19 15.3	5 58.9	14 15.3	19 50.5
28 W	8 25 57	5 44 15	12♐46 26	20 7 10	6 55.5	2 46.7	21 56.6	21 49.6	17 54.6	19 22.9	5 56.9	14 13.7	19 49.5
29 Th	8 29 54	6 41 36	27 31 55	4♑59 52	6 48.8	3 37.8	22 41.6	22 27.5	18 5.7	19 30.4	5 55.0	14 12.1	19 48.5
30 F	8 33 51	7 38 57	12♑30 6	20 1 29	6 39.7	4 25.6	23 27.5	23 5.4	18 16.9	19 38.0	5 53.0	14 10.4	19 47.6
31 Sa	8 37 47	8 36 19	27 32 49	5♒ 2 52	6 29.0	5 10.1	24 14.2	23 43.3	18 28.2	19 45.5	5 50.9	14 8.8	19 46.7

AUGUST 2004 — LONGITUDE

Day	Sid.Time	☉	0 hr ☽	Noon☽	True☊	☿	♀	♂	♃	♄	♅	♆	♇
1 Su	8 41 44	9♌33 42	12♒30 25	19♒54 17	6♉17.9	5♍50.9	25♊ 1.7	24♌21.2	18♍39.5	19♋53.0	5♓48.9	14♒ 7.2	19♐45.8
2 M	8 45 40	10 31 6	27 13 26	4♓26 59	6R 7.8	6 27.9	25 50.0	24 59.1	18 50.8	20 0.5	5R 46.8	14R 5.6	19R 45.0
3 Tu	8 49 37	11 28 30	11♓34 14	18 34 43	5 59.6	7 1.0	26 39.0	25 37.0	19 2.2	20 8.0	5 44.7	14 3.9	19 44.1
4 W	8 53 33	12 25 56	25 28 8	2♈14 23	5 53.8	7 29.9	27 28.7	26 14.9	19 13.7	20 15.4	5 42.6	14 2.3	19 43.3
5 Th	8 57 30	13 23 23	8♈53 36	15 25 59	5 50.6	7 54.5	28 19.2	26 52.9	19 25.3	20 22.8	5 40.5	14 0.7	19 42.5
6 F	9 1 26	14 20 51	21 51 55	28 11 54	5 49.4	8 14.6	29 10.3	27 30.8	19 36.9	20 30.2	5 38.3	13 59.0	19 41.8
7 Sa	9 5 23	15 18 20	4♉26 29	10♉36 16	5 49.3	8 29.9	0♋ 2.1	28 8.8	19 48.5	20 37.5	5 36.1	13 57.4	19 41.1
8 Su	9 9 19	16 15 51	16 41 55	22 44 5	5 49.2	8 40.4	0 54.5	28 46.8	20 0.2	20 44.8	5 33.9	13 55.8	19 40.4
9 M	9 13 16	17 13 24	28 43 28	4♊40 43	5 48.1	8 45.7	1 47.5	29 24.8	20 12.0	20 52.1	5 31.7	13 54.1	19 39.7
10 Tu	9 17 13	18 10 57	10♊36 28	16 31 21	5 45.0	8R 45.9	2 41.0	0♍ 2.8	20 23.8	20 59.3	5 29.4	13 52.5	19 39.1
11 W	9 21 9	19 8 32	22 25 56	28 20 45	5 39.3	8 40.6	3 35.2	0 40.8	20 35.7	21 6.6	5 27.2	13 50.9	19 38.4
12 Th	9 25 6	20 6 9	4♋16 17	10♋12 58	5 31.1	8 29.9	4 29.9	1 18.8	20 47.7	21 13.7	5 24.9	13 49.3	19 37.9
13 F	9 29 2	21 3 46	16 11 12	22 11 18	5 20.5	8 13.7	5 25.1	1 56.8	20 59.7	21 20.9	5 22.6	13 47.6	19 37.3
14 Sa	9 32 59	22 1 25	28 13 31	4♌18 5	5 8.4	7 52.0	6 20.8	2 34.9	21 11.7	21 28.0	5 20.3	13 46.0	19 36.8
15 Su	9 36 55	22 59 6	10♌25 9	16 34 50	4 55.6	7 24.9	7 17.0	3 12.9	21 23.8	21 35.1	5 18.0	13 44.4	19 36.3
16 M	9 40 52	23 56 47	22 47 13	29 2 20	4 43.4	6 52.7	8 13.7	3 51.0	21 35.9	21 42.1	5 15.7	13 42.8	19 35.8
17 Tu	9 44 49	24 54 30	5♍20 13	11♍40 52	4 32.8	6 15.5	9 10.9	4 29.1	21 48.1	21 49.1	5 13.3	13 41.2	19 35.4
18 W	9 48 45	25 52 14	18 4 17	24 30 29	4 24.6	5 34.0	10 8.5	5 7.2	22 0.3	21 56.0	5 11.0	13 39.6	19 35.0
19 Th	9 52 42	26 49 59	0♎59 28	7♎31 17	4 19.1	4 48.4	11 6.5	5 45.3	22 12.5	22 2.9	5 8.6	13 38.0	19 34.6
20 F	9 56 38	27 47 45	14 6 0	20 43 43	4 16.3	3 59.7	12 4.9	6 23.4	22 24.8	22 9.7	5 6.3	13 36.5	19 34.3
21 Sa	10 0 35	28 45 33	27 24 31	4♏ 8 32	4D 15.6	3 8.4	13 3.8	7 1.5	22 37.2	22 16.6	5 3.9	13 34.9	19 34.0
22 Su	10 4 31	29 43 22	10♏55 54	17 46 45	4 15.9	2 15.6	14 3.0	7 39.7	22 49.5	22 23.3	5 1.5	13 33.3	19 33.7
23 M	10 8 28	0♍41 12	24 41 12	1♐39 19	4R 16.2	1 22.2	15 2.6	8 17.8	23 2.0	22 30.0	4 59.1	13 31.8	19 33.4
24 Tu	10 12 24	1 39 3	8♐41 7	15 46 32	4 15.4	0 29.3	16 2.6	8 56.0	23 14.4	22 36.7	4 56.7	13 30.2	19 33.2
25 W	10 16 21	2 36 55	22 55 24	0♑ 7 27	4 12.6	29♌38.0	17 2.9	9 34.2	23 26.9	22 43.3	4 54.3	13 28.7	19 33.1
26 Th	10 20 18	3 34 49	7♑22 18	14 39 25	4 7.5	28 49.3	18 3.6	10 12.4	23 39.4	22 49.9	4 51.9	13 27.2	19 32.9
27 F	10 24 14	4 32 44	21 58 11	29 17 48	4 0.3	28 4.5	19 4.7	10 50.6	23 52.0	22 56.4	4 49.6	13 25.7	19 32.8
28 Sa	10 28 11	5 30 40	6♒37 27	13♒56 13	3 51.6	27 24.4	20 6.1	11 28.8	24 4.5	23 2.8	4 47.2	13 24.2	19 32.7
29 Su	10 32 7	6 28 37	21 13 12	28 27 27	3 42.6	26 50.0	21 7.8	12 7.0	24 17.1	23 9.2	4 44.8	13 22.7	19 32.6
30 M	10 36 4	7 26 37	5♓38 8	12♓44 29	3 34.3	26 22.2	22 9.8	12 45.2	24 29.8	23 15.6	4 42.4	13 21.3	19D 32.6
31 Tu	10 40 0	8 24 37	19 45 51	26 41 42	3 27.5	26 1.6	23 12.2	13 23.5	24 42.4	23 21.9	4 40.0	13 19.8	19 32.6

Astro Data Dy Hr Mn	Planet Ingress Dy Hr Mn	Last Aspect Dy Hr Mn	☽ Ingress Dy Hr Mn	Last Aspect Dy Hr Mn	☽ Ingress Dy Hr Mn	☽ Phases & Eclipses Dy Hr Mn	Astro Data
☽0N 8 10:40	☿ ♌ 4 14:53	1 2:54 ♇ ☌	♑ 1 18:02	1 20:52 ♀ △	♓ 2 4:35	2 11:10 ○ 10♑54	1 JULY 2004
♃⊼♆ 9 21:11	☉ ♌ 22 11:51	3 14:26 ☿ ☍	♒ 3 17:23	4 2:59 ♀ □	♈ 4 8:00	9 7:35 ☾ 17♈25	Julian Day # 38168
☽0S 23 3:48	☿ ♍ 25 13:59	5 2:16 ♇ ✶	♓ 5 18:27	6 14:00 ♀ ✶	♉ 6 15:27	17 11:25 ● 25♋13	Galactic Ctr 26♐54.8
♄⊼♇ 31 15:21		7 5:31 ♇ □	♈ 7 23:04	9 0:47 ♂ □	♊ 9 2:34	25 3:38 ☽ 2♏32	SVP 05♓11'59"
	♀ ♋ 7 11:03	9 12:53 ♇ △	♉ 10 7:52	10 20:00 ♃ □	♋ 11 15:21	31 18:06 ○ 8♒51	Obliquity 23°26'26"
☽0N 4 18:28	♂ ♍ 10 10:15	11 23:30 ☉ ✶	♊ 12 19:46	13 10:18 ♄ ☌	♌ 14 3:31		⚷ Chiron 24♑06.6R
♃□♇ 6 21:32	☉ ♍ 22 18:54	14 12:34 ♇ ☍	♋ 15 8:41	16 1:25 ☉ ☌	♍ 16 13:50	7 22:02 ☾ 15♉42	☽ Mean ☊ 8♉02.2
♄⚼♅ 7 8:27	☿ ♌ 25 1:34	17 11:25 ☉ ☌	♌ 17 20:57	18 7:16 ♃ ☌	♎ 18 22:10	16 1:25 ● 23♌31	
☿ R 10 0:34		19 18:51 ☿ ☌	♍ 20 7:45	21 1:40 ☉ ✶	♏ 21 4:38	23 10:13 ☽ 0♐37	1 AUGUST 2004
♃✶♄ 17 16:34		21 21:49 ♇ □	♎ 22 16:40	22 20:55 ♃ ✶	♐ 23 9:10	30 2:23 ○ 7♓03	Julian Day # 38199
☽0S 19 8:31		24 21:55 ☿ ✶	♏ 24 23:09	25 11:14 ☿ △	♑ 25 11:48		Galactic Ctr 26♐54.8
♇ D 30 19:39		26 10:49 ♂ □	♐ 27 2:49	27 2:59 ♃ △	♒ 27 13:09		SVP 05♓11'53"
		28 15:07 ♀ ☍	♑ 29 3:59	29 9:24 ☿ ☍	♓ 29 14:34		Obliquity 23°26'27"
		30 11:22 ♄ ☍	♒ 31 3:55	31 8:29 ♃ ☍	♈ 31 17:47		⚷ Chiron 22♑17.1R
							☽ Mean ☊ 6♉23.8

*Giving the positions of planets daily at noon, in LONGITUDE Greenwich Mean Time (UT)

Noon Planetary Ephemeris: GMT*

LONGITUDE — SEPTEMBER 2004

Day	Sid.Time	☉	0 hr ☽	Noon ☽	True ☊	☿	♀	♂	♃	♄	♅	♆	♇
1 W	10 43 57	9♍22 40	3♈31 42	10♈15 38	3♉22.9	25♌48.8	24♋14.8	14♍ 1.8	24♍55.1	23♋28.1	4♓37.6	13♒18.4	19♐32.7
2 Th	10 47 53	10 20 44	16 53 26	23 25 12	3R 20.6	25D 44.2	25 17.8	14 40.0	25 7.8	23 34.3	4R 35.2	13R 17.0	19 32.7
3 F	10 51 50	11 18 50	29 51 8	6♉11 33	3D 20.1	25 48.0	26 21.0	15 18.3	25 20.6	23 40.4	4 32.8	13 15.6	19 32.8
4 Sa	10 55 46	12 16 58	12♉26 53	18 37 36	3 20.9	26 0.5	27 24.6	15 56.7	25 33.3	23 46.4	4 30.5	13 14.2	19 33.0
5 Su	10 59 43	13 15 8	24 44 16	0♊47 29	3 22.1	26 21.7	28 28.4	16 35.0	25 46.1	23 52.4	4 28.1	13 12.8	19 33.1
6 M	11 3 40	14 13 20	6♊47 52	12 46 3	3R 22.8	26 51.5	29 32.5	17 13.4	25 58.9	23 58.4	4 25.8	13 11.5	19 33.3
7 Tu	11 7 36	15 11 34	18 42 41	24 38 25	3 22.2	27 29.7	0♌36.8	17 51.7	26 11.8	24 4.3	4 23.4	13 10.2	19 33.6
8 W	11 11 33	16 9 50	0♋33 52	6♋29 39	3 19.9	28 16.0	1 41.4	18 30.1	26 24.6	24 10.1	4 21.1	13 8.9	19 33.8
9 Th	11 15 29	17 8 9	12 26 19	18 24 26	3 15.7	29 10.1	2 46.3	19 8.6	26 37.5	24 15.8	4 18.8	13 7.6	19 34.1
10 F	11 19 26	18 6 29	24 24 29	0♌26 54	3 9.7	0♍11.7	3 51.4	19 47.0	26 50.4	24 21.5	4 16.4	13 6.3	19 34.5
11 Sa	11 23 22	19 4 51	6♌32 5	12 40 20	3 2.4	1 20.1	4 56.8	20 25.4	27 3.3	24 27.1	4 14.1	13 5.0	19 34.8
12 Su	11 27 19	20 3 15	18 51 56	25 7 4	2 54.6	2 34.9	6 2.3	21 3.9	27 16.2	24 32.6	4 11.9	13 3.8	19 35.2
13 M	11 31 15	21 1 41	1♍25 51	7♍48 21	2 47.0	3 55.6	7 8.1	21 42.4	27 29.1	24 38.1	4 9.6	13 2.6	19 35.7
14 Tu	11 35 12	22 0 9	14 14 35	20 44 30	2 40.5	5 21.5	8 14.1	22 20.9	27 42.0	24 43.5	4 7.3	13 1.4	19 36.1
15 W	11 39 9	22 58 39	27 17 59	3♎54 54	2 35.7	6 52.1	9 20.4	22 59.4	27 55.0	24 48.8	4 5.1	13 0.2	19 36.6
16 Th	11 43 5	23 57 10	10♎35 5	17 18 21	2 32.7	8 26.7	10 26.8	23 38.0	28 7.9	24 54.0	4 2.9	12 59.1	19 37.1
17 F	11 47 2	24 55 44	24 4 31	0♏53 23	2D 31.7	10 4.9	11 33.5	24 16.5	28 20.9	24 59.2	4 0.7	12 58.0	19 37.7
18 Sa	11 50 58	25 54 19	7♏44 46	14 38 29	2 32.2	11 46.1	12 40.3	24 55.1	28 33.8	25 4.3	3 58.5	12 56.9	19 38.3
19 Su	11 54 55	26 52 56	21 34 23	28 32 18	2 33.5	13 29.8	13 47.3	25 33.7	28 46.8	25 9.3	3 56.4	12 55.8	19 38.9
20 M	11 58 51	27 51 35	5♐32 5	12♐33 37	2 34.9	15 15.4	14 54.6	26 12.3	28 59.8	25 14.2	3 54.2	12 54.8	19 39.6
21 Tu	12 2 48	28 50 15	19 36 42	26 41 12	2R 35.7	17 2.6	16 2.0	26 51.0	29 12.8	25 19.1	3 52.1	12 53.8	19 40.3
22 W	12 6 44	29 48 57	3♑46 53	10♑53 32	2 35.2	18 51.0	17 9.6	27 29.6	29 25.7	25 23.8	3 50.1	12 52.8	19 41.0
23 Th	12 10 41	0♎47 41	18 0 52	25 8 32	2 33.3	20 40.2	18 17.3	28 8.3	29 38.7	25 28.5	3 48.0	12 51.8	19 41.7
24 F	12 14 38	1 46 26	2♒16 10	9♒23 21	2 30.1	22 29.9	19 25.3	28 47.0	29 51.7	25 33.1	3 46.0	12 50.9	19 42.5
25 Sa	12 18 34	2 45 13	16 29 35	23 34 23	2 25.9	24 20.0	20 33.4	29 25.7	0♎ 4.6	25 37.7	3 44.0	12 49.9	19 43.3
26 Su	12 22 31	3 44 2	0♓37 14	7♓37 38	2 21.5	26 10.1	21 41.7	0♎ 4.4	0 17.6	25 42.1	3 42.0	12 49.1	19 44.2
27 M	12 26 27	4 42 52	14 35 4	21 29 4	2 17.5	28 0.1	22 50.2	0 43.1	0 30.6	25 46.5	3 40.0	12 48.2	19 45.1
28 Tu	12 30 24	5 41 45	28 19 13	5♈ 5 11	2 14.3	29 49.8	23 58.8	1 21.9	0 43.5	25 50.7	3 38.1	12 47.4	19 46.0
29 W	12 34 20	6 40 39	11♈46 42	18 23 34	2 12.3	1♎39.1	25 7.7	2 0.7	0 56.5	25 54.9	3 36.2	12 46.5	19 46.9
30 Th	12 38 17	7 39 36	24 55 41	1♉23 3	2D 11.6	3 28.0	26 16.6	2 39.5	1 9.4	25 59.0	3 34.3	12 45.8	19 47.9

LONGITUDE — OCTOBER 2004

Day	Sid.Time	☉	0 hr ☽	Noon ☽	True ☊	☿	♀	♂	♃	♄	♅	♆	♇
1 F	12 42 13	8♎38 35	7♉45 46	14♉ 3 58	2♉12.0	5♎16.2	27♌25.8	3♎18.3	1♎22.3	26♋ 3.0	3♓32.5	12♒45.0	19♐48.9
2 Sa	12 46 10	9 37 36	20 17 56	26 27 58	2 13.3	7 3.8	28 35.0	3 57.2	1 35.2	26 6.9	3R 30.7	12R 44.3	19 49.9
3 Su	12 50 7	10 36 39	2♊34 27	8♊37 50	2 14.9	8 50.8	29 44.5	4 36.1	1 48.2	26 10.7	3 28.9	12 43.6	19 50.9
4 M	12 54 3	11 35 44	14 38 36	20 37 17	2 16.5	10 37.0	0♍54.1	5 15.0	2 1.1	26 14.5	3 27.2	12 43.0	19 52.0
5 Tu	12 58 0	12 34 52	26 34 27	2♋30 40	2 17.6	12 22.5	2 3.8	5 53.9	2 13.9	26 18.1	3 25.5	12 42.3	19 53.1
6 W	13 1 56	13 34 2	8♋26 32	14 22 39	2R 18.0	14 7.2	3 13.7	6 32.8	2 26.8	26 21.7	3 23.9	12 41.7	19 54.3
7 Th	13 5 53	14 33 15	20 19 37	26 18 3	2 17.5	15 51.1	4 23.8	7 11.8	2 39.6	26 25.1	3 22.2	12 41.2	19 55.5
8 F	13 9 49	15 32 30	2♌18 30	8♌21 31	2 16.2	17 34.3	5 33.9	7 50.8	2 52.5	26 28.5	3 20.6	12 40.6	19 56.7
9 Sa	13 13 46	16 31 46	14 27 37	20 37 16	2 14.4	19 16.7	6 44.2	8 29.8	3 5.3	26 31.7	3 19.1	12 40.1	19 57.9
10 Su	13 17 42	17 31 6	26 50 53	3♍ 8 50	2 12.2	20 58.3	7 54.7	9 8.9	3 18.1	26 34.9	3 17.6	12 39.6	19 59.2
11 M	13 21 39	18 30 27	9♍31 24	15 58 45	2 10.2	22 39.2	9 5.2	9 48.0	3 30.9	26 37.9	3 16.1	12 39.2	20 0.4
12 Tu	13 25 36	19 29 51	22 31 3	29 8 17	2 8.4	24 19.3	10 15.9	10 27.1	3 43.6	26 40.9	3 14.6	12 38.8	20 1.8
13 W	13 29 32	20 29 16	5♎50 25	12♎37 17	2 7.2	25 58.7	11 26.7	11 6.2	3 56.3	26 43.8	3 13.2	12 38.4	20 3.1
14 Th	13 33 29	21 28 44	19 28 38	26 24 8	2D 6.7	27 37.4	12 37.7	11 45.3	4 9.0	26 46.5	3 11.9	12 38.0	20 4.5
15 F	13 37 25	22 28 14	3♏23 24	10♏25 56	2 6.7	29 15.4	13 48.7	12 24.5	4 21.7	26 49.2	3 10.6	12 37.7	20 5.9
16 Sa	13 41 22	23 27 46	17 31 16	24 38 50	2 7.2	0♏52.8	14 59.9	13 3.7	4 34.3	26 51.7	3 9.3	12 37.5	20 7.3
17 Su	13 45 18	24 27 20	1♐48 6	8♐58 29	2 7.9	2 29.4	16 11.1	13 42.9	4 46.9	26 54.2	3 8.1	12 37.2	20 8.7
18 M	13 49 15	25 26 55	16 9 28	23 20 32	2 8.6	4 5.5	17 22.5	14 22.1	4 59.5	26 56.5	3 6.9	12 37.0	20 10.2
19 Tu	13 53 11	26 26 33	0♑31 12	7♑41 2	2 9.0	5 40.9	18 34.0	15 1.4	5 12.0	26 58.7	3 5.7	12 36.8	20 11.7
20 W	13 57 8	27 26 12	14 49 40	21 56 43	2R 9.3	7 15.6	19 45.6	15 40.7	5 24.5	27 0.9	3 4.6	12 36.7	20 13.3
21 Th	14 1 5	28 25 52	29 1 55	6♒ 5 0	2 9.3	8 49.8	20 57.3	16 20.0	5 37.0	27 2.9	3 3.6	12 36.5	20 14.8
22 F	14 5 1	29 25 35	13♒ 5 45	20 3 58	2 9.1	10 23.4	22 9.0	16 59.3	5 49.4	27 4.8	3 2.6	12 36.5	20 16.4
23 Sa	14 8 58	0♏25 19	26 59 30	3♓52 12	2 8.9	11 56.5	23 20.9	17 38.7	6 1.8	27 6.6	3 1.6	12 36.4	20 18.0
24 Su	14 12 54	1 25 4	10♓41 56	17 28 37	2 8.7	13 28.9	24 32.9	18 18.0	6 14.2	27 8.3	3 0.7	12D 36.4	20 19.6
25 M	14 16 51	2 24 52	24 12 7	0♈52 21	2D 8.7	15 0.8	25 45.0	18 57.4	6 26.5	27 9.9	2 59.8	12 36.4	20 21.3
26 Tu	14 20 47	3 24 41	7♈29 15	14 2 46	2 8.8	16 32.2	26 57.1	19 36.8	6 38.7	27 11.4	2 59.0	12 36.5	20 22.9
27 W	14 24 44	4 24 32	20 32 50	26 59 26	2R 8.9	18 3.0	28 9.4	20 16.3	6 50.9	27 12.8	2 58.2	12 36.6	20 24.6
28 Th	14 28 40	5 24 25	3♉22 35	9♉42 19	2 8.8	19 33.4	29 21.8	20 55.8	7 3.1	27 14.0	2 57.5	12 36.7	20 26.3
29 F	14 32 37	6 24 20	15 58 42	22 11 49	2 8.6	21 3.1	0♎34.2	21 35.3	7 15.2	27 15.2	2 56.8	12 36.8	20 28.1
30 Sa	14 36 34	7 24 17	28 21 51	4♊28 58	2 8.1	22 32.4	1 46.8	22 14.8	7 27.3	27 16.2	2 56.1	12 37.0	20 29.8
31 Su	14 40 30	8 24 16	10♊33 23	16 35 25	2 7.4	24 1.1	2 59.4	22 54.3	7 39.4	27 17.2	2 55.6	12 37.2	20 31.6

Astro Data	Planet Ingress	Last Aspect	☽ Ingress	Last Aspect	☽ Ingress	☽ Phases & Eclipses	Astro Data
Dy Hr Mn	Dy Hr Mn	Dy Hr Mn	Dy Hr Mn	Dy Hr Mn	Dy Hr Mn	Dy Hr Mn	1 SEPTEMBER 2004
☽0N 1 3:33	♀ ♌ 6 22:17	2 16:18 ☿ △	♉ 3 0:17	2 16:35 ♀ □	♊ 2 18:56	6 15:12 ☾ 14♊21	Julian Day # 38230
☿ D 2 13:10	☿ ♍ 10 7:39	5 6:57 ♀ ✶	♊ 5 10:26	4 10:29 ♇ ☍	♋ 5 6:55	14 14:30 ● 22♍06	Galactic Ctr 26♐54.9
☽0S 15 14:47	☉ ♎ 22 16:31	7 18:09 ☿ ✶	♋ 7 22:51	7 12:14 ♄ ☌	♌ 7 19:24	21 15:55 ☽ 28♐60	SVP 05♓11'49"
♃⚼♆ 15 21:00	♃ ♎ 25 3:24	10 4:43 ♃ ✶	♌ 10 11:07	9 10:44 ♇ △	♍ 10 6:01	28 13:10 ○ 5♈45	Obliquity 23°26'27"
☽0N 28 12:39	♂ ♎ 26 9:17	12 1:23 ♇ △	♍ 12 21:17	12 7:33 ♄ ✶	♎ 12 13:33		⚷ Chiron 20♑53.9R
♂0S 29 13:28	☿ ♎ 28 14:14	15 0:56 ♃ ☌	♎ 15 4:55	14 14:23 ☿ ☌	♏ 14 18:11	6 10:13 ☾ 13♋30	☽ Mean ☊ 4♉45.3
☿0S 30 14:54		17 1:33 ♄ □	♏ 17 10:26	16 15:44 ♄ △	♐ 16 20:59	14 2:49 ● 21♎06	
	♀ ♍ 3 17:21	19 12:25 ♃ ✶	♐ 19 14:31	18 15:47 ☉ ✶	♑ 18 23:08	14 3:00:23 • P 0.928	1 OCTOBER 2004
♃0S 6 19:14	☿ ♏ 15 22:58	21 16:20 ♃ □	♑ 21 17:36	20 22:00 ☉ □	♒ 21 1:39	20 22:00 ☽ 27♑51	Julian Day # 38260
♃⚻♅ 10 11:08	☉ ♏ 23 1:50	23 19:42 ♃ △	♒ 23 20:11	22 12:22 ♇ ✶	♓ 23 5:14	28 3:08 ○ 5♉02	Galactic Ctr 26♐55.0
☽0S 12 23:21	♀ ♎ 29 0:40	25 6:26 ♀ ☍	♓ 25 22:56	25 5:18 ♄ △	♈ 25 10:25	28 3:05 • T 1.308	SVP 05♓11'46"
♆ D 24 11:57		28 1:13 ☿ ☍	♈ 28 2:58	27 12:25 ♄ □	♉ 27 17:39		Obliquity 23°26'27"
☽0N 25 20:22		30 1:54 ♄ □	♉ 30 9:25	29 21:51 ♄ ✶	♊ 30 3:12		⚷ Chiron 20♑31.0
							☽ Mean ☊ 3♉09.9

*Giving the positions of planets daily at noon, in LONGITUDE Greenwich Mean Time (UT)

Noon Planetary Ephemeris: GMT*

NOVEMBER 2004 LONGITUDE

Day	Sid.Time	☉	0 hr ☽	Noon ☽	True ☊	☿	♀	♂	♃	♄	♅	♆	♇
1 M	14 44 27	9♏24 17	22♊35 22	28♊33 35	2♉ 6.4	25♏29.3	4♎12.1	23♎33.9	7♎51.3	27♋18.0	2♓55.0	12♒37.5	20♐33.4
2 Tu	14 48 23	10 24 20	4♋30 30	10♋26 32	2R 5.3	26 56.9	5 24.9	24 13.5	8 3.3	27 18.7	2R 54.5	12 37.8	20 35.3
3 W	14 52 20	11 24 25	16 22 12	22 17 59	2 4.4	28 23.9	6 37.8	24 53.2	8 15.1	27 19.3	2 54.1	12 38.1	20 37.1
4 Th	14 56 16	12 24 33	28 14 26	4♌12 7	2 3.8	29 50.4	7 50.7	25 32.9	8 27.0	27 19.8	2 53.7	12 38.5	20 39.0
5 F	15 0 13	13 24 42	10♌11 36	16 13 28	2D 3.7	1♐16.2	9 3.8	26 12.5	8 38.7	27 20.2	2 53.3	12 38.9	20 40.8
6 Sa	15 4 9	14 24 53	22 18 19	28 26 42	2 4.1	2 41.3	10 16.9	26 52.3	8 50.4	27 20.4	2 53.0	12 39.3	20 42.7
7 Su	15 8 6	15 25 7	4♍39 12	10♍56 19	2 5.0	4 5.7	11 30.1	27 32.0	9 2.1	27 20.6	2 52.8	12 39.7	20 44.7
8 M	15 12 3	16 25 22	17 18 32	23 46 16	2 6.2	5 29.4	12 43.3	28 11.8	9 13.6	27R 20.6	2 52.6	12 40.2	20 46.6
9 Tu	15 15 59	17 25 40	0♎19 51	6♎59 30	2 7.5	6 52.2	13 56.7	28 51.6	9 25.1	27 20.5	2 52.5	12 40.8	20 48.5
10 W	15 19 56	18 25 59	13 45 22	20 37 28	2 8.4	8 14.1	15 10.1	29 31.4	9 36.6	27 20.3	2 52.4	12 41.3	20 50.5
11 Th	15 23 52	19 26 20	27 35 38	4♏39 36	2R 8.6	9 35.0	16 23.5	0♏11.3	9 48.0	27 20.0	2D 52.3	12 41.9	20 52.5
12 F	15 27 49	20 26 43	11♏48 55	19 3 1	2 8.0	10 54.7	17 37.0	0 51.2	9 59.3	27 19.6	2 52.3	12 42.5	20 54.5
13 Sa	15 31 45	21 27 8	26 21 11	3♐42 35	2 6.4	12 13.3	18 50.6	1 31.1	10 10.5	27 19.1	2 52.4	12 43.2	20 56.5
14 Su	15 35 42	22 27 34	11♐ 6 16	18 31 17	2 3.9	13 30.4	20 4.3	2 11.1	10 21.7	27 18.4	2 52.5	12 43.9	20 58.6
15 M	15 39 38	23 28 2	25 56 37	3♑21 18	2 1.0	14 46.0	21 18.0	2 51.0	10 32.8	27 17.7	2 52.7	12 44.6	21 0.6
16 Tu	15 43 35	24 28 31	10♑44 23	18 5 3	1 58.1	15 59.9	22 31.7	3 31.0	10 43.8	27 16.8	2 52.9	12 45.4	21 2.7
17 W	15 47 32	25 29 2	25 22 34	2♒36 21	1 55.7	17 11.8	23 45.5	4 11.1	10 54.8	27 15.8	2 53.2	12 46.2	21 4.8
18 Th	15 51 28	26 29 34	9♒45 54	16 50 55	1 54.3	18 21.5	24 59.4	4 51.1	11 5.6	27 14.7	2 53.5	12 47.0	21 6.9
19 F	15 55 25	27 30 7	23 51 13	0♓46 41	1D 54.0	19 28.6	26 13.3	5 31.2	11 16.4	27 13.5	2 53.9	12 47.9	21 9.0
20 Sa	15 59 21	28 30 41	7♓37 22	14 23 21	1 54.8	20 32.9	27 27.2	6 11.3	11 27.1	27 12.2	2 54.3	12 48.8	21 11.1
21 Su	16 3 18	29 31 16	21 4 48	27 41 55	1 56.3	21 33.9	28 41.2	6 51.4	11 37.7	27 10.8	2 54.8	12 49.7	21 13.2
22 M	16 7 14	0♐31 52	4♈14 57	10♈44 8	1 58.0	22 31.2	29 55.2	7 31.6	11 48.3	27 9.3	2 55.3	12 50.7	21 15.4
23 Tu	16 11 11	1 32 30	17 9 44	23 32 1	1 59.2	23 24.4	1♏ 9.3	8 11.7	11 58.7	27 7.6	2 55.9	12 51.6	21 17.5
24 W	16 15 7	2 33 9	29 51 11	6♉ 7 28	1R 59.4	24 12.7	2 23.5	8 52.0	12 9.1	27 5.9	2 56.5	12 52.7	21 19.7
25 Th	16 19 4	3 33 49	12♉21 4	18 32 10	1 58.2	24 55.8	3 37.6	9 32.2	12 19.4	27 4.0	2 57.2	12 53.7	21 21.8
26 F	16 23 1	4 34 31	24 40 58	0♊47 35	1 55.2	25 32.7	4 51.9	10 12.5	12 29.5	27 2.1	2 57.9	12 54.8	21 24.0
27 Sa	16 26 57	5 35 13	6♊52 12	12 54 59	1 50.5	26 2.9	6 6.1	10 52.8	12 39.6	27 0.0	2 58.7	12 55.9	21 26.2
28 Su	16 30 54	6 35 58	18 56 3	24 55 37	1 44.5	26 25.5	7 20.4	11 33.1	12 49.6	26 57.9	2 59.5	12 57.0	21 28.4
29 M	16 34 50	7 36 43	0♋53 52	6♋51 2	1 37.6	26 39.7	8 34.8	12 13.4	12 59.5	26 55.6	3 0.4	12 58.2	21 30.6
30 Tu	16 38 47	8 37 30	12 47 20	18 43 5	1 30.5	26R 44.6	9 49.2	12 53.8	13 9.3	26 53.3	3 1.3	12 59.4	21 32.8

DECEMBER 2004 LONGITUDE

Day	Sid.Time	☉	0 hr ☽	Noon ☽	True ☊	☿	♀	♂	♃	♄	♅	♆	♇
1 W	16 42 43	9♐38 18	24♋38 35	0♌34 13	1♉24.0	26♐39.7	11♏ 3.6	13♏34.2	13♎19.0	26♋50.8	3♓ 2.3	13♒ 0.7	21♐35.1
2 Th	16 46 40	10 39 8	6♌30 23	12 27 30	1R 18.7	26R 24.1	12 18.1	14 14.7	13 28.6	26R 48.2	3 3.3	13 1.9	21 37.3
3 F	16 50 36	11 39 59	18 26 5	24 26 39	1 15.1	25 57.5	13 32.6	14 55.2	13 38.1	26 45.6	3 4.4	13 3.2	21 39.5
4 Sa	16 54 33	12 40 51	0♍29 43	6♍35 54	1 13.4	25 19.6	14 47.1	15 35.7	13 47.5	26 42.8	3 5.5	13 4.5	21 41.8
5 Su	16 58 30	13 41 44	12 45 46	18 59 54	1D 13.3	24 30.8	16 1.7	16 16.2	13 56.8	26 40.0	3 6.7	13 5.9	21 44.0
6 M	17 2 26	14 42 39	25 18 55	1♎43 23	1 14.3	23 31.7	17 16.3	16 56.8	14 5.9	26 37.0	3 7.9	13 7.3	21 46.2
7 Tu	17 6 23	15 43 35	8♎13 49	14 50 40	1 15.8	22 23.5	18 30.9	17 37.4	14 15.0	26 34.0	3 9.2	13 8.7	21 48.5
8 W	17 10 19	16 44 33	21 34 20	28 25 4	1R 16.7	21 8.1	19 45.6	18 18.0	14 23.9	26 30.8	3 10.5	13 10.1	21 50.8
9 Th	17 14 16	17 45 31	5♏22 59	12♏28 3	1 16.1	19 47.6	21 0.3	18 58.7	14 32.8	26 27.6	3 11.9	13 11.5	21 53.0
10 F	17 18 12	18 46 31	19 40 2	26 58 28	1 13.6	18 24.7	22 15.0	19 39.3	14 41.5	26 24.3	3 13.3	13 13.0	21 55.3
11 Sa	17 22 9	19 47 32	4♐22 43	11♐51 54	1 8.7	17 2.3	23 29.8	20 20.1	14 50.1	26 20.9	3 14.8	13 14.6	21 57.5
12 Su	17 26 5	20 48 34	19 24 57	27 0 40	1 1.9	15 43.1	24 44.5	21 0.8	14 58.6	26 17.4	3 16.3	13 16.1	21 59.8
13 M	17 30 2	21 49 36	4♑37 42	12♑14 40	0 53.8	14 29.6	25 59.3	21 41.6	15 6.9	26 13.9	3 17.9	13 17.7	22 2.1
14 Tu	17 33 59	22 50 39	19 50 14	27 23 5	0 45.6	13 23.9	27 14.2	22 22.4	15 15.2	26 10.2	3 19.5	13 19.3	22 4.3
15 W	17 37 55	23 51 43	4♒52 4	12♒16 12	0 38.3	12 27.6	28 29.0	23 3.2	15 23.3	26 6.5	3 21.1	13 20.9	22 6.6
16 Th	17 41 52	24 52 47	19 34 43	26 47 3	0 32.8	11 41.8	29 43.8	23 44.1	15 31.2	26 2.7	3 22.8	13 22.5	22 8.9
17 F	17 45 48	25 53 51	3♓52 50	10♓51 55	0 29.6	11 6.9	0♐58.7	24 25.0	15 39.1	25 58.9	3 24.6	13 24.2	22 11.1
18 Sa	17 49 45	26 54 56	17 44 21	24 30 17	0D 28.4	10 43.1	2 13.6	25 5.9	15 46.8	25 54.9	3 26.4	13 25.9	22 13.4
19 Su	17 53 41	27 56 1	1♈10 1	7♈43 56	0 28.7	10 30.1	3 28.5	25 46.8	15 54.4	25 50.9	3 28.2	13 27.6	22 15.6
20 M	17 57 38	28 57 6	14 12 28	20 36 7	0 29.6	10D 27.4	4 43.4	26 27.8	16 1.8	25 46.8	3 30.1	13 29.3	22 17.9
21 Tu	18 1 35	29 58 11	26 55 22	3♉10 43	0R 29.9	10 34.3	5 58.3	27 8.7	16 9.1	25 42.7	3 32.0	13 31.1	22 20.2
22 W	18 5 31	0♑59 17	9♉22 39	15 31 36	0 28.7	10 50.1	7 13.3	27 49.8	16 16.3	25 38.5	3 34.0	13 32.9	22 22.4
23 Th	18 9 28	2 0 23	21 38 1	27 42 16	0 25.0	11 13.9	8 28.2	28 30.8	16 23.3	25 34.2	3 36.0	13 34.7	22 24.6
24 F	18 13 24	3 1 29	3♊44 42	9♊45 36	0 18.5	11 45.1	9 43.2	29 11.9	16 30.2	25 29.9	3 38.0	13 36.5	22 26.9
25 Sa	18 17 21	4 2 36	15 45 15	21 43 52	0 9.3	12 22.8	10 58.2	29 53.0	16 37.0	25 25.5	3 40.1	13 38.3	22 29.1
26 Su	18 21 17	5 3 43	27 41 39	3♋38 48	29♈57.7	13 6.3	12 13.2	0♐34.1	16 43.6	25 21.1	3 42.3	13 40.2	22 31.3
27 M	18 25 14	6 4 50	9♋35 27	15 31 46	29 44.6	13 55.0	13 28.2	1 15.3	16 50.0	25 16.6	3 44.4	13 42.1	22 33.6
28 Tu	18 29 10	7 5 57	21 27 56	27 24 5	29 31.1	14 48.3	14 43.3	1 56.5	16 56.4	25 12.0	3 46.6	13 44.0	22 35.8
29 W	18 33 7	8 7 5	3♌20 26	9♌17 11	29 18.3	15 45.7	15 58.3	2 37.7	17 2.5	25 7.5	3 48.9	13 45.9	22 38.0
30 Th	18 37 4	9 8 13	15 14 35	21 12 55	29 7.3	16 46.7	17 13.3	3 19.0	17 8.5	25 2.8	3 51.2	13 47.9	22 40.2
31 F	18 41 0	10 9 21	27 12 32	3♍13 48	28 58.7	17 50.9	18 28.4	4 0.3	17 14.4	24 58.2	3 53.5	13 49.8	22 42.3

Astro Data	Planet Ingress	Last Aspect	☽ Ingress	Last Aspect	☽ Ingress	☽ Phases & Eclipses	Astro Data
Dy Hr Mn	Dy Hr Mn	Dy Hr Mn	Dy Hr Mn	Dy Hr Mn	Dy Hr Mn	Dy Hr Mn	1 NOVEMBER 2004
♀0S 1 1:21	☿ ♐ 4 14:41	1 1:22 ♂ △	♋ 1 14:54	1 4:29 ♄ ☌	♌ 1 10:51	5 5:54 ☾ 13♌09	Julian Day # 38291
♄ R 8 6:55	♂ ♏ 11 5:12	4 2:01 ☿ △	♌ 4 3:33	3 14:53 ☿ △	♍ 3 23:01	12 14:28 ● 20♏33	Galactic Ctr 26♐55.0
☽0S 9 9:17	☉ ♐ 21 23:23	6 8:46 ♂ ✶	♍ 6 15:01	6 2:29 ♄ ✶	♎ 6 8:47	19 5:51 ☽ 27♒15	SVP 05♓11'42"
♅ D 11 19:12	♀ ♏ 22 13:32	8 18:33 ♄ ✶	♎ 8 23:24	8 8:42 ♄ □	♏ 8 14:45	26 20:08 ○ 4♊55	Obliquity 23°26'27"
☽0N 22 2:09		11 4:03 ♂ ☌	♏ 11 4:06	10 11:04 ♄ △	♐ 10 16:55		⚷ Chiron 21♑18.6
♃△♆ 29 8:27	♀ ♐ 16 17:11	13 1:35 ♄ △	♐ 13 5:57	12 4:04 ♇ ☌	♑ 12 16:43	5 0:54 ☾ 13♍14	☽ Mean ☊ 1♉31.4
☿ R 30 12:18	☉ ♑ 21 12:43	14 15:59 ♇ ☌	♑ 15 6:34	14 11:45 ♀ ✶	♒ 14 16:11	12 1:30 ● 20♐22	
	♂ ♐ 25 16:05	17 3:08 ♄ ☍	♒ 17 7:40	16 8:34 ☉ ✶	♓ 16 17:25	18 16:41 ☽ 27♓07	1 DECEMBER 2004
☽0S 6 18:31	☊ ♈ 26 7:32	19 5:51 ☉ □	♓ 19 10:39	18 16:41 ☉ □	♈ 18 21:53	26 15:07 ○ 5♋12	Julian Day # 38321
☽0N 19 7:07		21 15:36 ☉ △	♈ 21 16:12	21 5:17 ☉ △	♉ 21 5:53		Galactic Ctr 26♐55.1
☿ D 20 6:30		23 18:48 ♄ □	♉ 24 0:17	23 13:42 ♂ ☍	♊ 23 16:33		SVP 05♓11'37"
		26 4:38 ♄ ✶	♊ 26 10:26	25 13:31 ♇ ☍	♋ 26 4:39		Obliquity 23°26'27"
		28 15:05 ☿ ☍	♋ 28 22:12	28 7:35 ♄ ☌	♌ 28 17:15		⚷ Chiron 23♑04.9
				30 14:55 ♇ △	♍ 31 5:34		☽ Mean ☊ 29♈56.1

*Giving the positions of planets daily at noon, in LONGITUDE Greenwich Mean Time (UT)

January

Sunday	Monday	Tuesday	Wednesday	Thursday	Friday	Saturday
				1	2	3
4	5	6	7	8	9	10
11	12	13	14	15	16	17
18	19	20	21	22	23	24
25	26	27	28	29	30	31

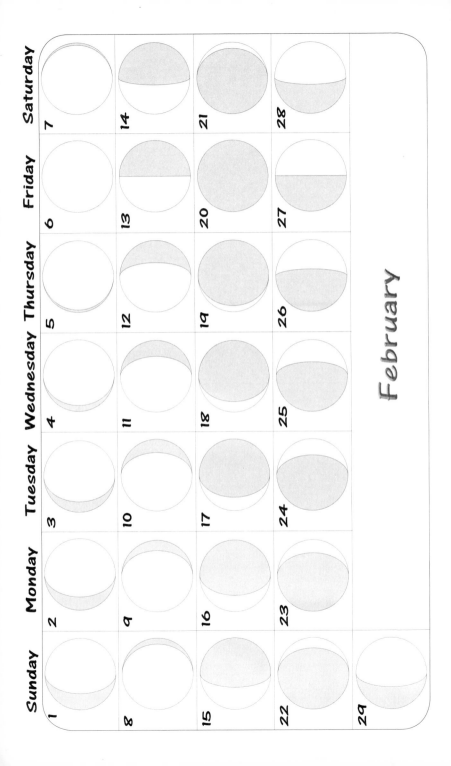

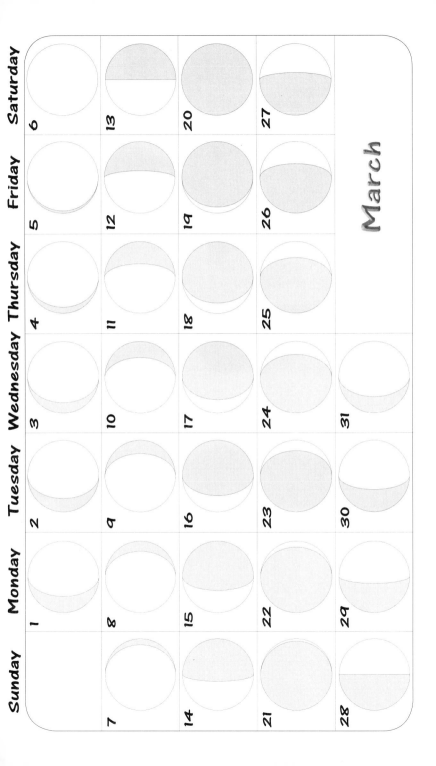

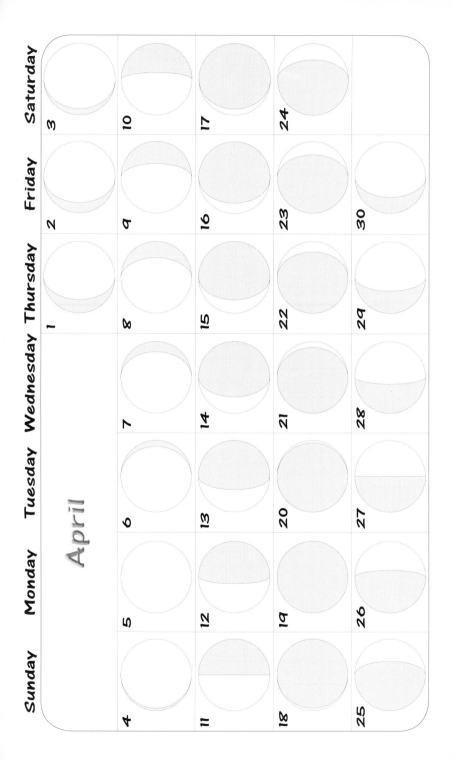

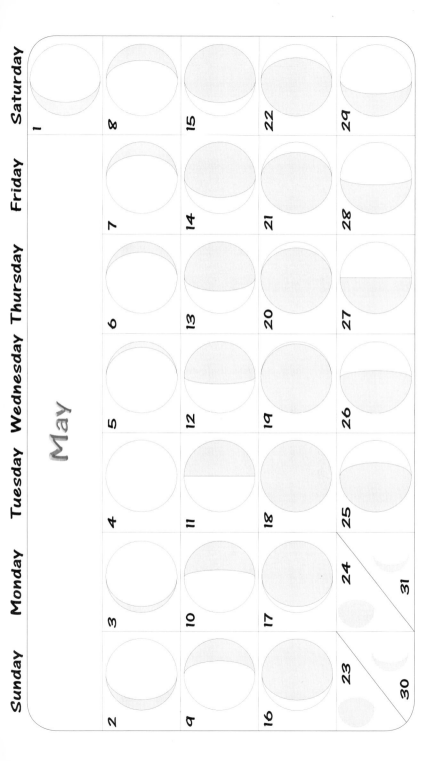

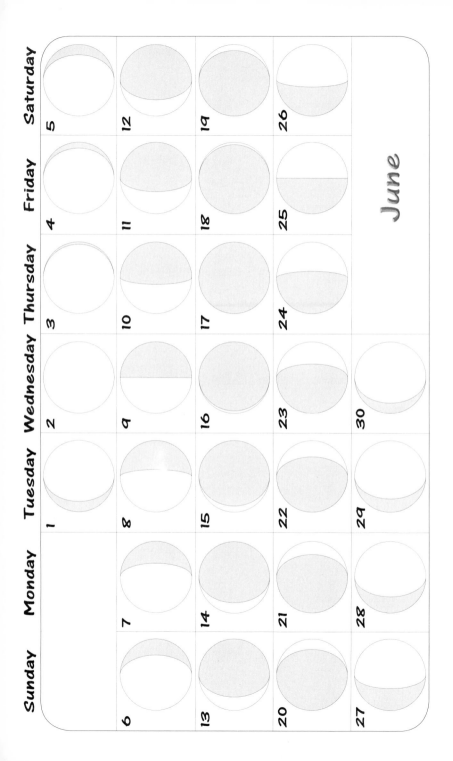

July

Sunday	Monday	Tuesday	Wednesday	Thursday	Friday	Saturday
				1	2	3
4	5	6	7	8	9	10
11	12	13	14	15	16	17
18	19	20	21	22	23	24
25	26	27	28	29	30	31

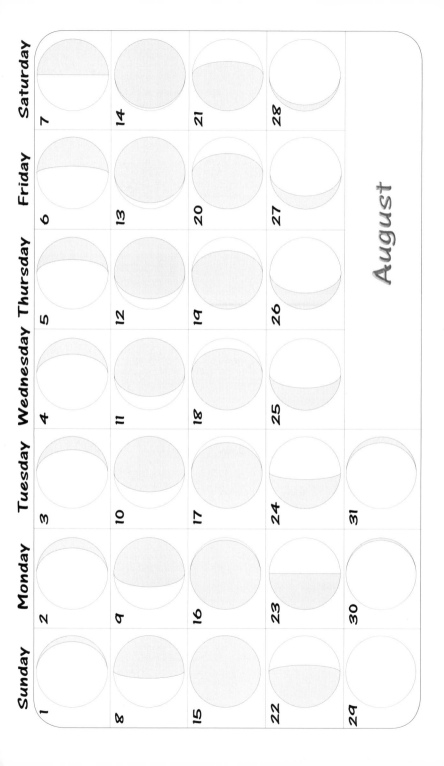

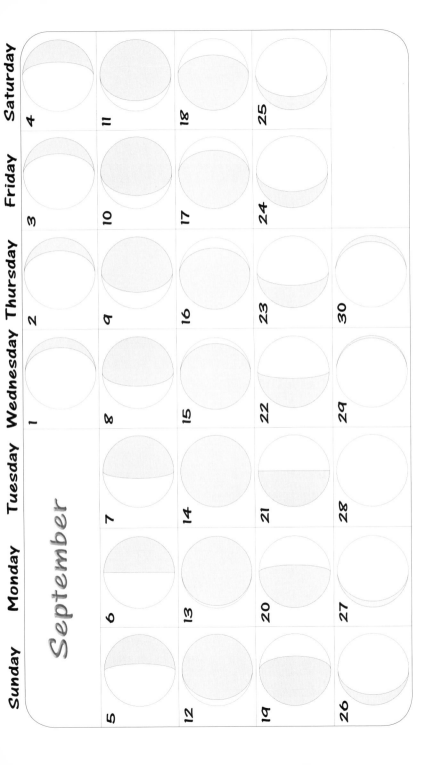

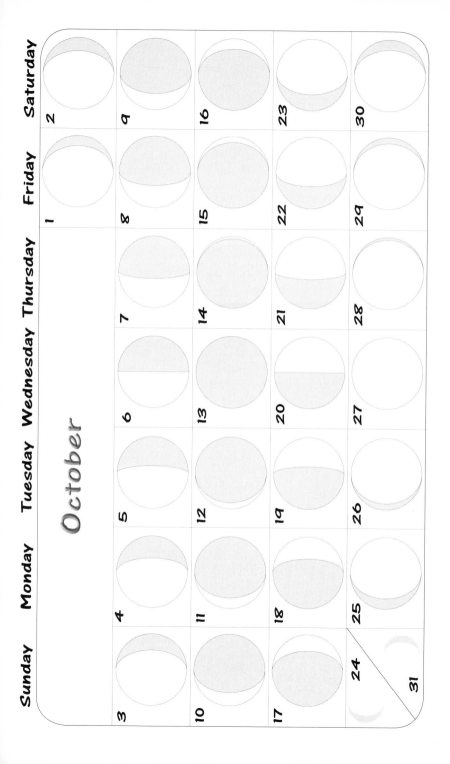

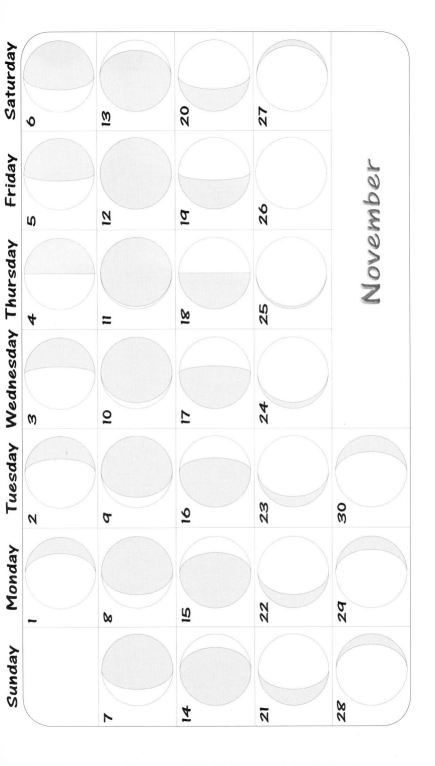

December

Sunday	Monday	Tuesday	Wednesday	Thursday	Friday	Saturday
			1	2	3	4
5	6	7	8	9	10	11
12	13	14	15	16	17	18
19	20	21	22	23	24	25
26	27	28	29	30	31	

JANUARY

S	M	T	W	T	F	S
						1
2	3	4	5	6	7	8
9	(10)	11	12	13	14	15
16	17	18	19	20	21	22
23	24	(25)	26	27	28	29
30	31					

MARCH

S	M	T	W	T	F	S
		1	2	3	4	5
6	7	8	9	(10)	11	12
13	14	15	16	17	18	19
20	21	22	23	24	(25)	26
27	28	29	30	31		

MAY

S	M	T	W	T	F	S
1	2	3	4	5	6	7
(8)	9	10	11	12	13	14
15	16	17	18	19	20	21
22	(23)	24	25	26	27	28
29	30	31				

JULY

S	M	T	W	T	F	S
					1	2
3	4	5	(6)	7	8	9
10	11	12	13	14	15	16
17	18	19	20	(21)	22	23
24	25	26	27	28	29	30
31						

SEPTEMBER

S	M	T	W	T	F	S
				1	2	(3)
4	5	6	7	8	9	10
11	12	13	14	15	16	(17)
18	19	20	21	22	23	24
25	26	27	28	29	30	

NOVEMBER

S	M	T	W	T	F	S
		(1)	2	3	4	5
6	7	8	9	10	11	12
13	14	(15)	16	17	18	19
20	21	22	23	24	25	26
27	28	29	30			

◯ = NEW MOON, PST/PDT

FEBRUARY

S	M	T	W	T	F	S
		1	2	3	4	5
6	7	(8)	9	10	11	12
13	14	15	16	17	18	19
20	21	22	(23)	24	25	26
27	28					

APRIL

S	M	T	W	T	F	S
					1	2
3	4	5	6	7	(8)	9
10	11	12	13	14	15	16
17	18	19	20	21	22	23
(24)	25	26	27	28	29	30

JUNE

S	M	T	W	T	F	S
			1	2	3	4
5	(6)	7	8	9	10	11
12	13	14	15	16	17	18
19	20	21	(22)	23	24	25
26	27	28	29	30		

AUGUST

S	M	T	W	T	F	S
	1	2	3	(4)	5	6
7	8	9	10	11	12	13
14	15	16	17	18	(19)	20
21	22	23	24	25	26	27
28	29	30	31			

OCTOBER

S	M	T	W	T	F	S
						1
2	(3)	4	5	6	7	8
9	10	11	12	13	14	15
16	(17)	18	19	20	21	22
23	24	25	26	27	28	29
30	31					

DECEMBER

S	M	T	W	T	F	S
				(1)	2	3
4	5	6	7	8	9	10
11	12	13	14	(15)	16	17
18	19	20	21	22	23	24
25	26	27	28	29	30	31

◯ = FULL MOON, PST/PDT

2005

Labrys
© Louise
Chambers
1989

225

WORLD TIME ZONES

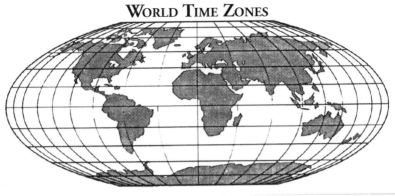

ID LW	NT BT	CA HT	YST	PST	MST	CST	EST	AST	BST	AT	WAT	GMT	CET	EET	BT	USSR Z3	USSR Z4	USSR Z5	SST	CCT	JST	GST	USSR Z10	ID LE
-12	-11	-10	-9	-8	-7	-6	-5	-4	-3	-2	-1	0	+1	+2	+3	+4	+5	+6	+7	+8	+9	+10	+11	+12
-4		-3	-2	-1	0	+1	+2	+3	+4	+5	+6	+7	+8	+9	+10	+11	+12	+13	+14	+15	+16	+17	+18	+19	+20

STANDARD TIME ZONES FROM WEST TO EAST CALCULATED FROM PST AS ZERO POINT:

IDLW:	International Date Line West	-4		**BT:**	Bagdhad Time	+11
NT/BT:	Nome Time/Bering Time	-3		**IT:**	Iran Time	+11 1/2
CA/HT:	Central Alaska & Hawaiian Time	-2		**USSR**	Zone 3	+12
YST:	Yukon Standard Time	-1		**USSR**	Zone 4	+13
PST:	Pacific Standard Time	0		**IST:**	Indian Standard Time	+13 1/2
MST:	Mountain Standard Time	+1		**USSR**	Zone 5	+14
CST:	Central Standard Time	+2		**NST:**	North Sumatra Time	+14 1/2
EST:	Eastern Standard Time	+3		**SST:**	South Sumatra Time & USSR Zone 6	+15
AST:	Atlantic Standard Time	+4		**JT:**	Java Time	+15 1/2
NFT:	Newfoundland Time	+4 1/2		**CCT:**	China Coast Time	+16
BST:	Brazil Standard Time	+5		**MT:**	Moluccas Time	+16 1/2
AT:	Azores Time	+6		**JST:**	Japanese Standard Time	+17
WAT:	West African Time	+7		**SAST:**	South Australian Standard Time	+17 1/2
GMT:	Greenwich Mean Time	+8		**GST:**	Guam Standard Time	+18
WET:	Western European Time (England)	+8		**USSR**	Zone 10	+19
CET:	Central European Time	+9		**IDLE:**	International Date Line East	+20
EET:	Eastern European Time	+10				

HOW TO CALCULATE TIME ZONE CORRECTIONS IN YOUR AREA:

ADD if you are **east** of PST (Pacific Standard Time); SUBTRACT if you are **west** of PST on this map (see right-hand column of chart above).

All times in this calendar are calculated from the West Coast of North America where it is made. Pacific Standard Time (PST Zone 8) is zero point for this calendar except during Daylight Savings Time (April 6–October 26, 2003 during which times are given for PDT Zone 7). If your time zone does not use Daylight Savings Time, add one hour to the standard correction during this time. At the bottom of each page EST/EDT (Eastern Standard or Daylight Time) and GMT (Greenwich Mean Time) times are also given. For all other time zones, calculate your time zone correction(s) from this map and write it on the inside cover for easy reference.

SIGNS AND SYMBOLS AT A GLANCE

PLANETS

Personal Planets are closest to Earth.
⊙ **Sun**: self radiating outward, character, ego
☽ **Moon**: inward sense of self, emotions, psyche
☿ **Mercury**: communication, travel, thought
♀ **Venus**: relationship, love, sense of beauty, empathy
♂ **Mars**: will to act, initiative, ambition
Asteroids are between Mars and Jupiter and reflect the awakening of feminine-defined energy centers in human consciousness. See "Asteroids" (p.199).
Social Planets are between personal and outer planets.
♃ **Jupiter**: expansion, opportunities, leadership
♄ **Saturn**: limits, structure, discipline
Note: the seven days of the week are named after the above seven heavenly bodies.
⚷ **Chiron**: is a small planetary body between Saturn and Uranus representing the wounded healer.
Transpersonal Planets are the outer planets.
♅ **Uranus**: cosmic consciousness, revolutionary change
♆ **Neptune**: spiritual awakening, cosmic love, all one
♇ **Pluto**: death and rebirth, deep, total change

ZODIAC SIGNS

♈	Aries
♉	Taurus
♊	Gemini
♋	Cancer
♌	Leo
♍	Virgo
♎	Libra
♏	Scorpio
♐	Sagittarius
♑	Capricorn
♒	Aquarius
♓	Pisces

ASPECTS

Aspects show the angle between planets; this informs how the planets influence each other and us. **We'Moon** lists only significant aspects:
☌ CONJUNCTION (planets are 0–5° apart)
   linked together, energy of aspected planets is mutually enhancing
✶ SEXTILE (planets are 60° apart)
   cooperative, energies of this aspect blend well
□ SQUARE (planets are 90° apart)
   challenging, energies of this aspect are different from each other
△ TRINE (planets are 120° apart)
   harmonizing, energies of this aspect are in the same element
☍ OPPOSITION (planets are 180° apart)
   polarizing or complementing, energies are diametrically opposite
⚻ QUINCUNX (planets are 150° apart)
   variable, energies of this aspect combine contrary elements

OTHER SYMBOLS

☽ **v/c**: Moon is void of course from last lunar aspect till it enters new sign.
ApG–Apogee: Point in the orbit of a planet that's farthest from Earth.
PrG–Perigee: Point in the orbit of a planet that's nearest to Earth.
D or R–Direct or Retrograde: Describes when a planet moves forward (D) through the zodiac or appears to move backward (R).

EFGH

IJKL

MNOP